DEVELOPMENT CENTRE STUDIES

PROFILES IN POPULATION ASSISTANCE

A COMPARATIVE REVIEW OF THE PRINCIPAL DONOR AGENCIES

by
Margaret Wolfson

DEVELOPMENT CENTRE
OF THE ORGANISATION FOR ECONOMIC CO-OPERATION AND DEVELOPMENT

Pursuant to article 1 of the Convention signed in Paris on 14th December, 1960, and which came into force on 30th September, 1961, the Organisation for Economic Co-operation and Development (OECD) shall promote policies designed:

- to achieve the highest sustainable economic growth and employment and a rising standard of living in Member countries, while maintaining financial stability, and thus to contribute to the development of the world economy;
- to contribute to sound economic expansion in Member as well as non-member countries in the process of economic development; and
- to contribute to the expansion of world trade on a multilateral, non-discriminatory basis in accordance with international obligations.

The Signatories of the Convention on the OECD are Austria, Belgium, Canada, Denmark, France, the Federal Republic of Germany, Greece, Iceland, Ireland, Italy, Luxembourg, the Netherlands, Norway, Portugal, Spain, Sweden, Switzerland, Turkey, the United Kingdom and the United States. The following countries acceded subsequently to this Convention (the dates are those on which the instruments of accession were deposited): Japan (28th April, 1964), Finland (28th January, 1969), Australia (7th June, 1971) and New Zealand (29th May, 1973).

The Socialist Federal Republic of Yugoslavia takes part in certain work of the OECD (agreement of 28th October, 1961).

The Development Centre of the Organisation for Economic Co-operation and Development was established by decision of the OECD Council on 23rd October, 1962.

The purpose of the Centre is to bring together the knowledge and experience available in Member countries of both economic development and the formulation and execution of general policies of economic aid; to adapt such knowledge and experience to the actual needs of countries or regions in the process of development and to put the results at the disposal of the countries by appropriate means.

The Centre has a special and autonomous position within the OECD which enables it to enjoy scientific independence in the execution of its task. Nevertheless, the Centre can draw upon the experience and knowledge available in the OECD in the development field.

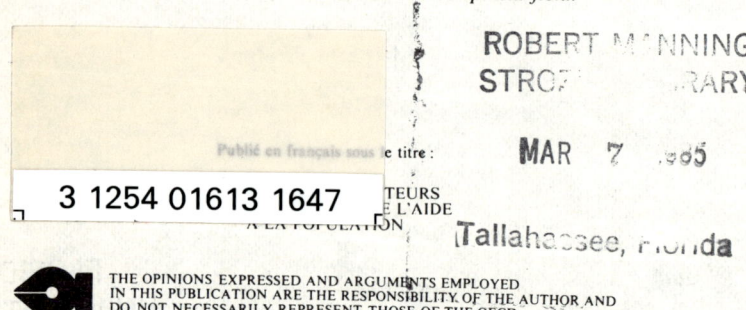

THE OPINIONS EXPRESSED AND ARGUMENTS EMPLOYED IN THIS PUBLICATION ARE THE RESPONSIBILITY OF THE AUTHOR AND DO NOT NECESSARILY REPRESENT THOSE OF THE OECD

© OECD, 1983
Application for permission to reproduce or translate
all or part of this publication should be made to:
Director of Information, OECD
2, rue André-Pascal, 75775 PARIS CEDEX 16, France.

CONTENTS

PREFACE	5
OVERVIEW	9
The changing scope of population assistance	9
The donors' views	18
The recipients' views	27
MULTILATERAL DONORS	43
UNFPA	43
The World Bank	67
BILATERAL DONORS	89
Norway	89
Sweden	103
The United Kingdom	119
The United States Agency for International Development	133
NON-GOVERNMENTAL ORGANISATIONS	155
The International Planned Parenthood Federation	155
The Pathfinder Fund	171

Also available

CHANGING APPROACHES TO POPULATION PROBLEMS, by Margaret Wolfson, OECD Development Centre in co-operation with the World Bank (January 1979)
(41 78 05 1) ISBN 92-64-11863-2   196 pages   £4.60   US$9.50   F38.00

COMPENDIUM OF AID PROCEDURES. A Review of current practices of Members of the Development Assistance Committee (May 1981). 'Document' Series
(43 81 02 1) ISBN 92-64-12195-1, 86 pages   £3.00   US$7.50   F30.00

DEVELOPMENT CO-OPERATION. 1982 REVIEW. Efforts and Policies of Members of the Development Assistance Committee (December 1982)
(43 82 01 1) ISBN 92-64-12392-X   256 pages   £9.50   US$19.00   F95.00

SOCIAL CONFLICT AND DEVELOPMENT. Basic Needs and Survival Strategies in Four National Settings, by Denyse Harari and Jorge Garcia-Bouza (January 1983)
(41 82 02 2) ISBN 92-64-12361-X   110 pages   £4.00   US$8.00   F40.00

Prices charged at the OECD Publications Office.

THE OECD CATALOGUE OF PUBLICATIONS *and supplements will be sent free of charge on request addressed either to OECD Publications Office,*
2, *rue André-Pascal, 75775 PARIS CEDEX 16, or to the OECD Sales Agent in your country.*

PREFACE

The ease and efficiency with which any development assistance activity actually gets carried out will depend to a considerable degree on the administrative procedures and practices applied by each of the two aid partners concerned — i.e. by the donor agency and the government of the recipient country. Donor agencies have long been aware of the bottlenecks for the implementation of aid programmes created by the limited administrative and managerial capability of developing country governments — even while recognizing that this is itself a function of underdevelopment. More recently, they have begun to take cognizance of the role played also by their own bureaucratic requirements and behaviour, and to consider whether these could not be modified in order to facilitate the implementation of the aid they provide.

In this spirit, the Members of the OECD Development Assistance Committee (DAC), in the late 1970s, worried at the widening gap between their aid allocations and the actual rate of disbursements, and concerned lest their own administrative arrangements might be partly, at least, to blame, undertook a novel and intensive examination of each other's aid procedures and practices. The problem of lagging aid disbursements, in fact, turned out to be only a temporary hiccup. The review of aid procedures, however, to which it gave rise, not only revealed "the bewildering variety of procedures and practices" which DAC Member countries applied in their respective aid programmes[1], but led to their adopting formal guidelines for the improvement of aid implementation in the future[2].

The guidelines are envisaged as constituting to some extent a list of "best practices" which DAC Members should aspire to and put into effect in their aid programmes, at the rhythm that their respective constitutional, legal and administrative constraints will permit. At the same time, they urge donors to strengthen the administrative capacity of their recipient countries for absorbing effectively the aid provided.

The present study by the OECD Development Centre is intended to carry the work of improving aid implementation a step further by examining in detail just what are the effects of different donors' aid-giving systems in the particular area of population assistance.

That population was the field selected for this purpose was the result of two separate but converging considerations. First, population assistance, as both aid donors and recipient countries are ruefully aware, is particularly difficult to implement effectively. Being designed to provide personal services to very large and often widely-dispersed target groups, population programmes are administration-intensive and require a considerable degree of effective decentralisation, backed by strong field-level structures. Since many of these features are common to all social development activities, albeit perhaps to a lesser extent, an analysis of the problems encountered in implementing population assistance was felt to be relevant as a guide to improving aid implementation in other social development sectors also.

The second consideration was the wish to give some practical follow-up to an earlier study undertaken under the joint sponsorship of the Development Centre and the World Bank on the evolution of population policies in the aftermath of the 1974 World Population Conference at Bucharest[3]. The Bank and the Development Centre had been

---

1. Compendium of Aid Procedures, OECD, 1981. Conclusions, pp. 70-71.
2. Adopted by the DAC High Level Meeting, November 1979.
3. "Changing Approaches to Population Problems" by Margaret Wolfson, OECD Development Centre, 1978.

discussing for some time the need to look at the way in which these policies were being actually put into effect. In particular, they felt it would be useful to examine the contribution of the various agencies providing population assistance to the implementation of the new population strategies in developing countries. A comparative review focussing on the aid procedures and practices employed by each of the main donors of population assistance was thus seen as a logical follow-up to the earlier review of population policies, and at the same time, as making a further contribution to the broader work initiated by the DAC to improve aid implementation generally.

In order to complement this enquiry into donors' aid requirements, the Centre felt that it was necessary also to try to throw a similar light on the corresponding arrangements employed by host governments. Two case-studies have, therefore, been carried out, one in Bangladesh, and one in Indonesia, which examine the implementation of population assistance programmes by the recipient country institutions concerned. In particular, they have sought to explore the way in which the public administration has coped with the additional responsibilities imposed by a major input of foreign aid and a vast expansion of government activities in a particular sector. The studies have been carried out by independent national research teams of the country concerned in order to explore the problems involved as the recipient itself sees them. In each case, the studies were preceded by discussions between the Development Centre and the government, not only so as to ensure the government's support and co-operation, but also its guidance, so that the focus would be primarily on the problems that the government itself considered of most immediate practical importance, in the light of its own programme and particular implementation problems.

The two country case-studies stand as separate reports and are not included in the present volume[4]. However, the findings and conclusions of all three studies have been brought together and an analysis of them presented to an international meeting of donor agencies and representatives of developing countries, organised jointly by the OECD Development Assistance Committee and the Development Centre in Paris, on 16th and 17th November, 1982[5]. The purpose of the meeting was to consider, on the basis of the experience revealed by this body of work, what both donors and recipients might do to improve the implementation of population assistance in terms of practical programme operations.

In making a comparative review of the principal donors of population assistance, it had first to be decided which of them should properly be considered as "principal". The selection presented certain problems. It was felt that the group of donors to be examined in depth should be representative rather than exhaustive, and should include multilateral donors and non-governmental organisations as well as the bilaterals, members of the DAC. While some agencies were obvious candidates because of the volume of the population assistance they provide, in other cases, a choice had to be made, sometimes arbitrarily, between agencies with programmes of roughly comparable importance. Since the main focus of the study was to examine different agencies' aid *procedures,* it was decided not to include those DAC donors who provide sizeable amounts of population assistance primarily in the form of contributions to the programmes of multilateral agencies. The Specialised Agencies of the United Nations, whose population programmes are funded by and undertaken on behalf of the UNFPA, were similarly excluded.

The donor agencies subject of this study accordingly cover the following: among DAC countries, the United States Agency for International Development (US AID), the Norwegian Agency for International Development (NORAD), the Swedish International Development Authority (SIDA) and the Overseas Development Administration of the United Kingdom (ODA); the two major multilateral donors of population assistance, the

---

4. They are to be issued shortly by the Development Centre for general distribution.
5. The report of the discussions has been issued by the Development Centre as a separate document, "The Implementation of Population Assistance Programmes", April 1983.

United Nations Fund for Population Activities (UNFPA) and the World Bank[6]; and two important non-governmental donors, the International Planned Parenthood Federation (IPPF) and the Pathfinder Fund. Since the aid procedures and practices that these agencies apply in the area of population assistance cannot properly be appreciated except in the context of the agency as a whole, each chapter begins with a brief description of the agency, its approach to problems of population, and the criteria that it applies to its population programmes.

The research for the study has been undertaken by means of interviews with each of the agencies concerned in order to learn details of their respective aid approaches and procedural arrangements. This information from agency headquarters has been supplemented by interviews in a number of recipient countries to ascertain the views of the officials directly concerned with the implementation of population programmes on the different approaches of their various aid donors, and to talk to the field missions of those donors. The countries selected for this purpose were Bangladesh, Egypt, Indonesia and Kenya, on the grounds that they all receive substantial population assistance, provided by a variety of aid donors. The agency chapters are accordingly based on the results of the discussions which the author held in capitals and in the field, up-dated as of April 1, 1983.

The author, as well as the Development Centre, would like to express their thanks publicly to the host of interested, sympathetic and helpful officials at every level, who took time out from their already crowded work schedules to answer innumerable and sometimes difficult questions in the search for significant detail. It is hoped that the results of their collaboration in this study will show the way in which both donor agencies and recipient governments can modify their respective aid arrangements in the future so as to make the work of aid implementation more rational and efficient.

In the Overview Chapter which follows and which sets forth some reflections on the analysis of the different donor agencies that are the subject of this study, the ideas presented are those of the author. They do not necessarily represent the views of the Development Centre or the DAC, or of the World Bank, with whose financial assistance the study was undertaken.

On behalf of the Development Centre, I would like to express my appreciation to the World Bank for the co-operation, encouragement and financial assistance with which they have supported the Centre's population work, and of which the present review and its companion case-studies are the latest fruits.

Just Faaland
President of the Development Centre
July 1983

---

6. Strictly speaking, of course, it is a misnomer to call the World Bank a "donor" agency, but we do so nonetheless, for convenience.

OVERVIEW

I. POLICIES AND PREFERENCES

The Changing Scope of Population Assistance

Population assistance defies definition — or perhaps has no need of it, being quite simply what any particular donor chooses to think it is. The aid response made by donor agencies to requests from developing countries wishing to effect some change in the demographic characteristics of their population (primarily, though not exclusively, a reduction in the rate of population growth) is known as "population assistance". Today, the range of activities that may be included under this heading is not only remarkably diverse, but would seem to be growing all the time.

Anomalies abound. UNFPA might provide training in manpower planning, and call it "population assistance": UNICEF (which does not consider itself a population assistance agency[1]) will provide training for traditional birth attendants in modern contraceptive techniques, and call it, not "population assistance" but, say, "community health care". These niceties of definition are problems only as regards statistical reporting. From the point of view of the recipient country, once the donor has agreed to contribute funding to the activity, they are immaterial. Irrespective of definition, developing countries know that (provided the funds are available) there are today few sound activities related to population, whether directly or indirectly, that are unlikely to find a taker among one or other of the agencies providing assistance in the population field.

Initially, "population assistance" was quite clear-cut, being limited to support for family planning programmes, sometimes accompanied by some form of direct motivational activity (family planning information, education and communication - IEC). Soon, however, it came to include some aspects of health care also, partly because of the obvious medical association with family planning, and partly because health care facilities provided a convenient vehicle for delivery of family planning services. All agencies providing population assistance moved naturally and easily into accepting this association, including the World Bank, which until then had never made loans for health activities, and whose assistance in this area in fact began in the form of health "components" in some of its loans for population. The one exception that may be noted to the general trend of family planning broadening out to include also health activities is UNICEF, where the progression went in the opposite direction. UNICEF, in accordance with its mandate, *began* by providing health care, specifically for the protection of mothers and children. It soon found, however, that to combat the problem of high infant mortality, it was necessary to encourage birth spacing, and was accordingly led to introduce family planning into its health programmes.

The real "opening up" of the scope of population assistance came in the mid 1970s, in the wake of the World Population Conference at Bucharest, with its defiant challenge that "development was the best contraceptive". After a period of — more or

---

1. UNICEF's mandate "to provide assistance to mothers and children" leads it to undertake numerous activities that spill over into what other agencies generally consider as "population assistance", viz: "improved nutrition for mothers and infants, safer child delivery and birth spacing, reduction of infant mortality, etc. UNICEF recognizes that though these are essentially "population" activities, they are often difficult to separate out statistically from the wider health care activities of which they are part.

less agonising — reappraisal of their population assistance policies, donors came eventually to accept the importance of the "development approach", and "population assistance" accordingly began to include, in addition to family planning and health care, support for a variety of activities of a social development nature, intended to tackle the presumed *causes* of high fertility. As was only natural, donors came to espouse the new "demand side" philosophy in their respective programmes at different rates and to a different degree. Some allowed themselves to be nudged into it almost reluctantly. With others, the enthusiasm was so total that it was difficult to be sure to what extent the initiative at the actual project level came from the developing countries themselves or from the donor agencies providing the assistance[2].

Today, there are few donor agencies whose population assistance does not include some "development type" activities such as income-generating projects for women, youth work, community-development schemes etc., in addition to the "core" population activities of family planning and health care (primarily, though not necessarily, mother and child health care). Norway and Sweden may perhaps be considered as exceptions — although not because they are unconvinced of the importance of the "beyond family planning" approach. On the contrary, Sweden now goes so far as to maintain that a "free-standing" family planning programme is not only likely to be ineffective, but is socially and morally wrong[3]. For the most part, however, Norway and Sweden have preferred to limit their population assistance to family planning and related health programmes, and to provide support for activities intended to alter the economic and social environment under their aid programmes in other development sectors (notably "basic needs" type programmes). Further, both countries follow a highly "responsive" posture with regard to their respective "partner" countries, and to date do not seem to have received much demand for population assistance of this type.

For other donors, even those whose whole mandate was initially to provide family planning services (IPPF and the Pathfinder Fund), there is today no difficulty at all about including also support for such diverse activities as seminars for parliamentarians, training of religious leaders, reform of the legislation relating to marriage and property, as well as a variety of activities related to education, improved health, environmental sanitation etc. Indeed, their readiness to do so is a matter of pride.

The agency which, as a matter of deliberate policy, has gone furthest in the breadth of its population assistance coverage is the UNFPA. Formally, UNFPA's assistance, whether directly through its country programmes, or indirectly through its regional and inter-regional activities, is grouped into five major categories of activity (the relative priorities between which have shifted somewhat from time to time). The categories are defined as follows: basic data collection; population dynamics (i.e. research and training into all aspects of demographic trends); population policy; population information, education and communication; and family planning — in short, virtually any activity held to touch on population in one way or another[4].

In terms of the diversity of actual population programmes, the other two "great powers" of the population assistance scene, the World Bank and US AID, are often not

---

2. At a meeting held at the OECD in Paris in May 1978, to discuss the change in the approach to population problems since Bucharest and their implications for population assistance, it was notable that whereas the heads of the donor agencies all spoke out loudly in favour of the "development approach", most of the representatives of the developing countries present wanted to receive assistance in the form of family planning and health services.

3. Sweden considers family planning to be an integral part of primary health care. It also considers the Alma Ata Conference on Primary Health Care organised by WHO and UNICEF in 1978 to be as important as Bucharest, if not more so.

4. Just how widely UNFPA interprets its population mandate may be seen from the following passage: It is "UNFPA policy for example" to give "special attention to certain groups of the population (women, youth, rural and disadvantaged sectors of the population), to the concepts of self-reliance and technical co-operation among developing countries (TCDC), to the recommendations contained in the (Bucharest) World Population Plan of Action, to the World Plan of Action of the International Women's Year Conference, to anti-poverty and basic needs strategies, to 'Beyond Family Planning' etc." Instructions for the Preparation of a Project Document, 1978.

far behind. Thus World Bank loans for population now include a variety of what it calls "software" activities that would have been totally unthinkable in the early years of the Bank, when its appointed function was to provide finance for major infrastructure investment. The second IDA Population Project in Bangladesh, for example, finds the Bank financing feature films (to promote the family planning "message"), women's projects, youth clubs, co-operatives etc., as well as continuing its traditional funding of health and family planning facilities and services. No less remarkable, in view of the fervour with which it once used to propound the "supply-side" approach to population problems, is the programme diversity now shown by US AID (viz — village development in Egypt, pilot nutrition programmes in Indonesia, health programmes in Africa, etc.). Like UNFPA, US AID has official policy instructions to apply a very broad approach to its population programmes, and notably to give "particular attention to the interrelationship between population growth and development[5]". Although operating on a much smaller scale, ODA received a similar directive from the government of the U.K.[6].

Most agencies, therefore, big and small, are today prepared to include various development-type activities in their population assistance, along with their support for family planning and health care. What is significant is perhaps, primarily, the fact that they are *prepared* to. In actual population assistance programmes, all donors still continue to give the lion's share to family planning. Thus even UNFPA, with its particularly broad interpretation of its population mandate, provides nearly 50 per cent of its aid as support for family planning programmes. (When in 1980, faced with a new situation of budgetary stringency, UNFPA was obliged to reassess its priorities for resource allocation, it restated the emphasis to be given to family planning). Family planning (and associated health care activities) accounts for some 75 per cent of the population programmes of US AID, and for the World Bank, the proportion is still higher. A similar preponderance is to be found in the programmes of the other bilateral donors providing population assistance and, of course, in those of the specialist non-governmental population assistance agencies.

Who Does What ?

Since nearly all the donors of aid have enlarged the scope of their population assistance in very much the same way, there would not, today, seem to be any a priori reason why, for any given activity, a requesting country should approach one donor agency rather than another. Certainly, there are often particular donor-client relationships. As regards the content of aid, however, division of labour in the population field, although part of most agencies' image of themselves, is in practice becoming increasingly blurred.

Donors do, of course, have their preferences, both positive and negative, as regards the type of aid that they will provide, to whom to provide it, in what amounts, and within what kind of aid relationship with the recipient. Few donors of population assistance, for example, want to spread their aid over quite so extensive a range of activities as UNFPA has done. Indeed, the very size and variety of UNFPA's programme encourages other donors to exercise a certain degree of specialisation in their own — on the grounds that they can hold back from certain areas because the need is being covered by the UNFPA (or possibly some other donor, supported by UNFPA funding).

Thus most donors prefer not to include in their bilateral programmes any sizeable aid for *demographic data collection*, surveys etc., nor for *bio-medical research*, although

---

5. Section 104(d) of the Foreign Assistance Act (1978), speaking of US overall development policy, notes the relevance for reducing the desire for large families of programmes in the areas of "nutrition, disease control, maternal and child health services, improvement in the status and employment of women, agricultural production, rural development" etc.

6. "...aid is needed first to relieve poverty, and raise living standards and to help create a social framework which is conducive to the practice of fertility regulation". "Future World Trends" — discussion paper, HMSO 1976.

they may contribute to regional and international research in these fields[7]. There are, however, exceptions. The U.K., for example, has a particular penchant for demographic research and training, and data collection, as a field in which it feels that U.K. university and research institutions give it a comparative advantage.

The area of *population policy*, another major UNFPA assistance category, sees donors deeply divided. For Norway and Sweden (and a large number of other DAC countries), the very idea of donor intervention in the sensitive area of population policy in a developing country is abhorrent. US AID and the World Bank, on the other hand, as well as UNFPA, consider that it is part of their role as population assistance donors, not only to help governments that have a population policy to improve their programme strategies, but to "educate" those that have not in the importance of the "population issue". IPPF and Pathfinder similarly devote considerable effort to building up a "constituency" for family planning in countries where the government is as yet unconvinced. While the World Bank's sphere of action is effectively limited to those countries where it is already supporting the national population programme, US AID has the possibility of using central funds from Washington to sponsor "consciousness-raising" activities for private groups, even in countries where there is no government-to-government programme covering population assistance; and UNFPA, because of its liberal interpretation of "population assistance", has an entrée even to countries whose governments may be hostile to family planning or to the need for a national population policy[8]. IPPF and Pathfinder, of course, as private agencies, can bypass governments altogether and undertake an activity anywhere there is a promising nucleus of private sector interest.

For the basic components of family planning programmes, i.e. *construction of facilities, equipment, provision of contraceptives,* and *training* of personnel, donors have certain preferences, but for the most part end up doing something of everything to a greater or lesser degree.

Training and *equipment* (including vehicles) are provided by all donors without notable specialisation, although only certain donors (e.g. UNFPA, the U.K., Pathfinder, for example) are prepared to accept requests for equipment or a training attachment outside of some broader population project to which they are providing support.

Construction, on the other hand, is considered to be pre-eminently the business of the Bank, with its tradition of making loans for infrastructure[9]. The Bank feels that "hardware" is a more appropriate object of lending than the other customary components of population programmes, and developing country governments, faced with the necessity of assuming a foreign loan for population, usually think so too. Other donors, therefore, like to leave it to the Bank as far as possible. Construction is for this reason one of the very few negative preferences applied by UNFPA, although it tempers the principle to the circumstances, and makes frequent exceptions. (It will even finance purchase). US AID, in principle, also prefers not to finance construction, but in practice often does, NORAD (the Norwegian Agency for International Development) and ODA (the U.K. Overseas Development Administration) seem quite pleased to do it, and SIDA (the Swedish International Development Authority), although it prefers today to make its major contribution to population programmes in the form of "software", does so too. IPPF and Pathfinder, on the other hand, will never cover construction, although IPPF, very exceptionally, has agreed to make a building *loan.*

For *contraceptive drugs and materials,* by far the biggest source of supply is US

---

7. US AID, for example, provides a large proportion of the funding for contraceptive and related research world-wide.

8. For example, when the Government of Bolivia reverted to an anti-family planning stance, UNFPA found other activities on which to spend the Bolivian allocation, which the Government would accept.

9. When the Bank began lending for population, over 90 per cent went for "hardware" (i.e. *construction equipment* and *vehicles);* in more recent loans, this element accounts for some 50-60 per cent.

AID, which not only provides developing countries with a large part of the requirements of the national programme of the government (including those parts of it financed by other donors), but also supplies the programmes of the private Family Planning Associations, either directly or indirectly. US AID is in an unusual position in that a considerable part of its aid (in all sectors) is undertaken through private U.S. bodies acting as intermediaries. In the field of population, this allows it to sponsor some activities, (e.g. study visits, seminars etc., undertaken with the idea of "sensitising" policy-makers) in certain countries where direct programmes would not be possible. Acting through the Pathfinder Fund as intermediary[10], it is also able to supply contraceptives to the (private) national Family Planning Association in some countries which have no national population programme (e.g. Brazil) or, where there is one, but the government has not asked US AID for direct support (e.g. Mexico).

There are other suppliers of contraceptives (for example, Norway, Sweden, the U.K. and IPPF[11]), although the amounts are declining, partly because countries get a large part of their needs from US AID, and partly because of their increasing capacity to supply (or package) their own contraceptive requirements. The Bank likes to leave supply of contraceptives to US AID where possible, but will include them as part of a Bank-financed project. However, it is exceptionally supplying, as straight commodity assistance, some of the contraceptive requirements for Thailand's large programme of commercially-based distribution.

Some donors have strong likes and dislikes as to the actual content of the government's population programme and the services that it provides. Thus, US AID will not support any programme that includes abortion. No other donor applies a total ban, but some would refuse to support a programme in which it was the sole method of fertility regulation provided (e.g. ODA). US AID takes an equally strong line with respect to any programme where there is an element of *coercion,* an attitude which is shared by Sweden. Many donors similarly are unhappy about incentive payments for sterilisation (whether made to the doctor or the client), an unease that has intensified since the Indian experience at the time of Emergency. However, at various times, they have agreed to them at the government's request, as the price for getting the programme moving, keeping the doctors interested etc. ("performance premiums")[12].

The interchangeability of donors' respective preferences regarding different forms of population assistance has, not altogether surprisingly, led to periodic expressions of concern in aid circles about the dangers of duplication. There have even, on occasion, been suggestions that it might be desirable for donors to work out an agreed division of labour in the population field. Leaving aside the fact that division of labour is not a feature of donor practice in any field of development assistance, and that in any case, not all donors are active in the same countries, nor even in the same areas of a given programme, it would seem that any such rationalisation would work to the detriment of the developing countries.

Admittedly, there are areas where different donors have decided, quite independently of each other, to do the same things (e.g. in Indonesia, two donors have separate programmes of "dukum" training – i.e. training traditional healers). But there is clearly room and need enough for both. Even if the methods and approach are different, the problem is one of co-ordination, not of duplication, for who can be sure, particularly in a new and unconventional endeavour, that only *his* chosen ways can do the job?

Present arrangements, moreover, albeit over-lapping, have the inherent advantage that in case of need, one donor can help another out to get a project started quickly,

---

10. US AID provides the main part of the annual budget of the Pathfinder Fund, to be applied to activities which are in concordance with US AID's broad priorities and for which it gives individual approval.
11. Which gets one-third of them from US AID.
12. Sometimes the payment has been made to the hospitals performing the operation, on a case basis, sometimes in the form of a salary supplement, and sometimes, exceptionally, as some form of compensation payment to the client. (The Bangladesh programme offers a "rickshaw allowance" and "surgical clothing").

or to keep one afloat, should funding unexpectedly dry up. Moreover, if a donor jibs at certain aspects of a programme, or, because of its particular rules and regulations, is unable to meet certain of its needs, there is a strong likelihood that another will supply the missing element. For example, the fact that a variety of donors, in addition to US AID, are prepared to provide contraceptives assures developing countries of a variety of type and brands[13]. US AID, for example, cannot provide Depo Provera (because of U.S. legislation requiring it to observe in its foreign aid programme the same rules that apply to the prescription of drugs within the United States), but the U.K.[14], Pathfinder and IPPF, to mention only a few, can. A similar kind of "dovetailing" is frequently resorted to when a donor cannot meet a specific request under the programme that it is supporting because of its requirements about aid "tying". Thus, when Indonesia wanted condoms from Japan, which could not be provided under the programme of US AID, UNFPA agreed to supply them.

A surprising amount of arrangements of this kind are in fact constantly taking place. IPPF and Pathfinder, for example, rivals in some situations, are found in others, either taking over from each other, when the funding period of the original donor comes to an end, or financing a bridging operation (sometimes for as long as two years) until the funds initially promised can be conveniently made available. Asked if they are prepared to take over projects initially funded by another donor, most agencies' initial response is to say that they are not[15]. Yet, not only do such arrangements seem to be made quite frequently, but much of the pioneering work done by IPPF to demonstrate the feasibility of some new approach or activity is predicated on just this possibility.

The major donors, admittedly, are less likely to take over from each other the funding of major projects, although such situations are not unknown. (When UNFPA announced that it would have to reduce by half its promised contribution to the Government's sterilisation programme in Bangladesh, the World Bank and the bilateral donors associated with it in the IDA Population Project conferred together as to how the shortfall could be made up). In general, it would seem that a donor's willingness to put funds into an activity already supported by another donor is partly a matter of budgetary flexibility, and partly a reflection of its *attitude* and *style*. A considerable amount of "interstitial" financing, if one might call it that, is provided by UNFPA, which unlike some other major donors (and some less major), does not seem to feel any special need for identification with particular projects, or for recognition of its own contribution as donor[16]. In fact, it often seems to prefer *not* to assume the sole external responsibility. (In Kenya, for example, UNFPA decided to use about half of the funds allocated to that country for support of programmes to be financed under the IDA Population Loan).

Who Assists Who?

In terms of the geographical criteria for population assistance, donors' preferences, while they do not coincide, similarly reveal a substantial degree of overlapping. Whatever the particular criteria applied, the countries that are at one and the same time the largest in size, the poorest and the most at risk because of their high rates of population growth have figured high up on most donors' priority list. (The recent accession of China as a new beneficiary of population assistance fits neatly with the prevailing priorities).

The largest priority group is that of UNFPA (40 countries) which, although

---

13. Sometimes too much variety, as US AID, which places bulk purchase orders, has occasionally changed the brands it delivers both to individual countries under its bilateral programmes, and to IPPF for its national Family Planning Associations.

14. ODA stipulates that the recipient government should be aware of the conditions pertaining to its use in the U.K.

15. At least, as it would seem from the interviews carried out by the author of this study.

16. The gift of over $ 15 million of computer equipment and related consultant services to China to assist in the 1982 Census was perhaps an exception to this low-profile approach.

based largely on demographic criteria, ends up as very much the same group as that designated by the U.N. as "the least developed". The World Bank's priority group is smaller (17 "key" countries), and consists essentially of the biggest countries with the biggest population problem (and where Bank assistance is likely to make the maximum global impact[17]). Most of these countries figure also on UNFPA's priority list and are therefore among the poverty group.

The poverty group has tended to be the favourite target for bilateral population assistance too, partly because, historically, the first countries to request population assistance happened to be among the world's poorest (India, Sri Lanka, Kenya, Pakistan and later Bangladesh), and partly because the concern for the relief of poverty, which became so important a consideration in aid policies in the mid-1970s, conveniently focussed donor attention on the very countries most in need of population assistance. Within the poverty group, countries have, of course, their own particular clients: US AID has its own mix of economic and political criteria; the U.K. gives preference to the countries of the Commonwealth (some of which happen also to be amongst the poorest, the biggest, and to have the most serious population problems); Sweden will assist only those countries whose political, economic and social policies it broadly approves of, etc. Both Sweden and Norway, although deeply committed to the cause of "the poorest" (and of population assistance), can only take on a limited number of "partner" countries under their respective country programming arrangements, although initially both Sweden and Norway were prepared to provide population assistance also to countries outside. Norway's partners (9) include a number of African countries that are not interested in population assistance (although they may be in "health", e.g. Botswana, Tanzania), and Sweden's include some countries that are found among everybody's "top ten", plus some others which are not (e.g. Viet Nam).

The donor that stands as an exception to this broad concordance of priorities is the Pathfinder Fund which, faithful to the purpose implied in its name, prefers ideally to concentrate its efforts on Latin America and Africa, where a pioneering role is still called for [18].

For population projects in countries outside the preferred and well-served circle of "the poorest", there are a variety of possible sources of assistance. The most promising are UNFPA, which is prepared to allocate one-third of its budget to countries outside its priority group, and IPPF, which provides funding to some 80 of its over 100 member Associations[19]. But the World Bank has made population loans to as many countries outside its "key" group as within it; US AID provides bilateral population assistance to 20 countries, of which several are outside the poverty group; and the U.K., which declares itself ready to support a population project in any country where there is a need (and with which it has an aid agreement), has population projects in widely-scattered countries outside of the Commonwealth.

With the shortage of funds that donors are facing today, it is possible that the primacy of *need* as the first criterion for population assistance may be challenged by the sometimes opposing one of the *effectiveness* with which the aid input is likely to be used. Thus IPPF, which until recently has distributed its resources on a largely pragmatic basis (an arrangement which tended to favour the more *experienced* of its national Associations), has made the decision to move away from the Associations of relative prosperity in favour of the less experienced and more necessitous newcomers. UNFPA, however, seems to have opted for the opposite approach, by introducing into its criteria

---

17. The Bank has a secondary group of 19 countries.
18. The avoidance of Asian countries, however, is not total: Pathfinder has vigorous programmes in Bangladesh and in Indonesia, for example.
19. Although IPPF, as a private body, is independent of government requests, its member FPAs often co-operate with the government in the national population programme. Some IPPF funding therefore is indirectly assisting the government programme as well as the Association's independent initiatives.

new considerations of *absorptive capacity*, government commitment and the assistance provided by others donors[20].

Big Projects or Small ?

When we look at preferred project size, the differences between donors, again, would seem to be becoming increasingly blurred. The Bank and US AID, big donors, have traditionally been associated with big projects. But the smaller bilateral donors like them too, rather than small ones, which represent a disproportionate administrative burden on limited staff resources. This is increasingly the view taken by NORAD and SIDA, whose smallest population projects are likely to be for several million dollars, but not by ODA, which feels that it can make a special contribution by picking up some of the small and unconsidered trifles (a single consultant assignment, for example) that might be unlikely to interest other donors concerned with broader activities.

Moreover, the big project is itself something of an illusion. One of the most remarkable features of population assistance today is the extraordinarily comprehensive nature of some population projects. A single World Bank project, for example, may include equipment, construction, consultant advice, training, management and logistics support, research and evaluation, and provide support for such varied activities as family planning, health care, information and motivation work, organising religious groups, raising the status of women, community development, youth clubs etc. US AID's population projects are similarly broad in their coverage, although they may be broken down into a number of separate agreements with each of the various implementing agencies concerned. In both cases, however, the likelihood is that if aid for some *small additional* activity should be required, it would be provided by either of these donors within the scope (and budget) of their already approved major population "project".

UNFPA's assistance, on the other hand, is made up of a very large number of separate and often very small projects, each with its own procedural requirements. Under its administrative procedures, UNFPA is obliged to treat each aid activity that it finances as a separate "project", even a simple training attachment or short-term consultant assignment. But the apparent separateness of these arrangements is often as misleading as the apparent "singularity" of the World Bank's population "projects", since UNFPA's individual projects may in fact be component parts of a single broad population programme. In fact, UNFPA has for some time been working to introduce a much greater coherence into its population assistance, and is now preparing country programmes, based on careful sector reviews, in much the same way as the Bank does.

One consequence of this ambiguity as to the size and scope of "projects" is that apart from IPPF and Pathfinder (the latter will fund an activity costing only a few hundred dollars), there is no correlation between agency size and project size. Another is that funds for small-scale experiment and innovation are as likely today to come from the larger donors, who will cover it as part of a major project budget, as from the smaller ones traditionally considered specialist in the path-finding function. For example, the World Bank, which embarked on lending for population with the idea that it would provide the large-scale funding required for replicating programmes that had already proved their usefulness, is now including in one of its Population Projects (Bangladesh) a special sum for funding small experimental projects proposed by *private* agencies.

If aid funding continues to be tight, the differences in function that donors initially ascribed to themselves may well become further obscured. With IDA funds hard to come by, the World Bank, for example, may find countries less keen to turn to it for large-scale programme support, when the price to be paid is a Bank loan at full or medium loan terms. Similarly, at the other end of the scale, donors who have preferred to finance innovation, may find it necessary to provide more of their assistance as

---

20. While both agencies maintain that the revised formulation of their criteria does not mean any significant departure from past practice, the implicit opposition between the two responses is nonetheless of interest.

support for regular government programmes, rather than see some promising endeavour founder for lack of the funds to keep it going. The ease with which donors have adapted their respective aid preferences to actual programme needs could in fact prove to be a major asset.

Is Anything Left Out ?

Reviewing the variegated pattern of donors' likes and dislikes in population assistance, and the way they tend to be applied in actual aid programmes, one is led to wonder whether there are any gaps in programme needs that present donor arrangements do not manage to cover, or cover only inadequately. Do donors between them now provide the full range of support that a government may need to develop the national population programme?

The answer would seem to be not entirely. One area, in particular, where donors have been notably reluctant to venture is that of sector aid for population (normally an arrangement whereby, after agreeing with the government on an overall strategy for a sector, the donor undertakes to provide a certain percentage of its cost). Only Sweden is prepared to assist population programmes in this way and is now providing six countries with sector aid for health and family planning activities jointly. Certain other donors have in fact got near to sector or "programme" aid, although without necessarily accepting the principle. For example, IPPF, which provides each of its member Associations with *budgetary support* for its annual programme of activities as a whole (each one of which must receive its prior approval, irrespective of the sources of financing), is in effect providing programme aid, albeit on a limited scale. And both NORAD and UNFPA have provided the Government of India with support for the national population programme as a whole. These are, however, exceptions, and most donors, even those who have been prepared to make sector aid available in other areas (e.g. agriculture or even health), have shown little inclination to do so for population. This reluctance is the more striking in that the concept of non-project aid seems to be viewed with increasing favour in discussions of the subject in international fora[21], and the view is frequently heard that development does not "happen" by means of projects.

The argument that "population" is not itself a sector can be quickly dismissed as most population programmes today include a wide area of activities along with family planning. A more serious objection is that made by the Bank, which has maintained that as population programmes are relatively new, the governments' policies are not sufficiently well-defined and sound, nor are the necessary local structures and experience available for carrying them out. In the absence of such conditions, and indeed with the express intention of helping to bring them about, the Bank has stuck to project lending for population, with a view to inculcating in the government services concerned the required financial and managerial discipline.

While this was no doubt generally true when the Bank first embarked on lending for population, one might question whether it is necessarily true today - and for all countries alike. In some of the countries which are by now into their second or even third population loan (Indonesia, Malaysia, Tunisia), it is reasonable to assume a fair degree of government commitment, the appropriate structures to be now in place, and a certain degree of experience built up. (If this is not the case, it would suggest that the Bank, by its own reckoning, has partly failed in its purpose).

By reluctance to provide countries with sector aid for combined health and population programmes in countries that might now be ripe for it, it would seem that donors have thereby closed an important door in their own face — namely, the possibility of exercising greater leverage with governments regarding their population strategies and the way in which they should be carried out. Some donors do in fact claim some such right simply by virtue of their project assistance. The World Bank, for example, when it sends its supervision missions to monitor the progress of the Bank-

---

21. For example, in the Development Assistance Committee of the OECD.

financed population project, is at the same time monitoring the progress of the whole national programme of which it is a part. US AID and UNFPA are similarly concerned with the government's population programme as a whole.

Where donors have provided sector aid, they have found that it almost inevitably brings with it a greater involvement in "policy" than was customary under their project assistance. This has not, however, deterred Sweden from accepting the more active role vis-à-vis the partner government that sector aid necessarily confers, despite its well-known views about policy being a matter solely for the government's determination, and population policy, most especially. Sector support for a combined health and population sector would seem to offer the further advantage of encouraging health ministries (traditionally more concerned to prevent deaths than to prevent births) to maintain a better balance between the "family planning" and the "health" aspects of their national programme and budgets.

Given the present emphasis on "policy dialogue", it seems unfortunate that developing country governments should not be given the broad assurance of continuing support that sector aid could provide. Donors certainly have often continued supporting particular countries' population programmes for very considerable periods of time (Sweden, for example, assisted the family planning programme in Sri Lanka from 1958 to 1981, and in India, its support began in 1968 and continued until 1980). Other donors, once committed to a country, similarly tend to make a long stay — partly because of mutual confidence and convenience, but partly also because projects usually take much longer to complete than was originally envisaged and planned for. Support for partial aspects of the programme and for overlapping periods of time, however, does not offer a government the possibilities for confident long-term planning, either for the expansion or even the regular operation of the national population programme as a whole. Yet it may be that the move towards more non-project aid for population would not be so dramatic a change as donors might think. Certainly, the fact that major donors now precede their population assistance to a country by making an intensive sector review, or something akin to it, and others have overall country programmes which are being continuously updated, suggests that the basis for a broader sector approach may already be there. Clearly, the first requirements are a greater degree of donor co-ordination and greater confidence as between donors — two elements which should prove mutually supporting. If aid funds remain tight, donors may find them both becoming inevitable.

II. THE DONORS' VIEWS

The Problems

Although sometimes highly committed to the importance of aid for population, all aid agencies, with the exception of the specialist population bodies, find it particularly difficult. It is surely significant that in no other field have donors chosen to provide so much of their funding through multilateral channels, in preference to financing their own aid programmes in particular developing countries. Even Norway, whose Parliament in 1971 decreed that about 10 per cent of Norwegian aid should be devoted to population activities, and which is thereby the only country to have declared an official aid target for population, by 1980 was giving three-quarters of its population assistance in the form of contributions to multilateral organisations[22].

The declining percentages of bilateral aid for population assistance over the past several years would suggest that the difficulties do not diminish with experience. Many agencies continue to view with suspicion the idea of bilateral aid for population, which, except by the staff immediately concerned, is still largely equated with family planning,

---

22. Comparable figures for other DAC countries in 1980 were: U.K. — 80 per cent; Sweden — approximately two-thirds; US AID—60 per cent (U.S. contributions to UNFPA and IPPF).

and as such considered unsuitable as a field for development assistance. Other and more informed objections that are variously heard are that population projects are difficult to measure, require heavy staff inputs for preparation and appraisal, are geared to unrealistic performance targets, have long lead times, are slow to disburse, and unpredictable as to their results. For some agencies, population projects have the further disadvantage that they do not include enough "hardware", that they often fail to reach the poorest and most vulnerable sections of the population, and are difficult to supervise effectively. As a consequence of this general unpopularity, despite sometimes the most convinced and consistent support for population assistance at the top agency levels (Mr. McNamara of the World Bank was the outstanding, but not the sole example), population projects have never gained much institutional acceptance within an aid agency as a whole. Organised usually on sectoral lines (as are government departments in developing countries), agencies have largely persisted in old-established habits of sectoral thinking, and it has accordingly proved extremely difficult both to insert a population "component" into aid projects in other sectors, and — despite the growing body of opinion that this was a desirable approach — to organize "integrated" projects in which population and other development problems were tackled as a single aid activity.

The agency staff responsible for population work usually share their colleagues' views as to the inherent difficulty of population projects. Indeed, based on their experience of actually implementing such projects in developing countries, they would probably add to the litany a number of additional problems that they have found are likely to be encountered at the receiving end. These habitually begin with the charge of faltering government commitment, and go on to include various deficiencies of organisational structure, managerial experience, administrative skills and competent "human resources" at all levels — in short, the complex of factors that go to make up a government's "absorptive capacity" for handling an aid project.

Reviewing these various problems, a number of questions immediately present themselves: first, to what extent are these problems special to population assistance? second, have aid donors modified their respective aid arrangements and practices in order to accommodate them? and third, are any further special arrangements indicated in order to improve the implementation and effectiveness of population projects?

At the very start, of course, population is "special" in the sensitivity of the subject, and thence, in the particular vulnerability of population projects to cultural and individual attitudes and emotions. This very obvious feature of population activities was not fully appreciated by many donor agencies in the first flush of enthusiasm for population assistance. While today, of course, this is no longer true, donors still perhaps tend to expect too much of the recipient country, and to assume an unrealistic constancy of commitment at all levels of the government, despite political, ethnic and other pressures. Some of the difficulties noted above (including the failure to reach the programme targets) derive in part, at least, from this failure of comprehension.

The other prime characteristic of population activities is their intensely personal character. Few other forms of aid activity are so *person-oriented* and, therefore, require the same high degree of *organisation* and *administrative efficiency* in order to deliver the services provided by the programmes to the intended beneficiary. The "target groups" in population projects are in fact not groups at all, but vast numbers of individuals often living in remote and scattered communities. Moreover, *preventive* programmes having less obvious appeal than other types of community activity, the populations concerned are sometimes not even particularly interested in the new services that are being developed for their benefit. To reach them, persuade them, keep them interested and supplied (and assisted medically should need arise), is far more administration-intensive a task than is common in other social development programmes (in education or rural development for example). Population programmes, or more precisely, family planning programmes which, as we have seen, still constitute their main component, are essentially *person-to-person* activities, involving not only the recruiting and training, but also supervising of great numbers of personnel, many of whom are at a low level of education and skill, and unused to operating in a structured work situation. If donors did not fully appreciate these special difficulties inherent in the very nature of population projects when they first embarked on population assistance, the slow and often disappointing implementation experience of many of their biggest population projects has assuredly brought the necessary understanding since[23]. Indeed, in some agencies it is readily admitted that the failure to take these factors adequately into account at the time of project preparation has been the biggest problem of all.

The following paragraphs review some of the ways in which donors have met the various challenges implied by the "special" nature of population assistance.

The Responses

i) Terms of aid

When they first approached the possibility of providing assistance for population, donors' concern, naturally enough, was to be able to make it available on terms that developing country governments would be likely to accept. Although no exceptional arrangements were made specially for population, the fact that the major recipients were often among the poorer countries enabled many of them to be offered population assistance on what were most agencies' most favourable terms. Thus the World Bank has made IDA credits for population (at 3/4 per cent interest over 50 years) to Bangladesh, India, Kenya, Thailand and the Philippines (First Population Project)[24]. US AID, although obliged to provide some of its development assistance in the form of loans, has successfully kept this requirement down to the minimum in the case of population assistance, and resorted to loan terms only occasionally, and then mainly for the contraceptives supplied to countries which have been long-term beneficiaries of its population assistance: very poor countries continue to receive population assistance entirely in the form of grants. Indeed, population stands out among U.S. aid programmes as being primarily grant-funded. Countries receiving population assistance from the U.K. similarly get it on grant terms, if they are among "the poorest". Others can receive a certain amount of contraceptives, vehicles and equipment on grant terms, as well, of course, as technical assistance which is always grant. In the case of Norway and Sweden, since their bilateral assistance is normally in grant form anyway, no special arrangements for population were necessary.

ii) Local and recurrent costs

Population projects are characterised by a high proportion of local expenditures of all kinds, and particularly of recurrent costs — a function of the peculiarly labour-intensive nature of family planning and related health programmes. For the specialist population agencies, this has presented no problem. UNFPA, for example, (partly because of the way it is itself funded from its member governments), is *pleased* to cover expenditures in local currency. It is quite happy also to include substantial amounts for recurrent cost expenditures (although it would not normally accept a project for recurrent costs alone). IPPF and Pathfinder, being concerned with what are essentially *domestic* programmes, fully expect to pay recurrent costs. In fact, IPPF feels that since its primary concern is to help its member Associations with their total programme of activities, its funding should more appropriately be applied to operating costs than to investment expenditure — an approach in sharp contradistinction to the classical donor view of the purposes of aid financing.

What is remarkable, therefore, is the extent to which other donor agencies have been prepared to adjust their normal aid arrangements to cover the special requirements of population assistance for this form of support.

---

23. As is evident from the comments made by some of the population staffs of the agencies interviewed.

24. The Dominican Republic received a Population Loan from the Bank's Third Window (at 5.6 per cent per annum). Population loans at the World Bank's current lending rates have been made to date to Indonesia, Jamaica, Malaysia, the Philippines (Second Population Project) and South Korea.

The DAC member countries, in the second half of the 1970s, had, with varying degrees of willingness, begun to show a new flexibility in their aid regulations as they came to include in their assistance programmes support for "basic needs" type activities, with their new and different aid requirements. The need for such flexibility was underlined by the issue by the Development Assistance Committee of Guidelines for, first, Local Cost and subsequently, Recurrent Cost Financing, which all DAC countries endorsed. While observance in actual aid programmes has been very varied, population on the whole has tended to be rather well served.

Most notable in this respect has been Sweden, whose whole approach to development co-operation was for years based on the principle of confidence in the partner country, and which accordingly felt that its aid contribution should be for the government to use as it saw fit. Sweden has therefore been prepared to cover *all* the local cost expenditures of population projects if required and, if necessary, the recurrent costs also. (One particularly striking illustration of the flexibility of the Swedish approach is its contribution to the IDA Population Project in Bangladesh, which is paid in convertible currency into the Government's account, for it to use to make up its own contribution to the Project. The Government of Bangladesh, not surprisingly, wishes that all its donors would behave in the same way[25].

Norway, similarly, says that it has gone further than the DAC Guidelines in some of its population projects, and has sometimes financed *all* the local costs, including such recurrent costs as the government has been unable to meet itself.

US AID has also shown itself sympathetic. It normally requires the government to put up at least 25 per cent of the total costs of a project, which means that it is itself prepared to cover a substantial portion of the cost in local currency; but where the 25 per cent requirement has been difficult for a government to meet, US AID has sometimes been prepared to waive it. Occasionally, it has accepted population projects consisting almost entirely of recurrent costs.

ODA, despite its acceptance of the DAC Guidelines, is more chary. It recognizes that a certain amount of local costs have to be accepted for social development projects (including population), and although it has agreed to finance a substantial amount of local costs in a project (special Treasury authorisation had to be obtained)[26], it dislikes it, and has now set a ratio for each country for local to recurrent costs, based on its economic situation, and applicable to all sectors alike. As for recurrent costs, the U.K. is still reluctant, on the grounds that these are properly the responsibility of the government. It may be prepared to accept them in exceptional circumstances and for limited periods, but is careful not to take on what might turn out to be an open-ended commitment.

The agency which has perhaps gone furthest in modifying its normal aid requirements in favour of population is the World Bank, accustomed to lending for the foreign exchange costs of infrastructure projects. As it came to make loans for social development projects also (including population), the Bank found itself obliged to apply its lending rules with a wholly new flexibility. Initially, like ODA, it had to advance special justification for including local cost expenditures. Later, it too set a percentage of allowable local costs for each borrowing country. While these arrangements were not introduced specifically for population, it is generally considered that it was population that led the way. The Bank's lending rules normally exclude recurrent costs altogether, but the Bank soon extended its coverage of local costs to include, under its population

---

25. Latterly, the Swedish Aid Authority (SIDA), has come to feel that its deliberately liberal approach has perhaps encouraged undue laxity at the recipient end, and that a tighter degree of donor control (what it terms "concerned participation") would not only enable the Swedish Government to follow more closely how its aid money is being spent, but would contribute to more effective project implementation as well.

26. The U.K. has currently one very big population project (the Orissa Project in India, £ 11.8 million) which is all local currency. This, however, is a special case, being funded out of part of India's debt arrears, after donors agreed to waive the outstanding debt of very poor countries under the Retrospective Terms Adjustment.

loans, various *incremental* operating costs also, which it was held the government would have to assume in order to implement the project (e.g. salaries of additional staff, training stipends, the costs of running additional vehicles, etc...). By this decision, the Bank was in fact opening the door very wide, the distinction between costs of this kind and the regular operating costs of a national programme being a fine one. The Bank has shown itself very flexible in the matter of interpretation, particularly for very poor countries with severe budgetary problems. Its practice of making second and third generation loans has, moreover, made it easier to carry recurrent costs as part of project implementation expenditures.

The underlying problem in the long-term is the likelihood of the recipient country being eventually able to handle its population programmes on its own. All donors, in theory, maintain that their assistance is designed to that end, by providing facilities and services that governments should be able to replicate and operate from their own resources. Donors are, of course, well aware that to accustom governments to look to foreign aid to cover a large proportion of staff salaries runs counter to the goal of self-reliance, or at the least defers its attainment. Some donors are accordingly firm about requiring governments progressively to take over recurrent costs and particularly salaries. (The Bank, for example, expects even the hard-pressed Government of Bangladesh to take over a growing proportion each year of the salaries and training costs of the 13,000 field-workers covered by the IDA Project). Most other donors, even if they write into their aid agreements that the government will assume responsibility for the project's recurrent costs on a phased basis (and not all of them invariably do — NORAD, for example, sometimes has not), have usually accepted the situation, if the government has proved unable to comply. Some donors (NORAD, SIDA, UNFPA) are now beginning to feel that they have been over-lenient in this respect, and have encouraged governments in bad habits both of dependence and lack of financial discipline. As aid funds get tighter, donors may be expected to become increasingly rigorous in requiring government "performance" as a condition of continuing aid disbursements.

Most donors would probably maintain that they would not agree to fund any project that was not likely to be sustainable once the aid input ceases. Most donors would also maintain, however, that this is so much a counsel of perfection that neither they nor the recipient even try to take it seriously. Despite great exercises of project appraisal, there is very little attempt to make any careful calculation either of the future operating costs of a proposed project in relation to its capital cost, or in relation to the government's likely budgetary possibilities[27]. Some of the reasons given are curious — for example, that this is for the government to work out, or that inflation in developing countries makes it impossible to anticipate realistically. The Bank, which does make some calculations of this kind, but admits that they are approximate only, maintains that in any case one effect of Bank population loans to a country is to increase the government's budgetary contribution to the health and population sector.

iii) Salaries and salary supplements

The biggest single element of local expenditure in population programmes is salary payments for local staff. Once having accepted the principle, donors have generally proved very liberal about financing them. Some (UNFPA, the Bank, US AID) have been prepared to cover the salaries of thousands of field-workers, in addition to paying for key project posts, something that most donors are prepared to do on occasion.

A more tricky problem is the payment of salary supplements, either as compensation to ill-paid government servants for assuming important project responsibilities, or as encouragement for service in rural areas, or as incentives to field-workers. Donors have mixed reactions. The World Bank, for example, is very ready (in all sectors)

---

27. The Bangladesh Planning Commission says that it has vetoed a lot of construction proposals, because it knows it would be unable to pay the salaries of all the staff that would be required to man them.

to pay salary supplements to attract talent to work on the Bank's projects (although it respects government policy on the subject), and UNFPA will sometimes attribute to senior staff certain "incremental functions" for which they can receive compensation (though in principle, it tries to limit salary supplements to 25 per cent of the corresponding government scale). US AID, on the other hand, is in principle opposed to any payments which would distort the government's regular salary structure, although it has occasionally made exceptions. ODA is also against incremental payments for local staff (although it is still making them to expatriates under the Overseas Service Aid Scheme).

Within the developing countries themselves, opinions are divided as to the desirability of donors paying preferential salary rates for work on their respective projects. Governments maintain that officials cannot be expected to assume important new responsibilities under a project (or at least to discharge them effectively) unless they are remunerated accordingly. At the same time, they are disturbed at the distortion of the national salary structure and at the emergence of a sought-after, donor-paid élite within the civil service. Donor-paid national "consultants" cause particular controversy, some people maintaining that the practice is encouraging "self-reliance", is an imaginative use of local resources and experience etc., while others resent it for the glaring differentials between consultant and national salary levels[28].

Since, however, developing countries' populations are continuing to grow, their needs for family planning and related programmes will continue to grow also. For many countries, and not only the very poor, this means that population assistance will continue to be required for a long time yet, not only to pay for the imports of contraceptives and equipment that the country cannot produce itself, but also to finance the enormous numbers of personnel who will be required to provide the services. The implications would seem to be, therefore, that it behoves donors to apply themselves to the question of how to make a more scientific calculation of whether the population programmes that they are assisting can be self-sustainable and in how long a period of time.

iv) Administrative and managerial capability

Although donors recognize that the administrative and managerial capability of the recipient country institutions is likely to be the key factor in the effectiveness with which their population assistance is implemented, they have been slow in coming to grips with the problem.

Some donors have a formal requirement to include an assessment of the capacity of the proposed implementing unit as part of the project appraisal exercise (UNFPA, US AID)[29], and some others (the World Bank and SIDA) also examine it with varying degrees of elaborateness. Even the World Bank, however, which regularly includes it as one of the elements to be covered in its appraisal reports, admits that it does not look at the likely administrative capacity of the potential borrower with anything like the rigour with which it examines its economic capacity.

One difficulty, as several donors have observed, is that there are few criteria for objective assessment. In the absence of quantifiable indicators, therefore, the approach must be largely subjective. Moreover, even if the exercise is undertaken with serious concern, as is today increasingly the case, no one can claim with certitude to know what the recipe for good management actually *is*, in any particular set of circumstances. Further, as donors again readily admit, to study the problem in the requisite depth, devise solutions and wait for the recommended structures to be put in place and start functioning, before allowing assistance to begin, would impose extensive delays on the

---

28. Perhaps unreasonably: private sector consultants in developing countries can often command fees comparable to those paid by international organisations.

29. Respectively, the Instructions for the Preparation of a Project Proposal, and the U.S. Congress's instructions to US AID to pay more attention to the administrative capacity of aid recipients among the poorer developing countries.

start of operations. For a number of reasons, neither donor nor recipient is usually willing to take that risk[30]. Even in cases where they have been aware, therefore, that the available administrative structures and experience were inadequate, donors have preferred to go ahead and get the programme started, in the hope that these would improve in the process of implementation, and that both donor and recipient would learn from experience and do better the next time round. (This is a view held notably by the World Bank, with its practice of making second and sometimes third generation loans, while the preceding one is still only part way through).

In its early population loans, the Bank tried to assure effective implementation of its projects by setting up special Project Implementation Units within the user department (current Bank practice in other sectors). Intended originally to manage the large civil works components of the projects (for which health ministries, unused to construction projects of such magnitude, generally lacked the necessary resources and experience), these Units, with staff paid by the Bank and with ample Bank funds at their disposal, came to occupy an anomalous position within the health ministry, and even in some countries to be more influential than the ministry itself. In all countries where such a Unit was established, it caused bitter (and lingering) resentment, although the Bank has since abandoned the arrangement. The Bank says that implementation of its projects has often slowed down in consequence.

Disappointment at the progress of implementation of a number of major population projects has eventually led all donors to the rueful recognition that it was necessary to take steps to assure a certain degree of implementing capability at the receiving end *before* starting operations. All donors have therefore been taking the problem much more seriously in recent years, sometimes including in their appraisal of the project specialist studies of various aspects of its implementation needs (e.g. training, logistics, etc.). In some cases, they are now making the strengthening of the administrative and managerial capacity of the implementing unit an important component of the project.

For some donors this has meant overcoming an initial delicacy of feeling about intervention in the machinery and processes of a developing country government[31]. This is the case notably of Norway and Sweden, and also of the U.K., which has been particularly hesitant for fear of being accused of lingering colonial attitudes (but which has nonetheless included a management study in its Project in Orissa). Other donors have not shared these inhibitions. The World Bank in particular has not hesitated to require major reorganisations of the structure of the administration, not only to assure the implementation of "the Bank project", but also that of the whole of the national population programme of which it is part. Certainly, as the range of the Bank's population assistance has widened, the organisation of project implementation has become increasingly complicated. Today, the user departments have been extended way beyond the health ministry (or family planning board), and may embrace the departments of social affairs, education, information, labour, rural development, etc. as well. Orchestrating these various power and interest groups adds a formidable new dimension to the problems of implementation. The Bank's attempts to resolve these problems by urging new structural arrangements within the machinery of government leads to criticism, not that it necessarily goes too far in its recommendations, nor that they were inappropriate, but that it does not allow them time to prove themselves before coming forward with alternative proposals.

All the major donors, where they have been large-scale contributors to a population programme, have variously had a significant influence on the institutional

---

30. Both donors and recipient fear to lose the initial momentum. Donors, in addition, are often under pressure from their own management to go ahead and make new projects, as well as being moved by the sincere belief that the very urgency of the problem justifies speed of action, even in the absence of some of the necessary conditions.

31. The IPPF is perhaps fortunate in this regard, since its "clients" are not sovereign governments but member Associations of the Federation, and as such, although independent, subject to some central guidance and control.

arrangements of the government departments concerned. In this respect, it would seem that a certain tacit division of labour as between donors' respective spheres of influence has generally been observed. Thus US AID, for example, played a major role in building up the managerial as well as technical strength of the newly-created Indonesian National Family Planning Co-ordinating Board (BKKBN), including helping it to simplify its linkages with other departments of government. UNFPA has done much the same for the Population and Family Planning Board of Egypt. Sometimes, too, the necessity to tackle the practical needs of project implementation has led to donors, almost inadvertently, making a major technical contribution to the national programme as a whole, as when US AID helped BKKBN to set up its data collection and logistics system in Indonesia, and the World Bank did something similar for the Population Programme in Bangladesh.

v) Maintenance

One area where it would seem that donors could make a greater contribution than in the past to developing countries' eventual self reliance is that of maintenance. With the exception of the World Bank^{32}, which has institutionalised attention to this problem as part of its post-audit procedures, donors have been somewhat slow to give the problem of maintenance the attention that it requires. Donors, as much as developing countries, have found it easier (and perhaps more impressive) to provide new buildings rather than to insist on the maintenance of existing ones. Admittedly, population assistance is today increasingly providing for the renovation and rehabilitation of existing facilities. Some donors (the World Bank and the U.K. to cite just two examples) have included facilities for training in maintenance of both buildings and vehicles in some of their population projects. There has been discussion also (in the Development Assistance Committee) of greater aid for maintenance and related training, as a form of non-project assistance. However, donors still make little systematic effort to check on the state of the buildings that they have financed, whether new construction or renovation, once construction has been completed. Certainly, they rarely, if ever, require proof of reasonable maintenance of the facilities they have already financed, as a condition of providing the country with some more^{33}. To encourage developing countries to become more maintenance-conscious and exercise greater discipline in this regard, would seem an elementary form of good housekeeping.

vi) Training

In all aid sectors, donors traditionally assume that the chief insufficiency of developing countries in respect of their "human resources" lies in technical skills, and they orient their training efforts accordingly. (US AID, for example, has provided advanced professional training for all the staff presently occupying senior positions with the BKKBN in Indonesia). Other donors, although they also generously fund training at senior level, do not generally do so in order to "groom" individuals for specific project posts, but prefer their training to be less "personalised".

But population assistance is perhaps special in the very large amount of training effort directed also to the sub-professional personnel required for actual service delivery at the client level. US AID and UNFPA in particular devote a considerable part of their population assistance to training large numbers of paramedical staff at all levels,

---

32. The Bank's "Project Performance Units", whose task is to check on the results of Bank projects, five years or so after completion, does include examination of maintenance, but it clearly cannot check on every facility nation-wide. Moreover, only 5 audits of population projects have been made to date.

33. They do not usually go and look, partly because the facilities are widely scattered throughout the country, and partly because agency staff, whether in the field or at headquarters, do not have the time.

including field staff[34]. The programmes of the World Bank and SIDA also have included substantial amounts of training for staff at the village level.

Despite the size of these training efforts, donors have generally been very tardy about making systematic efforts to evaluate the results. When they have had occasion to do so (and not always by design), the results have sometimes been disappointing. Either the government has failed to deploy the personnel as intended, or the staff, without satisfactory supervision, have proved unable to apply the skills they have been taught, or, at the higher levels (Asian doctors and nurses in particular), they have been lured away by the high salaries offered by the countries of the Middle East. The problem of the brain drain is clearly a particularly difficult one, for which there are no ready solutions. Taking the training effort overall, however, it would seem that more consistent arrangements are required to monitor the results of training as an integral part of project operations. To leave this monitoring to the national authorities concerned, as donors have been inclined to do, would seem to be imposing an unrealistic burden on an administration dealing often with a new programme and wholly new responsibilities.

In population projects, as indeed in aid in most other sectors also, training has been so heavily concentrated on the technical skills required that donors have tended often to overlook the management and administrative skills that are also required to implement a project or operate a national programme. Fellowships may be offered to senior staff in advanced management training etc., but the humbler skills that are indispensable to keep an activity going, book-keeping, record-keeping, procurement etc. — skills chronically in short supply in developing countries — are for the most part not included in the scope of the assistance.

The explanation is perhaps simply that donor agencies habitually operate at senior government levels, at which these more routine requirements are unlikely to come up for discussion. (As several donor agencies admit, they only begin to notice them once they find things going wrong in the course of implementation: then they may provide the services of an expert to straighten out the problem or train the local staff, or do both). The usual donor attitude, however, has been to leave the mobilisation of the necessary administrative substructure for the government to take care of.

Donors do, of course, make sporadic attacks on the problem of supporting skills — as difficulties arise, normally in the context of the particular aid project concerned[35]. The problem is rarely, however, tackled on the broader basis of strengthening the government's stock of such skills for the requirements of the administration as a whole. This may be one further consequence of the habit of *sectoral* thinking among donors. With the increasing recognition of the importance of administrative and managerial capability, perhaps it is time that donors considered the creation of an independent aid sector (and corresponding agency department) for public administration, which could help developing country governments to develop the staff skills needed for planning and operating development programmes and basic government services, not only at the senior echelons, but at the supporting middle and lower levels as well.

vii) Counterpart personnel and key project posts

Donors may or may not specify in their aid agreements that national "counterparts" are to be provided to work with (and presumably be trained by) foreign experts provided by the donors. Either way, they are realistic enough to recognize that the government will only produce them if it has the staff available and considers that

---

34. US AID, which is arranging training for large numbers of district-level staff for the Government's Population Programme in Bangladesh, is concluding the training course with three weeks with the BKKBN in Indonesia. This exercise in Developing Country Technical Co-operation has included bringing over from Bangladesh a large group of mullahs, with the idea of educating them by contact with their Islamic brethren who are supportive of family planning.

35. IPPF has organised workshops in some countries for field staff, at district and even village level, in such subjects as basic record-keeping, accounting, clinic-patient relationships etc.

particular project a priority. (They have sometimes had the experience of the government complying with the formal requirement by fielding the same official to serve as a counterpart simultaneously for several different population projects supported by different donor agencies).

The problem is more serious when there is no foreign "expert" involved, and the government is required to appoint qualified officials to fill key project posts. (The Bank's loan agreements, for example, normally require the post to be filled within 90 days). Donors generally specify the qualifications required and the terms of reference for the post, but leave the selection to the government. The problem lies not in the qualifications of the government's nominees, but in the fact that sometimes a government is unable to nominate anyone at all, or else that the official, once nominated and approved, leaves the post. In such cases, donors have found that there is little they can effectively do[36].

III. RECIPIENTS' VIEWS

The one constantly recurring comment that developing country officials make today about the various donor agencies that provide them with population assistance is not so much that they are assertive, exacting or even uncomprehending, but that they are impatient. After, in many cases, considerable experience of working together with particular donors, government officials in most countries seem reasonably confident that the broad strategies behind the population programmes that donors are assisting are their own choice and not donor-imposed[37], and that donors generally understand the principal problems that the government is up against. Nevertheless, the general complaint is that donors rarely allow sufficient time for their solution. This is not, of course, the only criticism of donors' attitudes and of the way in which their population assistance is delivered. It is, however, one of the most frequently heard.

The following paragraphs examine donors' aid procedures and practice in respect of programming; project preparation; field missions; consultants; procurement; disbursement; reporting, accounting and auditing; and also their arrangements for co-ordination of their population activities with those of other donors.

Programming

From the recipient country's point of view, the prime consideration in its relations with its donors is whether it can count on them to continue providing support, as promised, throughout the life of a project. The second is the likelihood of assistance being made available for new projects, as new needs arise.

With regard to the first point, it is to be noted that although donors have everywhere been talking of budgetary constraints, none, with the exception of UNFPA, have to date been obliged to cut back on their promises of support for a major population programme. This is the more remarkable in view of the fact that apart from the World Bank, all the agencies providing population assistance are themselves funded on an annual basis.

The bilaterals providing population assistance apply their normal programming arrangements as for aid in any other sector. Only very few donors (Sweden is one) are able to make legally-binding commitments for more than one year[38]. The others agree

---

36. In Kenya, for example, the post of Head of the Information and Education Division of the Programme was never filled for the whole life of the project, while that of Head of the Family Planning Centre was filled by a succession of different people for the first several years.

37. Not so true in the past, when donors tended to rush precipitously forward with population assistance before governments had had time to formulate their own population strategies, or even, in some cases, to consolidate the intention to carry out a national population policy.

38. UNICEF, however, can commit funds for three years and has on occasion given a country a pledge for five.

to provide funding for multi-year projects on the understanding that the amounts required for the activity in each successive year will in fact be forthcoming, although US AID and UNFPA's commitment to support projects extending over several years are made explicitly "subject to availability of funds". So far, recipients have found this de facto assurance of continuing support fully adequate.

Most donors' programming arrangements also allow them to accommodate good requests for new projects with varying degrees of ease. Thus, UNFPA's five-year country programmes are sufficiently broadly based as to constitute virtually an "umbrella agreement", within which specific projects are later worked out in consultation with the government and any UN specialised agency that may be involved (as source of technical expertise and subsequent "executing agency"). The bilaterals' country agreements cover aid for a given period in all sectors, and these are followed by further agreements covering population assistance, which are sometimes also in the nature of umbrella agreements. This is notably the case with US AID, which not infrequently commits an amount of money to a country to support its population programme without necessarily spelling out in advance all the specific purposes for which it is to be used. Discussions with the government may continue for some time on the details of the activities on which the allocation is to be spent. SIDA, whose "rolling" three-year country agreements are updated each year in annual consultations with the government, also provides a considerable margin for flexibility in the actual population activities to be supported, by means of the sector agreements which it makes for health and family planning activities over a broad front. In all these cases, while some of the total amount allocated will necessarily be applied to ongoing projects, the rest is available for new activities as may be subsequently agreed.

The opposite approach is taken by the World Bank, IPPF[39] and the Pathfinder Fund, all of which specify clearly at the outset the particular activities to which their assistance is to be replied. However, it is simple for IPPF and Pathfinder to look at new requests in each year's budget submission, while the World Bank, as previously noted, is often prepared to make a loan for a new and bigger project, while the current one is only part-way through.

The formal agreements covering population assistance vary as to the amount of detail that they include from one extreme to the other — not, as might perhaps be expected, according to different donors' aid practices, but according to the circumstances of the particular activity. Thus in the early days of project assistance, donors tended to draft agreements in such a way as to leave no ambiguity as to what the money was to be spent on. (One early Norwegian agreement for a population project went so far as to specify the amount that each clinic could spend on electricity). With increasing experience of population assistance, however, donors have come to recognize the need to allow for flexibility in implementation, and to draft their project agreements much less tightly. The same tendency is to be seen in the World Bank's loan agreements for population projects, which sometimes describe the activity to be financed in remarkably general terms, and leave the detail for working documents. (The Loan Agreement for the Second Population Project to India barely does more than indicate the broad project purposes).

In the matter of aid agreements, as in so many other aspects of donor-recipient relations, a donor's "style" is, to a considerable extent, a function of its *confidence* in the recipient's ability to handle the project and the aid funds provided for it.

Project Preparation

Developing countries commonly complain of the length and complication of donor agencies' processes of project appraisal. Here, it would seem that it is the developing countries themselves who are being impatient, since in some cases the

---

39. IPPF has recently introduced a system of "rolling" three-year programming also, as the basis of the annual budget requests by the member Associations. It will come into operation in 1984.

government's own procedures for approval of a new project and including it in the development budget are just as protracted[40]. What they find irksome is usually less the length of time involved than the heavy work input, and the demands that this imposes on already over-burdened government officials.

Curiously, developing country officials have not, as might have been expected, seemed unduly troubled by the differences in donors' respective requirements in the matter of the information and manner of presentation for a project request[41] – though whether this is because they have by now come to accept this as part of the price to be paid for development co-operation, or, more simply, because different officials tend to work with different donors, is difficult to guess. Certainly they recognize that each donor's requirements are designed so as to satisfy its own board of management of the soundness of the project proposal.

The non-specialist donors of population assistance all bring to the appraisal of population projects the same criteria and approaches as for their aid in other sectors, although they may apply them with varying degrees of flexibility. (Even the World Bank, which is often criticised for approaching the appraisal of a population project with much the same techniques as for a power plant, forbears to apply the criterion of cost-benefit, although it does try to demonstrate "cost-effectiveness"). Whatever the particular criteria used, however, the process of preparing a project proposal in such a way as to satisfy the particular agency's requirements for approval is almost invariably a formidable and time-consuming task for both donor and recipient.

The Bank maintains that the work of project preparation and appraisal is particularly labour-intensive in the case of population projects because of the "fluidity" of the sector and the lack of established methodologies. Certainly, the whole process, in the case of the Bank, is extremely demanding. It begins with an intensive sector study (UNFPA will have got this out of the way before preparing the country programme), and then goes on to a mammoth operation of data collection for the preparation of the project request, followed by a further lengthy exercise of project appraisal. The task of project appraisal is, of course, that of the Bank, but the responsibility for preparation of the project request is considered that of the government. In fact, it involves a tremendously exhaustive and exhausting effort on both sides[42]. The Bank maintains that this whole process takes about two years (the preparation of the First Bank Population Loan to Egypt is said to have required some 18 missions over a period of three years)[43].

The criticism is frequently heard that the Bank's population projects end up as being "over-designed". But other donors are also often extremely careful about the preparation of the project request. SIDA, for example, will sometimes spend two years on a major new request for a population project. US AID's requirements for the preparation of a project request end up in a basic "project document" which, if not as lengthy as a Bank report, is nonetheless a highly detailed description of the purposes and scope of the project, its inputs, implementation, scheduling, conditions, etc. So labour-intensive is the task of preparing the "project paper" that US AID often engages a specialist consulting firm to assist it. The Bank will advance funds out of the loan for this purpose – but to enable the *government* to hire extra staff or consultants to help it in the task.

---

40. They are also sometimes just as exacting. The Planning Commission of Bangladesh, for example, sent back for revision the proposed first IDA Population Project five times over a period of 28 months, and *after* the Bank had agreed the design for the project.

41. Or at least have not stressed it as a problem in the course of the present enquiry.

42. In the case of the preparation of the Second Health and Population Project in Kenya, an unusually difficult one, by the time of the author's visit in June 1981, the Government had prepared four drafts of the project request, in response to specific Bank requirements, which had been followed by the appraisal report prepared by the Bank team. The Kenyan officials involved were divided between admiration at the Bank team's round-the-clock working stints, and annoyance that they were expected to share them.

43. By the time the project appraisal report and draft loan agreement reach the Bank's Board of Executive Directors, the massive preceding input of effort has virtually guaranteed approval.

In practice, the extent to which the government concerned takes a substantive role in the drafting of the project request seems to vary considerably. Developing country officials recognize that the whole process of project preparation and appraisal is very educative and a valuable discipline for government planners. They not infrequently find, however, that donors' information requirements, based on their standard requirements for presentation of a project request, are often unrealistic as regards the reliability or even the availability of all the data demanded.

The Scandinavian donors are generally more understanding of the burden implied for the recipient country's administration in having to prepare a project request in the form the donor habitually requires. Thus NORAD was prepared to accept a request from the Government of Bangladesh submitted according to the Government's format for presenting a project for inclusion in the national budget. SIDA, also, is trying progressively to lighten its requirements in respect of the information and background documentation to be supplied. If it is satisfied as to the government's commitment, it is sometimes prepared to undertake itself the work of collecting the necessary background data, formulating the proposal and even preparing the project request.

Although the work burden for the recipient ceases with the presentation of the request to the donor's headquarters, there may still be a considerable wait before approval is finally given and work may start. In most cases, a small project will be approved quicker than a big one, which may have to obtain special top-level approval. UNFPA, for example, has to get the approval of the Governing Council for anything over $1 million, and NORAD has to get Cabinet approval for each major project, and parliamentary approval for very important ones. This obligation does not, however, necessarily delay the start of implementation. UNFPA, for example, exceptionally can authorize work to begin, up to a certain amount, pending formal approval of the

Small donors, as might be expected, can handle their usually much smaller requests with considerably greater speed. The Pathfinder Fund, for example, can process a project from inception of the idea up to final approval (including that of US AID for projects over $50,000) in from two to five months. US AID itself, however, is obliged to go through the hoops of its regular project procedures, even for the preparation of an activity costing only $100,000.

Most donors have the possibility of speeding up the process of project preparation and approval in cases of particular urgency and for "repeat" projects. Thus the World Bank made its Second ($46 million) Population Loan to India in 17 months. US AID can sometimes approve a "repeat" under a special procedure in as little as three months, although in other cases repeats have taken as much as a year.

It is not possible to make any precise comparisons as to the time taken by different donors of population assistance in the total process of project preparation and approval. One problem is to determine at what point the process may be said actually to start. In some cases, particularly if the donor has an active resident mission in the country, discussions may be well advanced on an informal basis well before any official approach is made to request financing. Further, although donors have their respective practices and procedures, which may be more or less time-consuming, they are all prepared to move faster when the field is familiar. Similarly, all tend to go slower in cases of doubt. (Norway, for example, not normally considered over-exacting in this regard, took three-and-a-half years before finally agreeing to the *extension* of its support for the Post-Partum Programme in India). It would seem, therefore, that the determining factor in how long a country may have to wait for approval in any particular case is determined very much by the circumstances of the project. If the donor has doubts about the proposal, it will inevitably be more cautious, sending more appraisal missions and demanding more data, than when it feels confident that the project is a good one, and that the necessary structures and experience are available for carrying it out.

Some donor agencies include in their agreements a proviso that disbursements can only start after certain specified undertakings by the government have been completed. The World Bank makes these a condition of its loans becoming effective. US AID specifies (not necessarily in the agreement itself but often in the accompanying letter which sets out all the conditions for project implementation) the actions that the government is expected to take to enable the project to start, normally allowing 90 days for the purpose (although, legally, disbursements can begin as soon as the agreement is signed). Other donors (UNFPA, NORAD, for example) usually make no conditions at all, and sometimes actually start making the first payments upon signature of the agreement and without waiting for the government to take whatever steps may be indispensable to get the work started (such as acquiring land or recruiting staff, for example).

In practice, it would seem that it makes very little difference whether the donor makes these a legal stipulation or not. The Bank, which does, had to delay the becoming effective of its First Population Project in India by a year, while its second and third loans to Indonesia began only two months after approval by the Board. UNFPA, which does not, has not only had some of its projects delayed for years because of the failure of the government to take the necessary initial action, but sometimes had meanwhile gone ahead and placed orders for equipment. In some cases, the explanation may be lack of commitment on the part of the government: in others, a lack of comprehension on the part of the donor of the practical difficulties of doing sometimes seemingly simple things in the particular political and other conditions of the developing country concerned — an example of donor "impatience", in fact.

Field Missions

Given the complexity of population projects, developing countries find the process of implementation is greatly assisted by the presence of a permanent donor aid mission to provide continuing contact and help in dealing with the unexpected. Only US AID and UNFPA maintain specialist population staff on their field missions. The World Bank has a Population Officer in Bangladesh for the co-ordination of the multi-donor IDA Project (the cost is met in part out of the bilaterals' contribution to the project), but not in other countries[44].

In this area of assistance, the donor arrangements that developing countries like best are those of UNICEF, which delegates a very wide area of decision-making responsibility to its field offices, once a country programme has been approved. Among our group of donors, the most decentralized are SIDA, which as a matter of policy, wants to bring "decision-making about Swedish aid, and responsibility for programme implementation closer to the scene in the developing country, where the relevant information is available"[45], and US AID, which delegates to the directors of its field missions a very wide degree of authority to make new financial commitments (now up to $20 million). (The extent to which this applies to population projects of course varies very much with the individual Mission Director, the mission strength and the importance of the population staff). The other extreme of management style is that of the World Bank, which operates through periodic missions sent out from headquarters, and by correspondence. The other donors come at various points in between[46].

For the recipient country, almost as important as the formal degree of authority delegated to field missions by the headquarters agency is the attitude of the individual population officer. There have been cases where the relationship between government and donor mission has changed radically following a transfer of personnel, bringing with it different personalities and approaches. To an extent, the attitudes of field staff reflect those of agency headquarters (for example, NORAD and SIDA staff are likely to take a sympathetic approach, since their respective agencies' aid philosophy is based

---

44. The Bank for a time had Population Officers in India and Indonesia, but the Banks' Resident Missions in those countries felt that the size of the population projects did not warrant a staff member for Population alone, and preferred to reallocate the posts to other sectors.

45. Statement made to the Development Assistance Committee.

46. IPPF has no local representation, the national Family Planning Associations in developing countries being independent bodies.

on confidence in the partner country). Where the aid agency is more centralised and bureaucratic, and has a large number of procedural requirements to be satisfied, the attitude of the field mission in interpreting them may be all-important. This is notably the case with US AID and UNFPA. For example, in some countries where the US AID population officer is a stickler for the rules (or has less than full confidence in the recipient government), government officials describe US AID as "painfully bureaucratic": in others, where he is more performance-minded and concerned to keep things moving, US AID is held up as a model of flexibility ("a simple phone call to the Mission is all that is needed").

Should it prove necessary to modify a project in the course of implementation (which, in the case of population projects, is more likely than not), US AID Mission Directors have recently been empowered to increase the amount of funding initially approved for a project by as much as 100 per cent (up to a ceiling of $20 million) and to extend the life of a project for up to 10 years. SIDA also allows its field missions full authority to re-allocate funds in any way that may be needed, even as between aid sectors, and to prolong aid agreements. UNFPA, on the other hand, allows its Co-ordinators only limited decision-making authority (up to 10 per cent within project categories). Although New York will usually accept the recommendation of the man-on-the-spot, the necessity to refer back to headquarters on even small matters (characteristic also of the U.K. and the World Bank) is resented by developing countries, partly for the delays involved, but also for the fact that it often requires them to write an official letter of request. Donors perhaps under-estimate the effort that this may represent for developing country officials (particularly since letters have usually to be written in the working language of the donor).

All donors' field missions assist with the practical problems of implementation, explaining their respective procedural requirements and helping with procurement, contracting, and preparation of progress reports and requests for disbursement. US AID can obviously provide the most help, partly because of its very large staff resources (at one time it was maintaining one officer in the field to two in Headquarters), and also because its management style (and often ability of the staff to work in the local language) enables it to operate at the middle level and in the field. Developing country governments appreciate the assistance that the US AID missions can provide, particularly in guiding them through the thickets of US AID's complex procedural requirements, but sometimes find the constant attention to the details of project implementation somewhat excessive — particularly the availability of mission staff to take off and look at projects anywhere and at any time!

One way in which countries find field missions an advantage is that they normally mean fewer special missions sent out from headquarters. The World Bank, without field representation, sends the most frequent, largest and the longest-staying visiting missions. US AID, on the other hand, uses its field staff for its rigorous and time-consuming exercise of project identification, supervision and evaluation, and does not, therefore, need to send many missions from Washington. UNFPA, similarly, only sends an occasional visitor from New York. NORAD and SIDA use their respective field staffs for low-key project monitoring, and to participate in the annual consultations, but may also send out specialist missions for appraising new projects and for project review. However, the presence of a field mission to provide the initial briefing at least relieves the host government's officials to a certain extent. Overall, there are still many more visiting missions (most of which require to see the same government officials) than developing countries can reasonably cope with. (The Deputy Secretary in charge of the national population programme in Bangladesh, for example, reckoned that at least 50 per cent of his time was devoted to receiving visitors).

Consultants

Whereas population assistance used to include large numbers of foreign consultants, they are not today an important feature of most population projects, except for short-term experts in specialised fields (communications, for example). Developing countries generally dislike foreign experts in population activities, partly because of their high cost (the Government of Bangladesh claims that a World Bank expert costs some fifteen times the salary of a corresponding Government official), and partly because with increasing experience they often feel that local expertise is likely to be just as good and probably more relevant. Nevertheless, a foreign consultant in a key project role can sometimes offer certain advantages over a national official. As an outsider, he is often better placed to see the whole picture, is not simultaneously preoccupied with other official responsibilities, and has the independence that may permit him to take initiatives and overcome bureaucratic obstacles in a way that a national might hesitate to do.

UNFPA, the World Bank and US AID used to be particularly criticised for making their population assistance consultant-heavy. UNFPA sometimes still is — particularly when a specialised agency of the UN is also involved. (Countries feel that the intervention of a specialised agency as source of expertise makes for an unnecessary additional layer of bureaucracy: they would prefer to go direct to the agency for recommendations, and then hire the consultants themselves). In the case of the World Bank, their consultants are not only more expensive than those of the UN, but their cost will eventually have to be repaid as part of the loan.

Where US AID includes consultants in its population projects, the recruitment process is nearly always particularly time-consuming because of the complicated contracting procedures. Contracts are a characteristic feature of U.S. assistance, and although the contract may be between the government and the contractor (US AID will sometimes engage a local firm to work with the U.S. consulting firm to gain experience), the contracts have to conform to US AID's regulations, and US AID itself is often very much involved. Even if only a single consultant is required, it has sometimes taken about a year to get him out into the field. If a team of consultants is to be engaged, the problems are compounded correspondingly. Moreover countries sometimes reject consultants chosen by US AID after a complicated tendering process, because of their high cost.

US AID has a variety of methods available to it for the recruitment of consultants, whether an individual or a team. It can either recruit directly (slow because of U.S. Government regulations), or indirectly, through private U.S. firms engaged for the purpose, which has the advantage of speed, but may add to the cost, or through a non-profit professional organisation, which often is less costly and works very well. US AID staff admit however that they find the recruitment of consultants the most difficult part of project administration (the "people part"), and that it is not unusual for important project posts to remain unfilled for as much as two years.

The practice of using private firms to hire consultants is used also by SIDA[47], although it does not provide many consultants in the population field (it does, however, in health, particularly in Africa). The firms need not necessarily be Swedish. Like US AID, however, SIDA finds the arrangement costly. US AID, SIDA and NORAD are prepared to provide third country nationals for consultant posts (US AID only when it recruits through U.S. firms or universities as intermediaries), but in practice none of them do so very often, partly because recruitment is usually done in the donor's capital, and partly because of the administrative complications of taxation, social security, etc.

Within the last few years, Norway and Sweden have made a new arrangement for recruiting expert personnel for developing countries, by setting aside a sum in the country's overall aid allocation for consultant salaries, and letting the requesting government make the actual hiring arrangements itself. The intention is to keep down the cost of foreign consultants and to use the money saved for other aid purposes. The idea has been warmly welcomed by developing countries, who see in it one further evidence of these donors' genuine desire to be helpful. The snag is that the potential consultants are sometimes hesitant to be hired directly by foreign governments.

---

47. In Viet Nam, for example, over 300 expatriates, mostly but not all Swedish, have been engaged in this way.

Procurement

Donor agencies' requirements in respect of procurement arrangements are a reflection partly of the agency's own administrative constraints, and partly of the need to respond to the conflicting demands of efficiency, speed, encouragement of local industry and accountability. There are few areas of project implementation where the recipient country is more keenly aware of the differences in the procedures and practices of their various aid donors.

Procurement is perhaps an especially awkward problem in the case of population projects, since they are likely to involve a lot of rather small items (thus multiplying the administrative burden) and a large element of local construction (necessitating numerous small local contracts). Developing countries often lack the necessary experience. Moreover, where the government is itself the purchaser or the contractor, it is not unusual to find that its own procedures are more complicated than those of the donor. Some donors are very understanding of these difficulties. (Both NORAD and SIDA have at various times undertaken procurement at a government's request, either because the government did not have the experience to do it itself, or to enable it to avoid its own bureaucratic procedures; NORAD has even done local purchasing on behalf of the government).

The World Bank requires the government to do the procurement itself, but gives advice on how to set about it[48]. UNFPA, on the other hand, does most of the overseas procurement on the government's behalf. Other donors come somewhere in between. The U.K., for example, either purchases direct through the Crown Agents (which charge a commission of up to 15 per cent), or the Crown Agents send the country details of what the market can offer and let it make its own choice.

Population assistance is not tied to goods and services produced in the country of the donor, except for the programmes of US AID and the U.K.[49]. US AID does allow waivers in certain circumstances – in the case of loans, goods manufactured in the recipient country or other developing countries may be permitted if significantly cheaper, and the same arrangements apply to grant aid for very poor countries[50]. Overall, however, US AID does not finance the purchase of goods of non-U.S. origin to any significant extent. (As against this, it offers the compensating advantage of being prepared to airlift goods if necessary).

The ODA is equally rigorous in its requirement that goods and services must be of U.K. origin. Its population projects permit national contractors, but it is very precise in its definition of what constitutes a "national" firm. (In Kenya, the effect of these rules tends to disqualify small local construction firms in favour of larger British ones, although it is recognized that this was not the intention).

The actual arrangements for the purchase of goods of foreign origin vary, not only as between donors, but also according to the particular circumstances. The World Bank, whose procurement procedures were designed for large infrastructure projects, requires international competitive bidding (ICB) where possible, but is pragmatic about where and when this may not be appropriate. Developing countries appreciate that the Bank's arrangements give them responsibility for the *choice* of contractor and supplier to a

---

48. If customs duty has to be paid, the Bank loan does not cover it, and if the government does not have the money readily available, there may be a lengthy delay at the docks. Under UN arrangements, goods and equipment imported for a project come in duty-free, but remain UN property: after five years, title passes to the government, and the depreciated value is not considered to require payment of import duty.

49. ODA maintains that U.K. aid is not entirely tied to U.K. goods and services since many U.K. manufactures include a foreign content, and are still eligible for aid financing. US AID allows some manufactures if the foreign components represent less than 50% of the total cost.

50. For this reason, officials of the Government of Bangladesh, for example, do not consider US AID's assistance as "tied".

greater extent than those of many other donors, but are not pleased at having to consult Washington at so many points[51].

UNFPA sometimes does procurement itself (or the executing agency does), and sometimes uses the UN's procurement services, or those of UNICEF. (Either way, ICB is required for all items costing over a certain amount). UNICEF procurement, which covers an enormous range of goods and equipment, tends not to be popular with developing countries, except for standard articles. Countries find that off-the-shelf goods from UNICEF stocks are sometimes unsuitable for their particular needs, shipping arrangements add to often already lengthy order and manufacturing delays, and since they themselves have no direct contact with UNICEF, they have no means of checking on the progress of their order until the stuff actually arrives. Because of the scale of its operations, UNFPA has numerous regulations intended to help it keep check on the purchases that it is requested to make. Developing countries accordingly find UNFPA's procurement procedures very complicated, and its quest for the most advantageous buy sometimes a cause of inconvenience and delay. However, in many cases, the UNFPA Co-ordinator is prepared to be flexible, and will sometimes allow local purchase where it is manifestly cheaper and speedier.

UNFPA projects, on the whole, do not include a great deal of local purchase[52]. The World Bank and the IPPF, on the other hand, actively encourage it. The former is prepared to allow a price preferential in favour of local manufacturers (15 per cent) and contractors (17 per cent). IPPF favours local purchase for reasons of convenience, but requires to see the pro forma invoice for each item, before the order is placed.

Large donors are probably better placed than small ones to examine the details of equipment requests, but not even the World Bank has the staff resources necessary to scrutinize every item it is requested to supply. Moreover, the donors' concern is primarily that of price and technical suitability. The actual substantive use that the country makes of the equipment once received seems to be either a lesser consideration, or donors feel that this is the government's business and not theirs[53].

When the government does the procurement, some donors (NORAD and SIDA for example) are content to let it apply its own rules and do things its own way. The major donors, in theory, may allow the government to apply its own rules of contracting, but in practice, follow closely every stage of the process, requiring to see the specifications (if not already agreed), the tender documents, the bids received, the winning bid, and sometimes also the reasons for the choice. the Bank has occasionally queried the government's award; UNFPA sometimes compares the award with prices and delivery dates that it could get from New York; and US AID not only checks the credentials of the winning firm, but sometimes also drafts the contract, sends it back to the country for approval, and participates in the contract negotiations.

The implementing agency in the developing country, which has, in addition, to go through all the hoops of its own government's procedures for purchasing and contracting, understandably sometimes finds these various requirements very irksome. On the other hand, it is equally understandable that donors are anxious to ensure that aid money is properly applied. Moreover, it is not uncommon for work on population projects to come to a halt because small building firms, contracted by the government, have proved insufficiently equipped to undertake construction jobs in remote parts of the country, and have gone bankrupt part way through the work.

---

51. Viz the health minister who complained that he could not "wait to get permission from the Bank every time he needed to buy a tap".

52. A complaint quite often heard is that the specialized agencies of the UN that act as executive agency for UNFPA projects are particularly prone to import from abroad, even when local manufacture would be adequate (for example, furniture).

53. In the case of highly specialized equipment provided by UNFPA (for example, audio-visual equipment for information and communication programmes), executing agencies may send follow-up technical missions to advise on maintenance. There is much less concern, however, to find out how the equipment is being utilised in actual programmes.

Similar difficulties arise with local firms contracted to produce furniture, etc. The task of synchronizing the readiness of the various elements that go to make up a population project (buildings, equipment, furniture, personnel, training) is generally considered that of the project manager. This would seem, on the face of it, a lot to ask of a developing country government. Certainly, the failure to achieve such synchronization is one of the major problems of implementing population projects. Both sides seem to miscalculate badly – a mixture, no doubt, of misplaced optimism and unrealistic scheduling, pressure to conclude new project agreements, and sometimes plain inefficiency – as well, of course, as the innumerable unanticipated hazards that will occur throughout the course of implementation. Extending the implementation schedule – almost a commonplace in population projects – is a symptom of the problem, but not the solution.

Disbursement Procedures

In their disbursement procedures, donors are trying to reconcile, on the one hand, the need for financial rectitude and accountability, and on the other, the danger of being so over-careful that nothing is allowed to happen. Whatever the broad arrangements decided on, the difficulty of striking the appropriate balance usually remains.

The problem lies not with payment for foreign goods and services, which most donors make direct to the suppliers, but with local costs. These may be covered either by reimbursement for expenditures that the government has already made using its own funds, or by advance payments at regular intervals[54]. The World Bank and the U.K. use only the reimbursement procedure. Sweden, UNFPA, IPPF and Pathfinder favour advances. US AID prefers reimbursement, but is prepared to do either, according to what is most convenient, as is Norway.

Reimbursement is usually the most difficult method, in that the donor requires very precise evidence of the expenditures incurred. The World Bank which, in the case of disbursement procedures, as for procurement, treats population projects in the same way as its loans in other traditional sectors, is the most demanding. The Bank requires pro forma statements to be completed for each major item, showing the contract category, sub-category and details of payment, to which have to be appended the supplier's invoice, evidence of payment, shipping documents, etc. It is extremely difficult for the project management to assemble all these documents. In one country, some 40 per cent of the construction work had been completed before the Bank had received a single request for reimbursement; in another, the Bank's supervision teams had to sit down with the project officers and reconstruct the bills. The Bank has now simplified its procedures to the extent that it will disburse on the basis of certified expenditure statements, without receiving the vouchers, which are to be retained in the country for spot-check by the Bank. This has not, however, solved the problem, since government officials cannot certify the financial statements, without themselves having the payment vouchers. In the case of projects dispersed among many different and often remote parts of the country, collecting all the vouchers is a difficult business at best, and there is often also a shortage of accounts officers to do the work. The government's own financial regulations sometimes further compound the difficulties by requiring requests for reimbursement to be submitted to the donor through the finance ministry. Some governments require that small requests under population projects should be grouped together (which causes delay for those requests presented earliest) and/or be presented in a certain manner. (In one country, a simple typing error in one of the documents necessitates the whole package being sent back). If donors worry about lagging disbursements, the explanation therefore is not necessarily physical delays in the progress of the project.

---

54. In addition, some donors pay certain types of local expenditures direct, for example, fellowships, seminars, etc.

Donors' actual requirements regarding requests for advances vary enormously. The formal requirements of UNFPA, for example, are as demanding for advances as for reimbursement, requiring completion of pro forma statements, accompanied by the actual payment vouchers. Recognizing that full compliance is virtually impossible, UNFPA Co-ordinators generally work out some compromise arrangements with the government.

US AID's arrangements, on the other hand, could hardly be more flexible. The requirements are adjusted to the particular country situation (sometimes there are pro forma statements to be completed, sometimes not). In some countries, therefore, US AID is considered tough: in others, very accommodating. In Indonesia, where, as already noted, the US AID Mission had established extremely close working relations with the BKKBN, the disbursement procedures applied by US AID were very much more flexible than those of the Government, with the result that BKKBN would turn to the Mission when it needed funds for some new activity and did not wish to go through the Government's protracted procedures[55]. US AID used often to make its advance payments in the form of one very large instalment at the outset, but it now tries to make regular quarterly payments if possible. It still, however, is prepared to be flexible about timing and amounts.

Sweden sometimes makes a single advance payment at the beginning of the year, or perhaps twice yearly. It not only has no pro forma statements to be submitted with requests for disbursement, but is realistically prepared to tailor its requirements to what it feels the particular country is likely to be able to produce. The prime consideration is usually not to hold up the progress of the work. (Sweden, unlike many other donors, is prepared to include among the items it will reimburse, work undertaken by the government on the project before the agreement was signed).

It is noticeable that in the past few years, the agencies which have generally taken a relaxed approach to the information they needed to have before making disbursements, have begun to tighten up. UNFPA, NORAD and SIDA have all on occasion withheld disbursements, and all are now seeking some formula which will provide more systematic and substantive information on how project funds are being spent.

Where agencies make disbursements quarterly against a careful disbursement schedule (often prepared several years earlier), there are not infrequently big discrepancies between the actual expenditures made on the project in any particular quarter and the scheduled instalment payment. In the case of UNFPA, if there is an unspent balance, the Co-ordinator sometimes allows the government to use the unspent balance as a handy interim source of funds. IPPF, on the other hand, carefully deducts the unspent amount from the scheduled instalment for the following quarter[56]. US AID includes in its agreements precise regulations obliging the government to refund to the U.S. Treasury the unspent balance of any project funds, within one month after the completion of the project, and also any interest payments that may have accrued on funds received from US AID during the life of the project.

Except for IPPF and the Pathfinder Fund, whose "clients" are private bodies, disbursements in local currency for population projects are normally paid not direct to the project unit, but to the ministry of finance of the country. There are some exceptions (UNFPA, for example, has sometimes worked out an agreement with the government whereby it can pay direct to the implementing department). Often, however, the necessity for most donors to pass through the ministry of finance represents an additional obstacle and cause of disbursement delays. The finance ministry

---

55. Eventually, these arrangements proved *too* flexible for the Government of Indonesia, which found itself unable to check on the progress of project expenditures against the national budget plan. It accordingly requested donor agencies to tighten up their respective procedures where necessary, in the interests of stricter budgetary control. (This probably represents one of the few cases where a recipient government has found its donors' procedures too lax, rather than the reverse).

56. In some countries, where programmes are not infrequently held up by some major calamity (civil unrest, floods, etc.), the national Family Planning Association complains that it thus receives at the end of a year considerably less money than its full allocation.

will have made the initial advance in local currency to the implementing unit for it to make payments under the project. The finance ministry cannot get reimbursed by the donor until it has received from the implementing unit all the necessary documents to be presented with the request for disbursement. But as we have seen, since the latter has itself already received the local currency it needs from the ministry of finance, it is not in any particular hurry to speed up the process whereby the finance ministry in its turn can be reimbursed by the donor.

A further simple, but nonetheless very real problem that makes it difficult for developing country officials to prepare requests for disbursement, is the fact that the government officials who actually have to do the job are not properly informed as to what is required. Donors generally explain their disbursement procedures before the project starts, often with printed manuals, etc. The explanations, however, are usually given to the senior officials with whom the donor has had contact in the course of the project preparation and negotiation, and it is expected that they will pass the necessary information down to the lower-level financial officers, who will do the actual work of collecting the receipts, filling in the forms, checking against budget schedules, etc. Sometimes, however, senior government officials are remiss about this, and there consequently arises a major communications gap within the recipient agency and between donor and recipient at the working level. (A problem of etiquette seems to be involved here, since it is sometimes considered inappropriate for the donor itself to make direct contact with the working level staff). Overall, the problems holding up disbursement would seem to be not the intrinsic complication of donors' disbursement procedures, but a number of practical difficulties at the receiving end, which donors often fail to appreciate fully, or at least fail to make realistic provision for.

Reporting and Auditing

Donors have markedly different attitudes to the monitoring of their population projects. NORAD and SIDA, for example, feel that it is unrealistic to expect developing countries to produce more in the way of information than they are required to do for the government's own reporting purposes. (SIDA missions will accept reports from East African countries written in Swahili if necessary). They therefore do not require more than whatever financial statements the recipient has to submit in order to obtain the next disbursement instalment. US AID, in some cases, also settles for the progress reports that must accompany requests for disbursement as and when funds are needed, but in others, has very demanding reporting requirements.

For many donors (e.g. US AID, the World Bank, UNFPA), reporting requirements are project-specific and worked out as part of the agreement. Most countries find the Bank's requirements particularly difficult, but the staff of the (usually six-monthly) supervision missions help in filling in the information requested. In the case of UNFPA, which is naturally concerned to introduce a measure of standardisation into the management of its multiplicity of operations, reporting requirements for all except minor projects are so onerous that UNFPA staff themselves recognize that to apply them literally would constitute an intolerable burden. The Co-ordinator therefore works out arrangements with the recipient in each particular case (and helps with them as may be necessary). The arrangements may themselves, however, be quite elaborate, as in some cases the recipient seems to feel that it is worth the investment of considerable time and effort to produce a report which will make a good impression[57].

Whatever the particular arrangements agreed upon, most donors recognize that written reports have severe limitations as an effective monitoring tool. First, they presuppose good project design at the outset. Second, in the case of population projects, quantitative data often does not convey any very substantive information. Third,

---

57. In one country, the preparation of the annual Progress Report to UNFPA takes from 4-5 months. The agency concerned, a beneficiary of important UNFPA assistance, takes the preparation of its reports to UNFPA very seriously and has engaged a full-time English-speaking report writer (paid by UNFPA).

donors do not have the staff to study the mountains of paper that frequent and detailed reporting would generate, still less to draw from them the implicit lessons for project implementation and decision-making. This is one of the reasons for the pragmatic attitude to reporting taken by some small donors. But it applies to the major donors also. (UNFPA, for example, has a requirement that on the completion of each and every project, the government or the executing agency should send a report to New York, via the Co-ordinator, who will add his personal comments: it would be impossible for New York to study all of them in detail, so the requirement is not always insisted on in practice).

For substantive monitoring, therefore, most donors rely mainly on direct observation and contact, through their field mission, if they have one, and/or visits from headquarters. The World Bank sends its "end-use supervision" missions, NORAD and SIDA hold their annual consultations, etc. The obligation to present regular financial statements and written reports, therefore, would often seem to be more of a disciplinary management exercise than a source of information for the donor.

When it comes to accounting and auditing, the problems are different. It might perhaps be expected that the fact that each donor requires the project accounts to conform to its particular financial year represents an additional burden for the finance officers of developing countries, who are obliged to maintain sometimes several different sets of accounts for the same project (if several different donors are providing funding), each beginning on a different date and covering a different 12-month period, as well as to keep a consolidated account to record cash flow. Surprisingly, finance officers seem to have adjusted to this necessity, and it has not been raised as a subject of complaint[58].

All donors require several audits during the life of a population project. Sometimes these are done by the donors themselves, sometimes by national firms of auditors acceptable to the donor, and sometimes by the government's own audit department, according to the arrangements worked out in any particular case. Some donors are prepared to pay for the audit to be done by a local firm, which is obviously the simplest arrangement, and the one that developing countries like best. (UNFPA will pay for this, but the World Bank will not include it as part of a loan). Where annual auditing is required, many donors find that the government's audit department not only is satisfactory on professional grounds, but is sometimes more exacting than the donor's own requirements (even, sometimes, those of the World Bank). The problem is that government audits are frequently badly delayed because of the insufficient numbers of qualified accountants and auditors in the government service, which results in a pile-up of projects awaiting audit at the end of the government's financial year. For final audit after project completion, some donors (for example, US AID and Norway) send auditors out from the general accounting office of their respective governments. Although, obviously, not every project can be checked in this way, just the knowledge that they might be is itself held to have a salutory effect. A quite different approach is taken by SIDA, which considers that it has no legal right to examine accounts administered by a recipient country government, and therefore leaves the auditing of project accounts to the country concerned[59].

As for broader post hoc evaluation of population projects, even those donors that have institutionalised procedures for assessing the impact of their aid activities (US AID, the World Bank, for example), seem somewhat daunted by the idea of evaluating their population assistance[60]. (The long-term nature of the activities, the difficulty of establishing causality, the problem of measuring results are variously

---

58. At least on the evidence presented to the author in the course of her discussions in developing countries.

59. SIDA's guiding principle is that the requirements for administering Swedish aid should not impose on the administration of a developing country demands that might be burdensome even for the government of a developed country.

60. US AID has done some — two general and one country evaluation.

advanced as reasons). The agency that probably takes evaluation of population assistance most seriously is the IPPF, which views it as an integral part of the programming, budgeting and reporting process. Like other donors, however, IPPF is well aware that it has yet to find a solution to the basic problem of how to arrange an effective mechanism for follow-up. Meanwhile evaluation studies, albeit highly professional, do not provide much help as a practical operational tool.

Donor Co-ordination

Where a country's population programme is supported by a large number of different donor agencies, the senior government officials concerned often deplore the "multiplicity of donors to be satisfied", and consequent likelihood of "more people being dissatisfied". Further, governments not infrequently criticise the tendency of donors to make each its own selection of the parts of the programme that it wishes to support. In the words of one leading ministry of health official, "donors come in like arrows, each aiming at their own particular targets"[61], and irrespective of the government's own priorities.

Happily, there has been a marked tendency in recent years towards a greater measure of effective co-ordination at the actual programme level. Indeed, actual co-ordination arrangements in a number of countries are probably better than might be suggested by discussions of the subject at top policy-level (where everybody is agreed that co-ordination is a good thing, but wishes itself to do the co-ordinating). It is recognized that whereas for overall development assistance, it is the Bank that plays the co-ordinating role, for population assistance a sort of gentleman's agreement between the Bank and UNFPA has accorded the role, in principle, to the latter. Which of the two agencies, in fact, exercises the leading role in any particular country, however, depends very much on the circumstances and the way in which donor support for its population programme has evolved.

The World Bank has a framework for co-ordination of population assistance in its Consultative Groups, which, exceptionally, include special discussion of aid for the country's population programme. UNFPA has also, exceptionally, invited donors to a meeting to mobilize support for population assistance for a particular country, and sometimes invites representatives of other donor agencies to participate in its Annual Country Reviews which take place in the country concerned.

The most effective efforts of co-ordination, however, have taken the form of joint financing for particular projects. UNFPA's association with bilateral donors in "multi-bi" arrangements (whereby it takes care of the implementation of the project, and one or more bilateral donors contribute part of the funding) have latterly been the subject of renewed interest, particularly on the part of the smaller bilaterals, which in this way are able to increase their aid for population activities without at the same time assuming an additional administrative burden[62]. The arrangements are slow to organize, however, which diminishes their attractiveness from the recipient point of view.

The World Bank has associated bilateral donors with it in a number of projects under "parallel financing" arrangements (whereby each donor contributes funds to part of the project according to its own aid procedures), or "joint financing" (which implies a certain amount of pooling of the donor inputs, with the Bank taking over the chief management responsibility). Both these arrangements offer the recipient the advantage of getting partial financing for the project on grant terms. They also provide some assurance that the participating donors are on broadly the same wave-length as regards the

---

61. The result has been in some cases to create a number of separate fiefs within the health ministry, headed by rival project managers, like so many war-lords.

62. The Government of Norway contributes joint funding to a large number of population projects, not only of UNFPA, but also of UNICEF, ILO and other international agencies. The Government of Italy, not traditionally a supporter of population assistance, has recently become interested in providing funds to UNFPA in this way.

strategies and approaches to be followed[63]. Joint financing has not, to date, spared the recipient country the burden of successive appraisal missions from each of the participating donors, but the example of the IDA Project in Bangladesh has shown that it can spare them separate review missions and the chore of separate reporting and procurement arrangements.

The example of Bangladesh, where the national population programme receives substantial external support in addition to the IDA Project, and where the local representatives of all the donors concerned meet regularly with the Governement's blessing, is instructive in a number of ways. First, it shows that co-ordination generally works best at the local level (the fact that the Bank has a resident Population Officer, of course, helps considerably). Second, it shows that donors' primary concern is with the development of the government's population programme as a whole, rather than with their own particular project. (For some of the activities, the World Bank is constructing the buildings, US AID paying the local salaries and UNFPA doing the training). Third, it suggests that exchange of information, also, is likely to be most useful at the local level. (Local aid missions report upwards to headquarters, but agency headquarters rarely pass on the information to other agencies to which it might be of interest[64]. At the local level, however, agencies have a common interest in dealing with the practical problems of implementation and, in addition, with new needs as they arise. How effectively donors will in fact get together in any particular case depends very much on the personalities in the individual aid missions. Where the representatives of the major population assistance donors are not genuinely interested in mutual exchanges of information, formal meeting arrangements are not likely to achieve very much.

Now that aid funds are getting tighter, it is likely that not only the need but also the prospects for greater donor co-ordination in the field of population assistance will increase. With fewer funds available, there will be less competition for "good" projects, and at the same time, with more experience (on both sides) of preparing and implementing population projects, the number of good projects should also increase.

Donor co-ordination, however, if it is to be a genuine working relationship, presupposes a certain degree of *mutual confidence* – both as between donors and as between donors and recipient. Without this, donors are unlikely to be prepared to make the necessary sacrifice of their habitual procedural and other requirements, in the interests of some more unified management arrangement. In particular, they need to feel a reasonable degree of assurance that the recipient has the capability to carry out the activity they are assisting, so that rigorous application of their individual aid procedures becomes less necessary as safeguards for their particular input.

It would seem therefore that the question of improved co-ordination of population assistance touches at several points on a number of other aid issues that have been raised earlier in these pages – notably, the need for more "non-project" aid for population, and for more assistance to help developing countries strengthen their management capability overall. By taking the emphasis off individual "projects" and joining, severally, with the government in support of its national population strategies, donors would be both harmonizing their own efforts, and economising those of the government (in respect of differing aid requirements). At the same time, by strengthening the administrative and managerial under-pinning necessary to put these strategies into effect, they would be helping to create the conditions that offer some assurance that the aid monies they provide would be effectively applied for the purposes mutually agreed upon.

---

63. A UNFPA report on one country which receives population assistance from several different donors showed that they had failed to co-ordinate their respective approaches on such matters as training, salary scales, incentive payments, etc.

64. Most headquarters officials maintain that the flow of written information they receive is already as much as they can cope with, and that the real co-ordination with other agencies takes place in the form of informal, personal contacts.

MULTILATERAL DONORS

THE UNITED NATIONS FUNDS FOR POPULATION ACTIVITIES[1]

I. INTRODUCTION

The United Nations Fund for Population Activities (UNFPA) handles some one-third of all the money made available each year for population assistance world-wide. Set up in 1967, in response, primarily, to a desire on the part of the donor community to strengthen international action to deal with population problems, the UNFPA is both more and less than a "donor agency". Its primary function is to act as a "broker" of population assistance funds, collecting contributions from interested governments and channelling them to developing countries, UN agencies, other international institutions and non-governmental organisations that wish to carry out population activities. The importance of UNFPA has grown with, and indeed has been a major cause of, the enormous increase in international assistance funding for population overall that has taken place over the past 12 years. As the size and scope of its financing has expanded, so has the number and diversity of its beneficiary institutions and activities. Today, the UNFPA may fairly be described, like the Ford Foundation in its heyday, as "a large body of money surrounded by people who want some"[2].

By 1980, UNFPA was receiving voluntary contributions[3] from 97 countries, more than two-thirds of which are themselves UNFPA beneficiaries, although in their case the contributions tend to be largely symbolic. (The People's Republic of China, for example, a new recipient to the tune of a $50 million commitment over a five-year period, has been contributing, on average, a quarter of a million dollars each year since 1979 and has pledged $300,000 for 1982). By far the largest proportion of UNFPA's funding comes from the DAC countries – one quarter of it provided by the USA alone. Indeed 30 per cent of the total population assistance provided by the DAC countries is given in the form of contributions to the UNFPA.

In 1980, UNFPA's annual budget amounted to over $147 million, it made commitments for projects amounting to $150 million (including some carry-over from the previous year), and approved nearly 400 new projects. Today, there is barely a country anywhere in the developing world that is not the scene of some activity financed by the UNFPA.

Despite the magnitude of the programme, UNFPA is a subsidiary organ of the United Nations[4] rather than a full-fledged agency, and, as its name indicates, is primarily a *Fund*, with more financing than operating responsibilities. It reports annually to the Governing Council of the UNDP, which has to approve its programme and budget for the coming year. The annual contributions (now pledges) from governments are made in a pledging conference held each year in November. Although it is rare for the Governing Council to disapprove any particular part of the annual programme of activities proposed by UNFPA, the Council does lay down broad directives for the orientation of its activities generally. UNFPA's programme is thus closely responsive to the views of the

---

1. Statistical table, see page 65.
2. Introduction to New Yorker Profile on the Ford Foundation.
3. Until 1979, the amounts were decided in bilateral discussions. Now countries give pledges at the annual pledging conference for other UN development activities. This resulted in 22 new countries pledging contributions for 1980.
4. General Assembly Resolution 34/104.

member countries of the UN, and has changed over the years in emphasis and approach, as development philosophies have changed in the UN forum.

Since it was not created to perform itself the functions of an implementing agency but built up international capacity through the United Nations system to respond to needs in the population and family planning fields[5], other agencies than the UNFPA itself are likely to be given the implementing responsibility for the activities that it finances. In this way, it has been able to promote its vast programmes with a total staff of less than 160 people, of whom only 78 are professionals. In addition, some 40 professionals are serving as UNFPA field staff, in countries where UNFPA is assisting large-scale programmes.

UNFPA allocates its budget partly to country-specific projects requested by the governments concerned, and partly to inter-country projects of various kinds. Country projects are submitted officially by governments. UNFPA arranges for the appraisal, preparation, negotiation and subsequent evaluation of the project requests. For implementation, however, it follows the practice of the UNDP, and usually calls upon one of the specialised agencies of the UN to act as "Executing Agency" and provide the necessary technical expertise. In principle, it is for the requesting country to designate the agency of its choice, but in practice, this is usually determined by the nature of the project. If there is no obvious specialised agency nor international personnel involved, or if the government feels that it is best equipped to handle the project, an agency of the national government itself may take on the implementation responsibility, in collaboration with UNFPA.

The necessity to build up expertise in population matters on an international basis took the form of additional posts within agencies ("infrastructure support", which provides technical backstopping in population matters), short-term expert posts for specific project assignments and, effective 1982, a 13 per cent charge for overhead expenditures. The arrangement has allowed the agencies to expand their work in the population field. However, the recipient countries — as they gained experience with population projects (and UNFPA assistance), and as technical assistance components were reduced to a minimum — began increasingly to feel that they could perform the role of executing agency themselves, and to question the intervention of another UN agency as an additional layer of bureaucracy. Today, a growing number of UNFPA projects (currently about one-third) are executed by the recipient country itself. These include most of the large projects in Bangladesh, India, Indonesia, South Korea, the Philippines and Thailand. In these cases, the UNFPA performs a co-ordinating role and helps the government with the practical details of project implementation as may be necessary. It is expected that the number of these projects will increase.

The inter-country projects funded by UNFPA (designated as "global", "inter-regional" or "regional") cover an enormous diversity of research, training, informational and technical backstopping activities. These are carried out by an equivalent diversity of implementing bodies. Some are undertaken by UNFPA directly (e.g. the Conferences of Parliamentarians on Population and Development)[6], as part of a continuing effort to feature an "awareness creation" activity every year or so. (For the next few years, the World Population Conference to be held in 1984 will provide a focal point). More often, however, UNFPA finances activities carried out by the various specialised agencies of the UN (e.g. the WHO Special Programme of Research Development and Training in Human Reproduction, or the demographic work of the Population Division of the UN), or by non-governmental institutions. The best-known example of the latter is perhaps the World Fertility Survey, but a considerable amount of UNFPA funding goes to assist research and training activities carried out by diverse population institutions, universities and statistical units, sometimes on a quite modest scale. Indeed, there are probably few institutions, public or private, anywhere in the world, concerned to advance the

---

5. Economic and Social Council 1763 (LIV).
6. Organised in collaboration with the Inter-Parliamentary Union.

state of knowledge on population matters, which have not at some time received international support by means of a grant from the UNFPA.

Today, UNFPA's inter-country activities represent some one-third of its annual expenditure. For many of these activities, the UNFPA contribution represents only a small part of their total budget. The intention, however, is to reduce their share to one-quarter only, in order to devote more resources to country projects. In the same spirit, regional projects are henceforward to be designed so as to provide support for country activities in the region concerned.

II. APPROACH AND CRITERIA

UNFPA sees its country and its inter-country activities as complementary in that one should enhance the other in carrying out its mandate to assist population activities. For the purposes of the present study, however, it is UNFPA's country projects that are of particular interest.

In the early years of its operations, UNFPA, as a matter of deliberate policy, cast its net very wide and tried to accommodate a great variety of approaches in respect both of the countries and the activities that it was prepared to support. Its aim was to win a firm political constituency for UNFPA as an institution dedicated to the cause of population assistance, and hence, to widen countries' awareness of the importance of "the population issue" in general. The breadth of this approach was much appreciated by developing countries, who often found a source of financing in UNFPA for diverse activities whose relevance to population was sometimes long-term and indirect, and which were not always easily assimilable under the current programmes of their other aid donors. When in 1974, the World Population Conference at Bucharest provided resounding endorsement of the broad "development approach" to population problems, UNFPA was able to say that this was what it had already been doing.

Despite the very wide range of activities to which it has been prepared to lend its support, UNFPA has sought to introduce greater coherence into its aid criteria by defining five major sectors for population assistance. These are "basic data collection"; "population dynamics"; "population policy"; "population education, communication and information" and "family planning"[7]. The relative priorities among these five have varied over time and the specific situations of the developing country. The order in which they have been set out above reflects no policy preference on the part of UNFPA. As thus listed, however, they constitute a logical sequence of population assistance activities.

Thus "basic data collection", notably demographic statistics and census-taking, has enabled UNFPA to undertake an important (and objective) demographic activity all over the developing world, including in some countries, notably in Africa, which are traditionally hostile to the idea of population limitation, and thereby to make countries aware of the existence, nature and magnitude of their respective population problems. "Population dynamics" covers research and training in respect of all aspects of population movements (i.e. fertility, mortality, morbidity, migration and urbanisation). The purpose is to provide informed material for policy-makers as to how population and development policy can interrelate. "Population policy" consists of assistance in the formulation and evaluation of population policies and programmes, an area where the bilateral donors of aid often hesitate to tread. UNFPA, on the other hand, sees a role for itself as assisting with both the formulation as well as the implementation of population policy, notably by working with governments "in appropriate institutional arrangements" to help them in better integrating population policies with development planning. To this end, UNFPA is supporting national efforts to prepare a series of

---

7. Other donors of population assistance have also accepted these categories for statistical reporting purposes.

"Population and Development Status Reports" which present the basic data concerned for different countries in a form easily available to policy-makers. The fourth classification, "Population education, communication and information", covers every possible kind of activity that offers a way of sensitising both the public and individuals to awareness of population problems. The thrust is both macro-level, i.e. the implications of population trends for society as a whole, and at the micro-level, in terms of the welfare of the individual family.

The major category of UNFPA's assistance, however, has always been that broadly described as "family planning". Before Bucharest, activities under this heading accounted for some 50 per cent of UNFPA's annual expenditures. Increases to other sectors in 1973 and 1974, in connection with the World Population Year 1974 and the World Population Conference, reduced the shares — although not the amounts — for family planning. By 1975, family planning accounted again for 50 per cent of expenditures. In recent years, "family planning" activities have fallen somewhat below this level, but together with projects of population education and communication, they still account for over half of UNFPA's total assistance. It should be remembered, however, that the classification "family planning" not only covers projects to establish and expand family planning services but also provides some funding to deal with sub-fertility and sterility, biomedical research and sociological studies. In recent years, a few service programmes have been presented in the context of social development activities that are designed to reach rural populations. (In Egypt, for example, the Population Development Project which UNFPA has been assisting covers village development activities which include family planning, UNFPA's assistance covering the other development activities and the family planning component on an equal footing).

The range of UNFPA's assistance criteria may be seen from the description given in 1978 in its "Instructions for the Preparation of a Project Document"[8]. This reads that it is UNFPA policy, "for example", to give "special attention to certain groups of the population (women, youth, rural and disadvantaged sectors of the population), to the concepts of self-reliance and technical co-operation among developing countries (TCDC), to manpower development and institution-building, to popular participation, to the recommendations contained in the (Bucharest) World Population Plan of Action, to the World Plan of Action of the International Women's Year Conference, to antipoverty and basic needs strategies, to 'Beyond Family Planning', etc."

Until now, UNFPA has been able to expand its activities over this very broad front, confident that its contributing countries would provide the funds necessary to put them into effect. With the 1980s, however, arrived a totally new situation of budgetary stringency which has obliged it to make a careful review of its funding priorities. The result has been a resounding re-emphasis on family planning as the main focus of UNFPA's activities[9]. Moreover, the definition given to "family planning" by the Governing Council in June 1981 would suggest that within this classification, the effort now is to be concentrated on the more traditional types of activity (family planning programmes and mother and child health care). It will be interesting to see how much diversity and innovation will continue to be supported in the context of UNFPA's new family planning projects.

i) Geographical criteria

By the mid-1970s, UNFPA had formulated a set of criteria, on the basis of which 40 countries were defined as priority for assistance. The underlying principle was

---

8. UNFPA 19 Rev. No. 2, October 1978.(This document is in the process of updating).

9. The UNDP Governing Council, at its meeting in June 1981, urged the UNFPA to strive for "a *substantial increase* in the proportion of resources for family planning and population education, communication and information, and for a substantial decrease as regards the share of basic data collection and population dynamics". Annex to the Report of the UNDP Governing Council (Document's own italics).

essentially to be the country's *need* for population assistance. Threshold levels were set for four demographic indicators (population growth, fertility, infant mortality and agricultural population density on arable land) and one economic indicator (per capita gross national product). A further 13 countries were classed as borderline countries. UNFPA's priority countries thus converged with the countries internationally recognised as "the least developed". The criteria and list of countries were reviewed a few years later, and it was decided that the designated priority countries should receive two-thirds of UNFPA's total country allocations. (So far, this goal has not been achieved[10], in part due to the advent of China in 1979 as a major new UNFPA recipient — a country outside the present priority list).

Faced today with the need to apply its resources with a new rigour, UNFPA has been requested by the Governing Council to make a review of its whole programme and report back. The Council has confirmed that priority countries should receive two-thirds of the total country allocation, but has asked UNFPA to reassess its priority country gradings. Criteria to be taken into account in making allocations in the future include, in addition to *need*, the magnitude of the population problem in relation to economic growth, population size and increase in actuel numbers, as well as the rate of annual increase. A new element has now been introduced, namely, the likelihood of being able to put population assistance to *effective use*. The considerations now to be taken into account include also the government's policies and programmes, its commitment to the declared national population policy, absorptive capacity, levels of other sources of population assistance, and actual and projected implementation rates.

ii) Size and types of project

UNFPA's rules provide that it can grant funds only for population "projects", that is to say for specific research, training, information or operational activities. It cannot, therefore, give straight budgetary subsidies, but can give funds to institutions for certain mutually-agreed project activities which must themselves conform to UNFPA's broad project criteria. Nonetheless, some of its longer-term beneficiary institutions have in time come to look upon UNFPA as one of their regular sources of financing[11]. Moreover, in some cases, (depending on the institution and the personalities involved), UNFPA has left to the institution a degree of latitude as to the precise substantive use of a particular research or training grant.

A UNFPA "project" may be of any size, ranging from the preparation, organisation and analysis of a national census (the figure for the China census is some $15.6 million), to a single brief consultant visit, a fellowship or study tour. A sizeable part of the annual budget is in fact spent on a large number of projects which individually may be considered as "small" — i.e. less than $100,000. Concentration within the country programmes on a few well-defined "big" projects is less frequent.

To an extent, the seeming fragmentation suggested by a list of UNFPA's ongoing projects at any given time is illusory in that individual fellowships, consultant visits, etc., although appearing as separate "projects", are in fact often undertaken within the framework of some larger UNFPA-financed activity. However, there are a number of other factors which operate in favour of small activities. One is the priority accorded to the poorer developing countries, many of which, particularly those in Africa, are unable to absorb large projects (though there are large projects in certain Asian countries). Another is that UNFPA often contributes to activities in which other donor agencies are also participating, rather than itself assure sole external aid responsibility for some major project or institution. Indeed, UNFPA, unlike most other donors of aid, usually prefers its assistance *not* to be identified with any particular project or institution. A further important reason is that UNFPA envisages its role as helping the government carry out its chosen population strategies and programmes. It is therefore willing to finance specific gaps in the national programme, or to come to the

---

10. The proportions for 1979 and 1980 were respectively 56 per cent and 42 per cent.
11. A confidence sometimes strained in the present tight budgetary situation.

rescue when funds previously supplied by other donor agencies are no longer available, or cannot conveniently be applied. (For example, when Indonesia wanted condoms from Japan, which could not be provided under the programme of US AID, UNFPA agreed to supply them). In this particular case the "project" thus agreed was a sizeable one, but it might equally be something quite small.

UNFPA does not have any special preferences as to the types of population activity that it is willing to support, but is prepared to finance any component of a population activity that meets its criteria[12]. There is perhaps a particular readiness to finance local cost expenditures (there is no rule fixing a proportion as between local and foreign exchange costs for UNFPA projects), and a number of its research and training projects consist solely of expenditures within the host country[13]. On the other hand, if a country does not need technical assistance, it will provide equipment alone (in India, at one point, it was only supplying vehicles), or commodity assistance (in Mauritius, UNFPA at one time supplied all the contraceptives required for the Government programme).

There are a few "negative" criteria. UNFPA does not provide budgetary support or "sector aid" for population or health activities, but only, as already mentioned, aid for "projects". However, a liberal definition of "project" has sometimes enabled it to come very close to sector support. (In India, in order to speed up the expansion of the service network, it agreed to "top up" the Government's population activities across-the-board). Also, as a general rule, it does not finance construction, preferring to leave this to other donors, in particular the World Bank. On the other hand, UNFPA is prepared to pay the rent for buildings or even, in rare cases, the cost of purchase, something that other donors hesitate to do. There is a tendency to be lenient in the case of a priority country with little or no infrastructure and to disallow this kind of assistance entirely for countries with established programmes.

III. CONTRIBUTION TO SELF-RELIANCE

The building up of national self-reliance in population matters (defined as "the ability of countries to cope, themselves, with "population problems" [14]) is the prime purpose of UNFPA assistance, and more particularly, the country programmes. To a large extent, these programmes are concerned with building up self-reliance in respect of different areas of *technical* ability (better integration of population and development planning; advice on population strategies and programmes; strengthening of infrastructure; manpower training; research; local manufacture of contraceptives; improved distribution systems, etc.). The projects are so designed as to make a *direct* contribution in the area concerned. UNFPA's evaluation studies are an attempt to assess to what extent they have been effective.

The following paragraphs consider the contribution (direct and indirect) made by UNFPA in respect of two other aspects of national self-reliance — namely *financial* ability and *managerial* ability.

---

12. Assistance normally conforms to the five "core" categories. Criteria include centrally-issued guidelines on specific sectors, decisions of UNFPA's governing bodies concerning priorities in allocations of resources, and the recommendations of international strategies having implications for the UNFPA programme of assistance. The guidelines are applied with flexibility to recipient countries which tend, at times, to be widely different, so that an activity which is deemed in one country to conform to the criteria may be disallowed in another.

13. Since its funding of UN agency projects is made in dollars, it is an advantage for UNFPA to be able to pay a large part of country project expenditures in local currencies.

14. A recent publication described "population problems" as consisting of "high or low fertility rates and internal or international migration". Population and Mutual Self-Help. Population Profiles, No. 12.

i) Contribution to strengthening financial ability: recurrent costs, salaries

UNFPA has been notably generous with respect to the financing of recurrent costs. While it is unlikely to take on a project that consists wholly of recurrent costs, many UNFPA projects consist in large part of recurrent costs. Normally, the project agreement provides that the government will itself assume responsibility for these costs on a phased basis, but where, for lack of budgetary resources, the government is unable to do so, UNFPA has not usually insisted. UNFPA staff are well aware that financing recurrent costs may seem to be encouraging an attitude of continuing dependence on foreign aid rather than of self-reliance. However, recent experience, no doubt influenced by UNFPA's own budgetary stringency, shows that it is beginning to take a much firmer line.

The major item of recurrent costs is salaries, or salary supplements. Salary supplements are defined as compensation for additional work and are based on local wages and hours of work. In Egypt, for example, these made up nearly one-quarter of the total cost of the UNFPA-funded Population and Development Project. UNFPA paid the full salaries of some senior staff (the project director, national "experts" and administrative support staff) directly brought in from universities and local research institutes, the Population and Family Planning Board submitting each year a list of persons to be thus remunerated. In addition, UNFPA provides salary supplements to staff members of the Board and other implementing agencies involved in UNFPA projects.

UNFPA maintains that where local expertise exists, engaging national experts not only contributes to eventual self-reliance but offers clear programme benefits also (relative cost, familiarity with the local environment, etc.). Further, in countries with very limited resources, it feels that taking on the responsibility for staff salaries may be the only way of getting a new activity off the ground. In Bangladesh, for example, when the Government proposed a programme to perform 400,000 sterilisations a year, UNFPA agreed to pick up the wage bill for the almost 3,000 field workers that would be needed. In principle, UNFPA tries to limit salary supplements to an increase of 25 per cent over the corresponding government salary. In practice, however, senior level staff, badly needed for key project positions, are sometimes given "consultant" status, or have new (and possibly nominal) functions added to their official duties, etc.

ii) Contribution to strengthening managerial capability

UNFPA points to the growing number of countries in which the government has taken over the role of "executing agency" previously exercised by one of the specialised agencies of the UN, as evidence of the increasing administrative and managerial competence of its recipients. Although for much of the practical work of programme implementation (preparation of reports, requests for disbursement, etc.), the government agencies concerned often receive substantial assistance from UNFPA staff in the country, they gain useful administrative experience in the process.

In its Instructions for the Preparations of a Project Request, UNFPA requires that "special attention should be paid to determining that the government implementing agency is adequately staffed and capable of implementing the project". In the absence of specific guidelines for assessment, the determination of the government's implementing ability has been made on the basis of largely subjective appraisals. Inevitably, therefore, UNFPA projects vary greatly in the extent to which they actually address this question and include specific measures to strengthen the services concerned.

In some countries, UNFPA has made the strengthening of the relevant population institutions a major feature of its assistance. Thus it has helped the Population and Family Planning Board of Egypt to take on additional senior and technical staff, has provided training for them at home and overseas, and supplied consultants in both advisory and line functions, thus building up capability at all levels. It has similarly helped strengthen the capacity of the National Statistical Office of Egypt[15] to undertake demographic work by providing administrative support personnel, consultants, training and equipment.

UNFPA's current programme in Egypt reflects a concerted effort to build up a strong national capability to cope with the country's population problems. In particular, it is trying to improve the planning capability of the different sector ministries so that population factors and objectives can be better integrated into the national development planning process. Approximately one million dollars is to be devoted to this purpose. A further one-half million dollars have been allocated for "various activities designed to improve the logistic and management aspects of the population programme". These include "ways to promote closer co-operation between ministries and the Population and Family Planning Board, contraceptive supply, pricing and distribution, the management information system, co-ordination and elaboration of the roles and responsibilities of the various types of personnel involved in the implementation of the population programme"[16].

In few other countries to date has UNFPA undertaken quite so comprehensive an effort. (It will be interesting in due course to see an evaluation of the effectiveness of UNFPA's contribution to building up Egypt's self-reliance overall — including financial self-reliance — in the population field[17]). Recently, UNFPA has re-emphasized its concern with countries' implementation capacity — to the extent of declaring that a positive assessment is henceforward to be one of the criteria for assistance. It is possible, therefore, that UNFPA will seek increasingly to address the problem of how to assure the administrative and human resources required.

When considering this problem on an individual project level, UNFPA's policy has always been to work through the existing administrative structure rather than to set up or require the setting up of special project implementing units. The recipient government is required to appoint a project manager and all other necessary personnel (their salaries may or may not be paid by UNFPA), and if UNFPA feels that the choice is less than satisfactory, it has no recourse other than to provide consultants to work with them.

Although, in principle, UNFPA would like its consultants to be supported by local counterparts, it does not insist. As a practical matter, it recognises that compliance is often nominal only, and that in countries where experience and talent are scarce, it is not uncommon for the same official to be designated as local "counterpart" to several different projects (funded by different donors) simultaneously.

UNFPA projects have a certain reputation of being "consultant-heavy", although UNFPA generally tries to avoid this. In Colombia, for example, a $10 million MCH project for which WHO/PAHO was the executing agency and provided the back-stopping services, had no outside project manager and only three months of foreign consultant time in seven years. On the other hand, there are instances where there has been no need of international consultants to backstop the project's management, but where UNFPA has suggested including in its aid a number of international short-term *advisers* as technical specialists. Although governments rarely refuse (and usually appreciate the quality of UNFPA advisers), they are becoming less keen on having UNFPA advisers, partly because of growing national self-confidence and expertise, and partly because of their

---

15. Central Agency for Public Mobilisation and Statistics (CAPMAS).

16. Assistance to the Government of Egypt: Comprehensive Population Programme, DP/FPA/12 Add. 13, April 1981.

17. At the time of writing, UNFPA had made nine evaluation studies of its assistance on an overall country basis, but not specifically from the viewpoint of its contributions to the eventual "self-reliance" of the country concerned. It has also conducted seven studies of regional or inter-regional programmes with implications for countries. Three more country studies and one regional study are scheduled at present.

high cost. (The full cost of UNFPA consultants is known, and comes out of the country's allocation[18]).

When UNFPA provides a consultant, his terms of reference are written by the government, and where possible, the government is given a choice among alternative candidatures. When a UN agency is responsible for the implementation of the project, the agency will send one of its own consultants or staff members. Countries recognise that this arrangement has the merit of filling posts much more speedily than can be done through UNFPA's central recruitment services in New York. They maintain, however, that it would be cheaper and more efficient simply to request agency advice on recruitment, and themselves hire the consultant direct, without the agency taking a role in the implementation of the project[19].

Three years ago, in an effort to improve the implementation of national programmes, UNFPA instituted an annual training course for national personnel working in directly-executed projects. The course covers assessments of major population issues, new developments in national policies and programmes and a review of the assistance provided by the UNFPA. The course is held in New York, and visiting project officers are given the opportunity to become acquainted with other United Nations organisations (as well as the UNFPA) and New York-based and non-governmental organisations active in the population field.

IV. PROGRAMMING ARRANGEMENTS

The Agreement-making Process

Although UNFPA is still likely to have a large number of separate projects in any country in which it is particularly active[20], there has for some time been a move in the direction of country programming. Comprehensive country reviews (entitled "Needs Assessment for Population Assistance") are progressively being carried out for each recipient country in order to provide a coherent framework for future UNFPA assistance. By the end of 1982, 70 countries have been the subject of such reviews, and more are planned at the rate of some 20 a year. The purpose of the Needs Assessment Missions (undertaken by teams of outside consultants) is to identify the country's requirements in terms of technology, manpower, training and finance, in the light of the government's population policies and programmes, and the resources available for carrying them out. Although the Mission Reports review the situation as a whole, including the contribution of other aid donors, and make recommendations for new strategies and programmes, the prime intention is not to offer the government a blueprint for its future population activities (and, hopefully, to provide one for other donors), but specifically, to identify areas where UNFPA might assist.

The Needs Assessment Report, which is presented to the government and must receive its approval, does not normally include cost estimates for specific projects[21] and does not, of itself, constitute a country programme. For the preparation of the country programme, UNFPA sends a small follow-up mission from New York who work out together with the government a number of specific projects to be implemented over a five-year period. A document, broadly describing the purpose of each activity, the nature and amount of the UNFPA input to each, and the amount to be contributed by the government is then presented by UNFPA for Governing Council approval. Approval

---

18. There is virtually no difference in the cost of consultants supplied by UNFPA, UNDP and other UN agencies.
19. Views expressed to the author by recipient country officials.
20. In 1980, for example, it had 20 ongoing projects in Indonesia, 34 in Bangladesh, etc.
21. Exceptionally, the Needs Assessment Reports for Rwanda and Guinea did include estimates of cost.

"subject to availability of funds" is usually assured, although sometimes, the Council has requested more information.

Once approved, the terms of country programmes have been considered binding, and the money allocated for a country programme has not been used elsewhere. (In Bolivia, for example, when, after a number of population projects had been agreed, the Government suddenly reverted to a strong anti-family planning stance, UNFPA looked for other population activities that would be acceptable to the Government on which to spend the Bolivian allocation). If at the end of the programme period, any of the country allocation is still unspent, UNFPA agrees to the country using it for some population activity not specified in the original programme. Only very exceptionally, such as in Iran when all UNFPA activities were stopped, has the balance of a country's approved budget reverted to UNFPA.

Until recently, UNFPA assistance to a multi-year country programme, approved by the Governing Council, could be counted on as an effective assurance of funding in the amount agreed for the given period. The proviso "subject to the availability of funds" had been considered as purely a juridical formality. Towards the end of 1980, however, when UNFPA's own sources of financing fell below expectations, it suddenly assumed a wholly new and uncomfortable reality. Countries were informed that the money that they had been promised for the following year would be sometimes drastically reduced, programme schedules would need to be extended accordingly, and sometimes activities postponed or even dropped altogether.

Under UNFPA procedures, the five-year country programme, as approved by the Governing Council and signed by the government, constitutes a sort of "umbrella agreement", providing a broad framework for future co-operation. The substantive details of the individual projects are the subject of a much more intensive process of consultation and preparation, involving the government, UNFPA and the UN executing agency, if any. Technical specialists participate as appropriate. This sometimes leads countries to complain that the consultants sent by UNFPA or the UN specialised agencies for the task of project appraisal are not always familiar with the country and its programme.

The whole process, from initial discussion of a project proposal, through appraisal and preparation of the formal request, to approval by UNFPA in New York may take anything from 4 to 18 months. The formal request, embodied in a lengthy project document, may actually be drafted by UNFPA, but in close collaboration with the department of government which will have the implementing responsibility. Once the document has been submitted to New York, consideration may last from three to six months, depending on the size of the project. If an executing agency is involved, the request will go to its Headquarters, also, for examination. Requests up to $100,000 can be approved within one to two months; larger projects have to be examined by UNFPA's Project Review and Allocation Committee who look closely at the substance of the request and its relevance to the UNFPA mandate, and whose recommendation for approval cannot be taken for granted. (For example, the Population and Development Project in Egypt was approved by the Review Committee with the proviso that certain modifications be adopted). Requests above $1 million have first to be recommended for approval by the Project Review and Allocation Committee and then submitted to and approved by the Governing Council. However, the system allows for emergency requests to be dealt with quickly. (A request from Thailand to make good a shortfall in the contraceptive supplies provided by other donors was approved within 15 days).

Once approved and signed, the official request becomes the Project Agreement ("project document") between the government, UNFPA and the executing agency, if there is one. The project document, which rigorously follows a standard UNFPA format, contains a very detailed description of the activity, the various inputs, and the manner and schedule of its implementation (the Plan of Operations). Recipient countries sometimes complain that the project document is *too* detailed, and does not contain sufficient built-in flexibility to permit changes to be made easily as the course of implementation may make necessary. On the other hand, UNFPA staff working in the country have occasionally been heard to complain that in some cases they are not clear enough. Because of a UN regulation that no Governing Council document may exceed 30 pages, the country programme, on the other hand, is often very general as regards the individual projects in the broad summary document submitted to the Governing Council, and this sometimes leads to ambiguities. Generally, when funds have permitted, UNFPA has tried to respond sympathetically to requests for substitution if they can be accommodated within the budget categories of existing projects. On the other hand, a request from the Government of Viet Nam which involved a change of programme category (a computer instead of a consultant), although it amounted to less than $40,000, had first to be examined by a consultant sent specially from ESCAP and then approved by New York.

Although the process of project appraisal and approval is complicated and protracted[22], this does not necessarily mean significant delays in the start of implementation. In Indonesia, for example, while the work of project appraisal was still underway, the Indonesian project agencies (the National Population and Family Planning Co-ordinating Board and the Central Bureau of Statistics) were preparing their respective requests in the format required by the Government of Indonesia, and processing them through the Government's administrative machinery for its approval.

More important, once projects are ready to start, they do not, in practice, have to wait for the Governing Council to give its formal approval. The Council's annual meeting is in June, and in theory, this could delay a project for almost a year. However, UNFPA's Executive Director is empowered to authorise "pre-project funding" for activities which are within the approved programme to an amount equal to 40 per cent of the total. Thus in Indonesia, the $30 million, five-year programme was recommended for approval by the Project Review Committee in October 1979, and the Executive Director authorised work to start the following January on those projects that were ready, up to an amount of $8 million. Normally, expenditures on the project made by the government during this "pre-project" period are not reimbursed by UNFPA, but there have been occasional exceptions (Viet Nam).

The project agreement will specify in some detail the responsibilities of the government, including the actions to be taken to get the project underway. In most cases, however, UNFPA does not make compliance a pre-condition for making the first disbursements. Some projects have been delayed for years because of failure of the government to carry out the necessary administrative arrangements, procure sites, provide labour, etc. (In some cases, UNFPA had meanwhile gone ahead and placed orders for equipment).

Project Implementation and Local Representation

In 1980, UNFPA had local representatives (known originally as "Co-ordinators") in 37 countries[23], including, now, China. In the days when most of the projects funded by UNFPA were implemented by different agencies of the UN, or even outside bodies, UNFPA obviously needed some means of keeping track of them. It accordingly stationed a representative to "co-ordinate" the various UNFPA projects in the country and act as liaison between the government and UNFPA Headquarters in New York.

Initially, the Co-ordinator's functions were largely advisory (he was described as "senior adviser on population matters to the UNDP Resident Representative", who is himself the official Co-ordinator of the projects of all UN agencies in the country). With the increasing number of directly-executed projects, however, the function of the Co-ordinator has evolved significantly. The change has recently been given formal

---

22. For all except *very* small projetcs, for which there is no proforma, and a one to two-page description with cost breakdown will suffice.
23. Plus three serving as regional liaison officers.

recognition in a change of title. In 1981, the "Co-ordinator" became "Deputy Representative and Senior Adviser for Population". The difference is a substantive one[24].

At present, the arrangements determining the relationship between the UNFPA Co-ordinator and the UNDP Resident Representative are so loosely defined as to permit, in practice, a wide variety of situations, depending on the circumstances and personalities concerned. In all cases, however, it is the Co-ordinator (to continue to use his old title) who takes the substantive decisions. When a project has been approved by New York, UNFPA sends a letter to the Resident Representative authorising him to sign the Project Agreement with the government and to open a project account. It is the Co-ordinator, however, who decides when disbursement may be made from the account, and (on behalf of the Resident Representative) signs the request to the UNDP Financial Officer to release the necessary funds.

The Co-ordinator today usually has a small staff consisting of one or more programme officers, an administrative officer, a financial officer, etc., some of whom will probably be nationals of the country. The Co-ordinator and his staff generally establish close working relations with local officials, at operational as well as senior policy levels, and are likely to be closely involved in the actual project implementation, although here too, the degree of practical involvement varies from country to country.

Most Co-ordinators, with their close and continuing experience of the country, feel that it is their role to interpret its needs to UNFPA Headquarters in New York and frequently act as spokesmen on its behalf. The Co-ordinator formally has only limited decision-making powers: he can authorise reallocation of funds as between project categories up to 10 per cent, and approve new requests up to $5,000. For anything above this, he has to seek approval from New York. Although many Co-ordinators go to great pains to influence New York to react sympathetically, and in most cases, New York will accept the substantive advice of the man-on-the-spot, the necessity to refer back to New York tends sometimes to irritate recipient country governments — in part, perhaps, because the process has to be initiated by a formal letter of request from the government[25].

In most cases, recipient countries find the presence of the Co-ordinator's office a tremendous help in overcoming the procedural problems that beset the course of project implementation, in facilitating changes and in getting a favourable reception for new project ideas. It has the additional advantage of providing convenient, low-key possibilities of project monitoring, without necessity of special visits from Headquarters. Few countries receive visits from New York more than once, or at the most twice a year, and then rarely from more than one or two people at a time.

Until recently, the office of the Co-ordinator was treated as a "project" within the country allocation. It is now financed as part of UNFPA's administrative overheads.

V. IMPLEMENTATION PROCEDURES

In view of the multiplicity of its operations, the number of countries and actors involved, and the variety of projects being funded at any one time, it is natural that UNFPA would seek to exert a degree of unifying control by means of its rules and procedures. UNFPA's procedures for project implementation are accordingly numerous, detailed, tough and complicated. Like its funding criteria, they are also subject to frequent revisions.

Since each recipient country is likely to have a large number of UNFPA projects ongoing at any one time, the task of complying with UNFPA procedural requirements could be a severe administrative burden. In practice, however, it generally is not. In

---

24. Discussions are currently being held in New York regarding the new role and responsibilities of the UNFPA Co-ordinator.
25. Some governments compare UNFPA unfavourably in this respect with UNICEF, which leaves a wide area of decision-making responsibility to its local representatives.

some cases, the requirements are simply not met, or not met in full, and UNFPA has not insisted. In others, the Co-ordinator or the executing agency either takes over much of the burden or substantially assists. The situation varies, however, from country to country. In some, the Co-ordinator translates UNFPA forms into the local language, makes a point of training local officials in both the detail and the meaning of their use, etc. In others, governments complain that UNFPA simply hands over its written "Standard Procedures" and does not bother explaining them until things go wrong.

If some of UNFPA's rules and procedures are tough, the spirit in which they have been applied generally has not been. In 1974, UNFPA wrote: "Perhaps the greatest hurdle external aid programmes have to surmount is the long time-lags in delivering assistance. Consequently, the Fund's operating policies have been directed towards avoiding bottlenecks resulting from too complicated procedures, and towards being as *responsive as possible to governments' wishes* and *needs*[26]. UNFPA was speaking, here of its decision to move away from using outside bodies as executing agencies in favour of more direct project execution, but as a statement of policy, it could apply equally to most of its regulations and procedures.

Inevitably, in so vast a programme, the way in which the rules are applied varies greatly. In general, however, UNFPA is recognised by both developing countries and its institutional recipients as being essentially accommodating. When, on occasion, it has taken a more rigorous approach, the reaction of surprise and dismay has been all the greater.

Budgeting and Disbursement

UNFPA has a very high level of disbursement for its programmes overall. Country and inter-country programmes together are disbursed at an average rate of some 80 per cent a year (of programmed expenditures)[27] due partly to overprogramming, partly to the nature of certain activities such as conferences, etc. which are easy to disburse in full, and partly because UNFPA counts as "expenditures" certain disbursements to UN agencies and other institutions. For the country activities, the rate of implementation has generally been considerably lower, although in many cases it has risen significantly in the last two to three years.

Each country is given a notional expenditure figure for the year, based on the budgetary requirements of ongoing and new activities, as mutually agreed between the government and the Co-ordinator[28]. The programming arrangement in fact provides a considerable degree of built-in flexibility since the annual programme is intended as a framework of activities rather than as a set of scheduled commitments. The progress of implementation is reviewed every six months, and the budget revised accordingly.

For projects implemented by recipient governments, project budgets[29] are set out in the letter of approval which New York sends to the UNDP Resident Representative. The country (or the executing agency) is entitled to spend funds against project allocations covering two to three years, allocations being in fact authorisations to spend funds.

The Resident Representative opens an imprest account for the project's local currency expenditures. Foreign currency expenditures (equipment purchases, salaries of expatriate consultants, etc.), are paid direct by UNFPA in New York. For local

---

26. International Population Assistance : the First Decade. (Author's italics).

27. UNFPA uses the term "pipe-line" to denote, not project funds awaiting disbursement, but project requests awaiting approval, and the term "commitment", not in the sense of a financial engagement but as an approved budget.

28. Countries that have a high disbursement rate find themselves today in the position of having no margin for making the cuts now demanded in view of UNFPA's own budgetary situation.

29. Some countries complain of inflexibility in that UNFPA budgets do not include an item for contingencies. However, there have been occasions where the "sundries" item has been used at the discretion of the Co-ordinator to provide a margin of manœuvre in difficult situations.

currency expenditures, funds are remitted to the government by UNDP in the currency of the country[30].

For the local costs of a project, UNFPA can make disbursement in three ways: by means of advances (usually quarterly[31]); by reimbursement of expenditures already made; and by direct payment by the UNDP local office (for minor equipment, travel, per diems, etc.). The most usual method is quarterly advances, but reimbursement is sometimes more convenient, particularly if the project contains a large amount of local cost expenditures. (In Bangladesh, for example, some 75 per cent of the UNFPA programme has been funded in the form of reimbursement).

Advances have usually been the simplest procedure from the point of view of the recipient. Whereas reimbursement can only be made against presentation of actual payment vouchers, etc. — often a formidable administrative hurdle, and one of the factors making for delays in disbursement — advances were, until recently, made without any such documentation. For the first two quarters, advances are made automatically. Requests for the third and subsequent quarters have to be accompanied by a progress report and financial statement showing what has been spent against the approved budget, item by item. The forms for this purpose[32] are short and straightforward. They nonetheless sometimes pose problems, either because of deficiencies in the government's accounting, or because project budgets, prepared at the time the project document is written, may differ substantially from the actual pattern of implementation several years later. It is therefore sometimes genuinely difficult for project managers to know just how much they have in fact spent compared to the agreed budget schedule, and for UNFPA to follow how its money is being disbursed. Further, in many cases, the situation as perceived by the project accounts officer does not correspond to the actual progress of implementation as perceived by the project manager.

In principle, requests for advances should be accompanied by full supporting documents[33], a requirement which would make the system of advances as difficult as that of reimbursement. However, even without supporting documents, many countries are unable to meet the requirements for accurate financial statements satisfactorily. UNFPA has therefore rarely insisted on strict compliance.

Occasionally, it has insisted. (In one case, funds were withheld for six months because the Co-ordinator insisted that the financial reporting system should be functioning effectively before funds were to be released). Sometimes the Co-ordinator provides "technical assistance" to get the financial reporting and requests for advance established on a satisfactory basis. Thus in Egypt, the operation of UNFPA's financial reporting system called for an extensive effort of training and adaptation involving the UNFPA office and the administrative and financial departments of the national implementing agencies of all the UNFPA-assisted population projects. In Indonesia, the Co-ordinator has stationed a UNFPA-financed officer to work part-time in the financial services of the National Family Planning Co-ordinating Board and part-time in project monitoring.

Latterly, UNFPA has been taking a more rigorous approach to the financial monitoring of its projects. However, it recognises that to insist on full compliance with all the documentation officially required for requesting advance payments would be impractical. The usual arrangement is for the Co-ordinator to work out together with the government a practical system for reporting expenditures and obtaining funds, using

---

30. Only 2 per cent of the contributions received by UNFPA are in non-convertible currencies. UNFPA changes its convertible currencies into non-convertible in the proportion needed to pay for the actual expenditures incurred in the field. UNFPA eventually reimburses UNDP in the equivalent amount of convertible currency at the rate of exchange effective when the advance took place.

31. For a one-time activity (e.g. a seminar), UNFPA will advance 80 per cent of its contribution at the outset.

32. Form A — request for advance; Form B — statement of previous expenditures for that calendar year and previous years.

33. Supporting documents should include disbursement vouchers and receipts, monthly payroll and time records, suppliers' invoices, travel tickets, receipts for daily allowances, etc.

some compromise formula that takes into account the government's own administrative constraints and financial practices[34].

In theory, any unspent balance from one quarter's advance should be deducted from the amount requested for the following quarter. It is tempting, however, for governments to use the balances as a handy interim source of financing. Sometimes Co-ordinators allow this on the understanding that the amount will eventually be made good for the same or subsequent projects. On the other hand, they are naturally reluctant to have advances lying idle, possibly earning interest in the recipient's bank account.

The actual process of payment is simple and rapid. For directly-executed projects, once the Co-ordinator has authorised disbursement, funds are released immediately from the imprest account which the Resident Representative has opened in a local bank and are paid to the implementing agency (or central government) within a few days. (New York has only to be kept informed). Where there is an executing agency, the latter will disburse according to its procedures, but any differences are slight.

When government regulations permit, UNFPA will make payment direct to the implementing agency concerned, rather than to the central treasury for it to redirect to the project. (In Indonesia, the Co-ordinator obtained once-for-all authorisation from the Central Government Co-ordinating Body — BAPPENAS — to do so). This greatly facilitates project implementation, as otherwise implementing agencies may sometimes have to wait months before they finally receive from the Treasury the local funds corresponding to the donor's aid contribution.

Until 1981, UNFPA allowed a 10 per cent increase on an annual project budget for unforeseen costs or price increases. This flexibility allowance has now been reduced to 2 per cent with a maximum limit of $5,000. Where a currency devaluation occurs, however, the matter is more complicated. In Egypt, for example, the value of the Egyptian pound was practically halved in relation to the U.S. dollar in the course of the project. As project budgets are recorded in dollars, this would have generated about twice as much funds in local currency as was originally approved for local costs. The recalculation of budgets on the basis of the initial approval and the new exchange rate resulted in savings on the programme in Egypt amounting to about $700,000, and the Co-ordinator persuaded New York to let this be used for other activities within the country programme.

Procurement

The goods and equipment requirements for UNFPA projects are carefully reviewed and costed as part of the process of project preparation, either by the executing agency (in the case of specialised equipment) or by UNFPA. Once the list has been agreed, the actual procurement may be done by a number of different agencies.

For directly-implemented projects, the receiving government can be given authority to purchase, if UNFPA is satisfied that it has the necessary technical expertise[35]. Government procurement, however, is generally not encouraged and tends to be rare. The more usual arrangement is for procurement to be done by the executing agency, if there is one, by UNFPA itself, by the UN[36] or by UNICEF.

UNICEF has been extensively used as a procurement agency both by the UN and UNFPA. It has specialist expertise in a number of procurement fields, and because it

---

34. In Indonesia, for example, the Co-ordinator has agreed to authorise advances upon receipt of vouchers for up to 60 per cent of the money spent, and consisting of a combination of receipts and commitments.

35. An ad hoc procurement committee, chaired by the UNDP Resident Representative and of which the UNFPA Co-ordinator is a member, is set up to assess which items can be purchased by government procurement and to decide the procedures to be followed — which may be either those of the government or the UN.

36. Procurement by the UN is done through the UN Purchase and Transportation Unit. Recently, UNDP has set up its own International Procurement Agency, for which suppliers often quote special terms.

buys up large stocks of certain goods and equipment, it is often able to provide goods quickly from "off-the-shelf". UNICEF's comprehensive printed catalogue giving technical details of available goods and equipment is much appreciated in developing countries as a practical form of technical assistance. Despite these various advantages, however, UNICEF procurement is often unpopular. Sometimes off-the-shelf purchase proves unsuitable for the particular country concerned (e.g. wrong cycle and voltage in the case of electrical equipment). Sometimes it is difficult to ensure installation and local servicing for equipment purchased abroad. There is the further complaint of the absence of direct contact between UNICEF and the implementing body concerned. The latter is therefore not kept informed of the progress of the order, and sometimes is not even told the final choice of supplier or likely delivery date.

Although there is no official policy on the matter, UNFPA is becoming increasingly inclined to undertake international procurement itself. This would eliminate both the time involved in using UNICEF as a middleman (which is sometimes swamped with orders from other agencies). It will also reduce the cost — UNICEF charging a fee of 3 per cent for goods up to a value of $100,000. UNFPA is continuing, however, to take advantage of UNICEF's expertise for purchase of contraceptives and medical supplies. A UNICEF staff member is attached to UNFPA for this purpose.

Whoever the procurement agent used, the same broad rules should be followed. For items costing under $1,000, the country specifies what it wants, and UNFPA will pass the request to the UN or UNICEF, who will compare available supplies and prices and decide what to buy. (If there is an executing agency, its headquarters will do this). For items over $1,000, international competitive bidding[37] is required and there should be at least three bids. For major items, approval has to be sought from the Contracts Committee of the agency concerned (for purchases over $20,000 in the case of UNFPA, for those over $10,000 for UNESCO and some other specialised agencies). These rules apply equally to purchase by UNICEF which has its own Contracts Committee.

Recipient countries generally find UNFPA's procurement arrangements very complicated. Certainly, UNFPA is very particular in the matter of specifications[38], and its quest for the most advantageous buy may cause delays or inconvenience at the recipient end. On the other hand, UNFPA is prepared to facilitate matters by allowing local purchase for greater speed or where it may be cheaper. (In Egypt, for example, where, under President Sadat's "open-door" policy, many foreign manufacturing companies have set up local agencies, UNFPA found that the local agent could sometimes provide the goods at half the c.i.f. price of those quoted by the foreign supplier, and with immediate delivery).

Local purchase (which may include "regional" purchase) is however hedged about with a number of safeguards. The implementating agency (ministry of health, university, etc.) is authorised to place orders itself only up to an amount of $250[39]. The Co-ordinator's office then pays the supplier direct. Local purchases up to $1,000 for any single item can be approved by the Resident Representative of the UNDP (on the advice of the Co-ordinator), without reference to New York. For more important purchases, UNFPA in New York requires first to see the specifications and to have detailed information as to the intended use, and then to receive copies of the three best bids received. It then compares with the prices and delivery dates it could obtain by purchasing from New York. If it appears a clear case, a cable of approval can be sent immediately. At other times, it may contact a supplier overseas.

---

37. International competitive bidding (ICB) can sometimes lead to some unexpected situations. Fifteen major computers were requested for the China census. The UN (the Executing Agency) after ICB chose IBM, the model that China had asked for in the first place. But under NATO rules, a technical committee has to give approval for the provision of highly-advanced equipment, and this took about a year.

38. In some cases, UNFPA has held up funds on the whole project pending submission of additional information.

39. Furniture is usually purchased locally under this arrangement. It is therefore annoying to recipient countries that some executing agencies buy furniture abroad too.

Where purchasing is done locally, UNFPA is intimately involved in the whole process of calling for bids and examining the tenders. Countries usually appreciate this, because although UNFPA procurement requirements are likely to be more complicated than their own, the Co-ordinator helps. Most implementing agencies already have a Tenders Committee for important purchases. Under UNFPA procedures, this has to include a representative of the Resident Representative's office (usually their Purchase Officer) and the Committee is chaired by the Co-ordinator. This is generally considered to be helpful rather than restrictive.

The amount of local purchase that actually takes place, of course, varies with the country and the nature of the goods required. In Egypt, as we have seen, there is now a considerable amount. In Indonesia, on the other hand, the only major item purchased locally is cars, for which the Government has banned imports. In general, however, UNFPA seems to be increasingly favouring local purchase where this appears to offer practical advantages.

Although UNFPA does careful screening of purchase requests and has rigorous purchase requirements, once orders have been placed, it is generally much less demanding about follow-up. Where the government does the purchasing itself, it is not required to send in invoices or the actual receipts (even to the office of the Resident Representative). In principle, receipts are supposed to be made available to the Resident Representative and the UN auditors, but many governments do not bother about keeping them. All that is required is an annual Inventory Report (a physical listing of the equipment received) to be prepared by the implementing agency and sent to New York after certification by the Resident Representative. In practice, even these are not always submitted.

UNFPA is well aware that these arrangements have erred on the side of over-flexibility. Occasionally, it cracks down and requires a special detailed and substantiated account of the equipment that has been provided. (In one country, UNFPA finally demanded a full and complete accounting of all the equipment supplied since the beginning of UNFPA aid to the country. It then made its own listing and compared the two, its final report including 36 attachments).

Overall, UNFPA is trying generally to exert a tighter degree of control over what happens to the equipment that it supplies. The task is not easy in that it is often sent to widely-dispersed destinations, and once arrived, the actual use made of it is difficult to check on. Further, the inventory forms used by UNFPA for reporting the physical and financial facts of purchase and delivery, although they specify the physical location of the equipment, do not convey any substantive information as to the purpose for which it is being used or by whom[40].

Goods financed by UNFPA and imported into the country from abroad are exempt from customs duty and legally remain the property of UNFPA for five years. After this time, the goods are deemed to have no more useful life and can pass into the possession of the government tax-free. For this reason, many countries prefer UNFPA procurement to that of donors who give immediate custody to the government, but require it to import itself in the normal way.

Reporting and Auditing

The spirit and practice of UNFPA's reporting and auditing procedures are well summed up in the following quotation from one of UNFPA's basic manuals: "All procedures are intended to provide a *standard method of operation*. However, it may be necessary to *modify the procedures in cases where previous arrangements have been agreed to for ongoing projects or because of particular circumstances* regarding new

---

40. In the case of highly-specialised equipment (e.g. audiovisual equipment for information and communication programmes), executing agencies may send follow-up technical missions to advise on maintenance. There is sometimes little effective concern, however, to find out the substantive use being made of the equipment in actual programmes.

projects. All such deviations from the procedures should receive the approval of UNFPA Headquarters[41]".

The purpose of the procedures is to provide a periodic review of accomplishments and problems "for use in decision-making". To this end, a series of "core" reporting arrangements are provided for: specifically, a Project Progress Report – to be submitted twice a year for each and every project; an annual Tripartite Project Review for all major projects, undertaken jointly by the government, UNFPA and the executing agency, if any; and an Annual Country Review, for those countries where UNFPA has either a country agreement or two or more major projects (over $100,000). In addition, the Co-ordinator is expected to be doing continuous monitoring, preparing substantive quarterly reports on progress and identifying any special problems. On project termination, a final report should be presented. There may, on occasion, if there are special technical problems, be a Mid-Term Review as well.

The Project Progress Report consists of two pages of pro forma to be completed, to which, for all except very small projects, should be appended a narrative description under six headings[42]. Preparing it is meant to be the responsibility of the executing agency, or the government, in the case of a self-executed project. The report is sent to the Co-ordinator for transmission to New York. Recipient countries and Co-ordinators alike maintain that, strictly observed, this requirement would constitute an intolerable burden. In practice, therefore, the reporting arrangements to be followed are agreed between the government and the Co-ordinator at the time the project document is signed. They therefore vary greatly from country to country.

The reports (two a year) need not be more than three to four pages per project (no pro forma) but simply follow the agreed project plan. They show the activities that have been implemented in the previous six-month period, those which have not been implemented and why, and how the programme should be re-phased for the following period. The reports are produced each January and July and constitute a work plan for the next six months[43].

In Egypt, for large-scale government-implemented projects, UNFPA has agreed to accept only one major project report as an annual progress report. This system conforms with the Egyptian Government's own reporting requirements. On the other hand, for relatively small projects or for those that are executed by a United Nations specialised agency, project reports are presented every six months. Notwithstanding this flexible approach, and although the Co-ordinator participates in the preparation of the Annual Progress Report, the exercise remains a major production, exhausting the Egyptian services concerned. The Population and Family Planning Board prepares at least two drafts in English, preceded by several versions in Arabic, before agreeing to a final version, and the whole process takes from four to five months[44].

"Tripartite" Reviews – also project-by-project, but for major ones only – may in fact be bipartite if there is no executing agency involved. It is then for the Co-ordinator to decide whether a review is in fact needed. (Headquarters does not necessarily participate). The government has the formal responsibility for writing the report on the meeting, and the Co-ordinator sends it to New York with his comments. UNFPA recognises that these reviews, if held annually, are often cursory and partial (being conducted by the interested parties concerned), they rarely include field visits, and are sometimes mounted primarily as an exercise to attract additional funding. In other

---

41. Financial Procedures for the Execution of UNEPA Projects by Recipient Governments. (Author's italics).
42. In one country, the implementing agencies received 8 pages of explanation plus 14 attachments.
43. The Indonesian National Family Planning Co-ordinating Board has three staff members engaged full-time in preparing reports to its three principal donors. (The Government pays their salaries). Even so, most donors help fill in their respective report forms – at least at the beginning.
44. The Board, beneficiary of important UNFPA assistance, takes the preparation of its reports to UNFPA very seriously. It has engaged a full-time English-speaking report-writer (paid by UNFPA), and in 1979 presented a comprehensive report of 100 pages.

cases, they have lasted several days and constituted a hard-headed appraisal of the problems encountered. All parties know that there is always the ultimate sanction of a cutting-off of funds.

The final report, on project termination, should be prepared either by the executing agency or the government three months before actual completion of the work. The report (no format) is to be sent to the Co-ordinator, who then has to add his personal assessment of the project's results and makes suggestions for utilisation and follow-up. Final reports are officially "mandatory" for the executing agency and the donor agency. In practice, the conclusion of a project has not always been followed by the preparation of a final report, although in recent years, the situation has improved. The reports are filed with the UNFPA library and abstracts are published.

The Annual Country Review is programme-oriented and brings together all the areas of activity which UNFPA is assisting. It accordingly has contributions from every project manager. In the case of Egypt, for example, it is put together by the Monitoring and Evaluation Department of the Population and Family Planning Board, and then goes to the Board of Directors for its approval before being presented to UNFPA. A good month's work at senior staff levels goes into its preparation. The country reviews can be valuable, however, as providing an *overall* examination of goals and achievements and enabling decisions to be made about special action needed to speed implementation, re-programming, etc. It is also one of the few occasions when UNFPA-sponsored activities are reviewed in relation to the country's broader development plans and priorities. These meetings are normally chaired by the government, and someone from UNFPA Headquarters may attend. The basic document is a country brief prepared by the Co-ordinator. In practice, Annual Reviews tend not to be held as a regular event, even in countries which have major UNFPA projects. As with the other monitoring and review requirements, assiduous observance would seriously encroach upon the conduct of operational responsibilities.

These various monitoring arrangements, if strictly followed, should catch out any problems in performance, delivery, timing, etc., and decide such remedial action as may be necessary. UNFPA officials recognise, however, that they are generally not effective in doing so. They give several reasons. Good monitoring presupposes good project design (not always the case); reports are sometimes written by people seeking primarily to make a good impression; and as we have seen, the system is only irregularly applied. To a very large extent, good reporting, in practice, depends on the interest and ability of the individual Co-ordinator. There is, further, the built-in anomaly that UNFPA Headquarters would be totally unable to deal substantively (or even read) the flood of paper that would engulf it if its official reporting requirements were strictly observed. A computerised system is accordingly currently in preparation.

Auditing requirements seem to be considerably less exacting. Implementing agencies usually keep two sets of accounts — one according to the government's regulations and one according to UNFPA's. There are sometimes differences in the methods of registering expenditures and keeping books, which makes reconciliation at the end of the financial year somewhat awkward, but in most cases, these problems would seem to be minor. Even the fact that some governments have different financial years from that of UNFPA does not seem to cause major problems for the accountants accustomed to keeping two sets of accounts (or even several, where an agency is being funded by several different donors).

Most countries find UNFPA the most relaxed among their various donors in the matter of auditing. In Bangladesh, for example, UNFPA was prepared to accept the regular government audit done one year after the end of the Government's financial year, but since the Government auditors have been unable to cope with the volume of work, UNFPA has appointed a commercial auditing firm (paid for, not out of project funds but out of the general fund of the Co-ordinator). In Egypt, commercial firms are contracted by UNFPA to audit the annual accounts of directly-executed projects, and their audit reports are adjoined to the Government's annual financial reports to UNFPA. However, in view of the large number, complexity and size of the activities implemented by the Population and Family Planning Board, the external auditors examine the Board's accounts every quarter.

UNFPA does not *itself* do an audit until a project has been completed. At this time, all the accumulated vouchers covering perhaps four years of expenditures are supposed to be presented for audit. This audit, undertaken by the UNDP Auditing Service, which spends most of its time travelling, as a practical matter, cannot be applied to each and every one of UNFPA's projects. It is therefore done on a spot-check basis only[45].

VI. CO-ORDINATION WITH OTHER POPULATION ASSISTANCE DONORS

UNFPA has consistently sought co-ordination with other donors at headquarters level. It has sponsored a number of meetings at which the heads of most of the major donors of population assistance have been invited to consider how the goal of co-ordination may be pursued more effectively — sometimes as a general policy issue, sometimes in the context of the needs of a particular developing country. Thus in April 1981, UNFPA took the initiative of assembling all potential aid donors to consider the resumption of population assistance to Pakistan following the publication of the Government's new Family Welfare Programme, and to try to get some indication from each of the likely measure of its support.

As a political reality, however, UNFPA, as it well recognises, can go only so far in these endeavours. The main problem, as was plainly pointed out at the Geneva meeting, is that every donor is happy to co-ordinate provided that *it* can be responsible for the co-ordinating. While the smaller bilateral donors may be prepared to come in under the umbrella of UNFPA, the two other "great powers" of the population assistance scene, the World Bank and US AID, generally are not. A further difficulty is that UNFPA's Needs Assessment Reports, being aimed at identifying areas of assistance for UNFPA, do not always serve as the basis for other donors for selection of projects. (Most bilateral donors say that they find these reports useful, but as background information only).

The "great powers" usually prefer either to "go it alone" or to take the lead in associating other donors with their programmes. Occasionally, however, UNFPA has scored a notable success in achieving a practical measure of co-ordination. Thus in Bangladesh, UNFPA persuaded the World Bank and US AID to organise their respective Review Group and Aid Evaluation Missions into a *Joint Mission* with the UNFPA Needs Assessment Mission in order to save the time of senior Bangladesh Government officials.

As a general rule, where UNFPA has been most effective in introducing some co-ordination of population assistance activities has been at the country level. For example, in Egypt (where the population assistance donors had never all sat down together with the Supreme Council for Population and Family Planning), UNFPA took the initiative and invited all the major population assistance donors to attend their Annual Country Review meeting[46]. (UNFPA was particularly concerned to take steps to effect some co-ordination of population assistance in Egypt, and for this purpose, commissioned a study which revealed the numerous inconsistencies and anomalies resulting from the absence of dialogue between Egypt's several population assistance donors[47]). On the

---

45. All directly-executed projects are expected to be audited by the government auditors or by a legally-recognised external auditor in the country. In addition, all projects are subject to audit by the UNDP Internal Audit Service which conducts, on an annual basis, a few selected audits on behalf of UNFPA. Projects are also subject to audit by the United Nations Board of External Auditors who report directly to the General Assembly. Projects executed by United Nations specialised agencies are audited by the agencies themselves in accordance with their own internal auditing procedures. All agencies provide to the Fund year-end audited accounts certified by their own External Auditors.
46. The World Bank did not attend.
47. Donor Assistance to Family Planning in Egypt, Nataraja, January 1980.

other hand, UNFPA does not normally participate in meetings of the World Bank's Consultative Groups, even when population is on the agenda[48].

How effective UNFPA is in practice in co-ordinating with other population assistance donors at the country level is very much a function of, on the one hand, the individual Co-ordinator (or possibly UNDP Resident Representative), and on the other, the circumstances of the particular country. In Kenya, for example, where UNFPA has a relatively small programme, there are no regular co-ordination arrangements, but UNFPA is prepared to use some half of the total allocation to support the health activities to be financed by the World Bank Group. Indeed, in a number of countries, UNFPA funding is used to complement the activities of other donors, either by picking up components that are difficult to accommodate under the other donors' programmes, or by helping with local costs, etc. A considerable degree of quiet dovetailing of different donors' population programmes is in fact going on in this way. Thus in Bangladesh, for example, the Bank constructs buildings, UNFPA pays staff salaries, and US AID does the training[49]. In Egypt, the Population and Development Project, which started with assistance from UNFPA, is now the subject of a collective effort from three external donors, — UNFPA, the Government of the Netherlands (by a special grant which is channelled through UNFPA under the "multi-bi" scheme) and US AID.

A different form of co-ordination favoured by UNFPA is association with bilateral donors in joint-financing of selected population activities. In common with many other UN agencies, UNFPA has entered into "multi-bi" financing arrangements with a number of bilateral donors. Under these arrangements, the bilateral donor provides funds for agreed population activities in addition to those financed under its bilateral programmes, with UNFPA undertaking the administrative and management responsibilities on behalf of both the funding parties concerned. In the mid-1970s, UNFPA entertained high hopes of being able to undertake a major increase in its activities through "multi-bi" arrangements. Apart from some of the Scandinavian donors, the response was at first somewhat slow, although a number of joint projects are being undertaken. (In some cases, donors hesitate because they are already participating in joint financing of population projects with the World Bank in the particular country concerned[50]. In others, they wish to choose which particular project component they will assist, to undertake their own appraisal and monitoring, apply their own procurement procedures, etc.). It recognises that the various practical problems of co-ordination and conciliation involved make "multi-bi" more suitable for large-scale activities which justify the additional complications of organisation and implementation.

Recently "multi-bi" seems to be showing an up-turn. The first such activity, undertaken in 1976, was a grant of funds-in-trust of $2 million from Sweden for a sex education project in Mexico. As of June 1982, the cumulative total of allocations for funds-in-trust stands at $13.8 million, the principal donors being Denmark, Finland, Italy, the Netherlands, Norway[51] and Sweden. The OPEC Fund has recently agreed to a $1.5 million grant for Pakistan. New arrangements for "multi-bi" are currently being negotiated and UNFPA expects substantial additional financing by these means, with

---

48. In 1979, for the first time, it attended the meeting of the Bangladesh Consultative Group as an observer.

49. Bangladesh is perhaps a country where unofficial co-ordination arrangements work unusually well. The population assistance donors meet informally once a month and the representatives of the three principal donors then call on the Deputy Secretary of the Ministry of Health to present an oral report. Previously, there were monthly donor meetings presided over by the Deputy Secretary, but he now attends only if specifically invited.

50. In 1980, UNFPA hoped to organise some $25 million of assistance for Bangladesh through multi-bi arrangements. In the event, only a few donors were willing to participate, as most of them were already contributing to the IDA projects.

51. The Government of Norway has contributed $5.7 million towards the cost of UNFPA Needs Assessment Missions as well as a number of primary health care and family planning projects in particular countries (Jamaica, Peru, Sri Lanka, Nepal).

additional contributions from Italy and other countries. One reason why interest in multi-bi arrangements has suddenly quickened is probably that countries realise that they offer an easy means of increasing their bilateral aid for population without the administrative burden involved in working up independent bilateral programmes.

UNFPA

AID FOR POPULATION ACTIVITIES
($ US million)

i) Total volume of population assistance expenditures through 1981   851.3

ii) Annual expenditures on population assistance, 1975-1981

1975	71.2
1976	75.8
1977	72.1
1978	95.7
1979	131.6
1980	147.5
1981	136.5

iii) Division of total expenditures on population assistance by major population sectors.

	1975	1976	1977	1978	1979	1980	1981	Total	%
Basic data collection	11 761	13 126	10 504	11 624	20 951	27 451	32 992	128 409	17.6
Population dynamics	4 858	6 819	6 506	8 396	13 308	16 835	14 648	71 370	9.8
Formulation and evaluation of population policies and programmes	3 981	2 542	2 731	4 075	9 488	9 187	9 652	41 656	5.7
Family planning	35 123	37 935	36 420	48 980	57 622	60 554	43 265	319 899	43.8
Communication and education	8 900	8 319	8 562	11 607	16 773	19 564	19 526	93 251	12.7
Multisector activities	6 590	7 040	7 408	11 017	13 440	13 927	16 450	75 872	10.4
Total	71 213	75 781	72 131	95 699	131 582	147 518	136 533	730 457	100.0

THE WORLD BANK[1]

I. INTRODUCTION

The World Bank entered the field of population at the end of the 1960s, following important public statements by President McNamara in which he argued that a high rate of population growth was "the greatest single obstacle to economic and social development"[2], and was, moreover, undermining the effective employment of scarce development funds. The first Bank loan for population – a $2 million trial project in Jamaica – followed in 1970.

Providing on average about one-tenth of the total international financing made available each year for population activities, the World Bank is the third major donor of population assistance after US AID and the UNFPA[3]. As the third of the "great powers" in the population assistance field, the significance of the Bank lies, however, less in terms of overall financial flows than in its contribution to the programmes of certain individual developing countries. A large part of the World Bank's funding for population activities has been concentrated on a relatively small number of recipient countries, for whom the presence of the Bank has proved of enormous importance as a source of massive and continuing support for the national population programme. Some countries have received Bank loans for population to the tune of $30 million or more, often receiving a second loan for a similar or greater amount while the first is still running. Indonesia, for example, is already into its third population loan from the World Bank. Further, the Bank has in some cases used its influence to mobilise other donor agencies to co-ordinate their aid for population to provide additional funding for the population programmes supported by the Bank.

Since its decision to provide assistance for population activities was made in order to tackle the problem of population growth, "population" for the Bank has tended to be synonymous with "over-population", and the prime objective has been to assist programmes designed to limit fertility, primarily through family planning. The Bank's early population projects, therefore, began simply as support for family planning programmes. Later, they came to cover assistance for health activities also, as some developing countries felt that an improved health infrastructure offered the most convenient carrier for family planning, and because of the obvious relationship of family planning to mother and child health care. As its programmes developed, however, the Bank, like most other agencies providing population assistance, began to include also certain activities designed to increase the *demand* for family planning, and support for the institutions who were to design and implement the country's population programmes. From quite early on, therefore, Bank population projects have included activities in the area of population information, education and communication, research and monitoring arrangements to test their effectiveness, and a sizeable effort of institution-building.

In addition to providing funding for population projects, the Bank envisaged that it could make a contribution to tackling the problem of population growth on a broader front also – specifically, by creating a wider awareness of the population problem, providing technical assistance and by research. In the case of the latter, the World Bank as an institution has taken a much broader approach to the problem of population than does the World Bank as an agency providing population assistance.

---

1. Statistical table, see page 88.
2. Address to the University of Notre-Dame, 1969.
3. Which provide roughly one-half and one-quarter respectively.

The Bank's Development Economics Department includes a Population and Human Resources Division which carries out basic research into demographic statistics and the inter-relationship of demographic movements of all kinds (i.e. mortality and migration as well as fertility) and economic and social variables. Some of these aspects are covered by the Bank in its lending in other development sectors (e.g. migration under Urban Projects). The Bank's "Population" projects, however, have continued to focus on the central concern of fertility.

As a lending institution, the World Bank, unlike other population assistance agencies, can only provide funding for population activities in the form of loans. However, in population as in other sectors, the poorer developing countries have qualified for IDA credits (at 3/4 per cent interest over 50 years) — viz, Bangladesh, India, Kenya, Thailand and the Philippines (First Population Project). The Dominican Republic received a Population loan from the Bank's Third Window (at 5.6 per cent per annum). Population loans at the World Bank's current lending rates have been made to date to Indonesia, Jamaica, Malaysia, the Philippines (Second Population Project) and South Korea.

Today, IDA funds are shrinking, the Third Window facility no longer exists, and the Bank's current interest rate is in the neighbourhood of 11-12 per cent. Developing countries' understandable resistance to borrowing for population is likely to increase proportionately. Perhaps, coincidentally, the Bank's public speeches on the importance of the population "issue" have also ceased.

Obstacles to Bank Lending for Population

When the World Bank, the titan of international development financing, first entered the area of population assistance, it was seen as a major breakthrough both for population assistance and for the promotion of population policies in developing countries. In terms of overall volume of aid, these hopes have not been realised[4]. For a number of reasons, the Bank has found it unexpectedly hard to make loans for population.

First, of course, is the fact that Bank aid is only available on loan terms. From the developing country point of view, population projects are not good candidates for external borrowing — their outcome is long-term and uncertain, they are particularly susceptible to the influence of local conditions and cultural factors (often unpredictable), and it is difficult to obtain valid quantifiable results. Further, borrowing from the Bank for a population project involves not only the financial obligation of debt and interest repayment, but a protracted and difficult burden of preparatory work before the money can begin to flow. In this respect, a "soft" IDA credit is as burdensome as a Bank loan on normal "hard" terms.

When it was first decided that the Bank should make loans for population, it was also decided as a matter of policy that there would be no special arrangements, but that the Bank's standard lending procedures should apply. Many observers, including some within the Bank, have questioned this approach. However, the rationale at the time was that these procedures, which the Bank likes to think of as "perhaps (its) unique contribution to the theory and practice of development finance[5]" would inject a valuable element of discipline and rigorous performance into population projects. The Bank has thus had to handle complicated and diffuse activities designed to provide a person-to-person service, involving a change in the most intimate aspect of individual human behaviour, using the same procedures as had been evolved for lending for major infrastructure investment.

---

4. Barely 1 per cent of the total amount of funds provided annually by the World Bank for development activities is for population, although of course it was never envisaged that population activities would come to rival major infrastructure projects as subjects for Bank lending.

5. E.K. Hawkins: "The Principles of Development Aid".

While the Bank does not go so far as to make a cost-benefit analysis before agreeing to lend for population projects, but only applies criteria of cost-effectiveness[6], it nevertheless builds into the project various performance targets which the recipient government is expected to meet[7]. The result has often been to make manifest the sometimes disturbing gap between officially agreed schedules of operations and the realities of project performance.

It is sometimes suggested that the tendency towards procedural orthodoxy which marked the Bank's approach to the new area of population assistance may have been strengthened by the arrangements set up within the Bank for handling population work. Since there was no population experience among existing Bank staff, when a new Population Projects Department was created (consisting mainly of talent from outside)[8], it was placed under the general supervision of the Central Projects Staff — the Bank's "quality assurance unit".

Perhaps the Bank's greatest handicap, however, has been less loan terms and inappropriate procedures than the fact that its population work has received little institutional support within the organisation itself. There are several convergent reasons. First, as a cost-conscious financial institution, the Bank judges operations in terms of their "manpower co-efficient" (i.e. the input of staff time in relation to the amount of the loan), a standard by which population (with three times that of the hardware sectors) emerges as way above average. Second, population projects tend to have a large element of local currency costs — whereas the Bank traditionally feels that its lending should be primarily for foreign exchange needs. Third, and partly as a consequence, they tend also to be slow to disburse compared to quick-disbursing infrastructure activities — a grievous defect in an institution that rates its operating effectiveness in terms of the amounts of money lent and disbursed each year. Finally, population projects, by their nature, tend to be difficult for the Bank to supervise effectively. For Bank staff outside of the Department immediately concerned, therefore, "population" has been seen as at best a risk venture, and rarely as a subject to be vigorously promoted in their own relations with the Bank's borrowers. The strong commitment to population of President McNamara "did not permeate the institution[9]".

The Bank is itself very conscious of these problems and has undertaken various initiatives to try to remedy them, including major policy reviews undertaken by leading outside experts in the field. (Population is the only sector of the Bank's work to have been thus examined). An external Advisory Panel (headed by the late Dr. Bernard Berelson) emphasized the need to bring population closer to other sectors of Bank lending, and suggested that the Bank seek to introduce population "components" into activities in other social sectors. While agreeing that the Bank should continue to support family planning programmes, it urged the desirability of promoting a more multi-sectoral approach, and of giving greater emphasis to activities likely to encourage the demand for family planning services.

The Bank continues to find it difficult however to "mesh" its population work with its work in other sectors. The reorganisation of the Population Projects Department into the Department of Population, Health and Nutrition[10] was made largely

---

6. "Project presentations are supposed at least to demonstrate that the project is the 'least cost' way of achieving the government's population objectives". World Bank Lending Policies and Procedures in the Population Sector, World Bank, 1977.

7. The Bank's early population loans tried to estimate a "cost per family planning acceptor", but this practice has since been dropped.

8. The Bank's lending operations at Headquarters are divided into six Regional Offices, each responsible for lending in all sectors within the Region. Population, together with three other sectors, has been placed with the Central Projects Staff as being too small to be divided among the Regional Offices.

9. Dr. Bernard Berelson and Ronald Freeman: "Review of the Implementation of the Recommendations of the External Advisory Panel on Population", 1978.

10. Nutrition had already become a subject for Bank lending and has shifted from an initial association with Population Projects to Agricultural Development, and then back to Population. Health facilities however had previously only figured in Bank loans as convenient carriers for family planning services.

with the idea of offering new and non-clinical bridges to family planning. The Bank's work in population in fact opened the way to Bank lending for health activities (starting with population-related delivery systems), and some of the Bank's projects have been for both family planning and health services (e.g. Kenya). The Bank has also had some success in introducing a population education component into its education loans in some countries. However, some of its recent health lending has not included a family planning element (e.g. Brazil), and it has not yet proved possible to introduce a population component into loans for rural development, urban projects, etc.

II. APPROACH AND CRITERIA

The Bank has always maintained that as a source of (loan) funds for population, it is likely to be "the donor of last resort". Nevertheless, it sees a special role for itself, first, because of the large resources that it can muster, and second, for the access that it enjoys to developing country governments at the highest levels. Indeed, in many respects, the Bank has acted rather as "donor of first resort".

Thus in certain cases, the promise of a Bank loan has encouraged governments to embark on population programmes at a time and on a scale that they would have been unlikely to have undertaken without Bank persuasion. The first IDA Population Project in Egypt is one. Another is the IDA Population Project in Kenya, where the Bank opened the way to a multi-donor participation in an ambitious health and population programme. In both cases, the country's population strategies had barely had time to crystalise, but the intention was to help build up a strong "constituency" for family planning within the government and create a structure for health and family planning service delivery on a national scale.

Where a government has once formulated its population strategies and started a national programme, a World Bank-size loan can have the effect of a significant scaling-up of the level and speed of activities (as in Tunisia, Indonesia and the Philippines). Where a national programme is beginning to flag, whether for lack of finance or because of faltering government commitment, the injection of World Bank money can have a valuable revivifying effect (e.g. in Malaysia). Where a government feels that it is useful to demonstrate international support for its population policies, a Bank loan is the obvious answer[11].

Unlike other donors who hesitate to get involved in the area of national population policy[12], the Bank hoped that it could use its influence and prestige (and promise of loans to follow) to establish a dialogue with governments on population matters in countries where no national population policy as yet existed or, in countries which officially had a population policy, to improve its drive and direction. While it has been undoubtedly effective in this latter goal in those countries where it is a major source of funding to the government population programme, it has been disappointed in its hopes of making governments as yet unconvinced more aware of the seriousness of the population problem.

One reason is that the strong and influential relationship which the Bank as an institution has built up with developing country governments has traditionally been with their economic decision-makers — heads of the finance or the planning ministries. For these officials, population is rarely a priority problem — or at least not to the extent of their wishing to incur large-scale foreign indebtedness to finance family planning pro-

---

11. Association of the national population programme with support from the World Bank can, on the other hand, sometimes have quite the contrary effect. The Government of Mexico eventually rejected the courtship of the Bank and decided against a Bank loan for population, after several years of intensive and painstaking negotiation. In India, also, Bank support for the Government's Population Programme at the time of Emergency subsequently became something of an embarassment.

12. The Bank includes in its definition of "population work", "setting explicitly or implicitly, government demographic policy and targets". Bank Lending Policies and Procedures in the Population Sector.

grammes. The problem of the population growth rate may be raised by the Bank's economic missions, but it would not usually seem to be pushed very hard — perhaps because the mission members themselves do not consider it that important. (One of the recommendations of the Berelson Report was that the Bank's country economists should be more involved in population questions and that there should be greater stress on population in the regular country economic reports). Although in some countries, the Bank has now built up a special clientèle within the health ministry (or other body responsible for the national family planning programme), these bodies rarely have a great deal of influence on the determination of national development priorities. As a consequence, the Bank's relations and influence with a country's top economic policymakers and with the health ministry tend to run in parallel rather than be mutually reinforcing.

Geographical Preferences and Size

Having begun with a number of small population loans (to small recipient countries — Jamaica, Trinidad, Tobago and Tunisia[13]), the Bank quickly went on to make bigger loans to bigger countries. Partly because of the heavy input in project preparation, which is the same for a small loan as for a large one, the Bank applies to population its traditional preference for big projects. It similarly prefers to make its population loans to big countries (which are able to absorb big loans), and where it hopes that its assistance will make an impact not only on the demographic situation of the borrowing country, but also in terms of the *global* problem of population growth.

The Bank accordingly designated 17 countries as "key" countries for its population assistance — the criteria being a population of over 20 million and a rapid rate of demographic growth[14]. (A further group of 19 was designated as second priority on the grounds that though their growth rate posed serious problems, their size offered less potential for effecting a "global" impact: the Advisory Panel, however, advised the Bank to stick to the 17 "key" countries).

The Bank's key countries, being big countries with a big population problem, overlap with but do not coincide with the UN's list of "least developed" countries, nor with the 40 countries designated by the UNFPA as its priorities for population assistance. While some countries figure as most deserving of population assistance on everybody's list, the Bank list includes some others also (Brazil, Colombia, Mexico, Turkey and, until recently, Iran). The Bank has to date made population loans to seven countries on its "key" list (to several of them more than once) and to another seven outside.

The Bank's recent population projects (other than those in small countries) have received loans of $25 million and above. The term "project", however, is somewhat misleading in that, in fact, a Bank population project encompasses a considerable number of separate activities, representing support for different elements of the national population programme. Together these are supposed to be "sufficiently coherent to form a justifiable whole",[15] though they do not of course represent self-contained projects in the sense that the Bank's infrastructure projects do. The Bank's population projects not only combine different *types of assistance* — physical facilities, equipment, advisory services, research, training — but also a variety of different *functions* and *purposes*. A typical example is the Population Project in the Philippines, which includes two major training components, two major motivational programmes, management support, a management information system, logistics support (procurement and distribution) and a small research and evaluation component, which together represent half the total cost. The other half is for what the Bank calls "service support", i.e. construction and equipping of health centres and training units in different areas of the country and at different levels of operation.

---

13. $2 million, $3 million and $4.8 million respectively, the latter supported by a further $4.8 million provided by the Government of Norway under co-financing arrangements with the Bank.
14. The criteria include also population policy and mortality rate, but end up as being essentially population *size*.
15. World Bank: World Bank Lending for Population.

Although most of its major population loans are for comprehensive "projects" of this nature, the Bank has resisted the suggestion that it make "sector" loans for population — one of the few recommendations of the Berelson team that it did not adopt. The Bank does provide sector loans in some other fields, e.g. agricultural development[16], where it feels that the sector is sufficiently advanced and the government's policies are well-defined and sound. In the case of population, however, it feels that the necessary local structures and experience are still not yet sufficiently developed. It has therefore stuck to its faith in project lending as a means of inculcating financial and managerial discipline[17]. (The view is sometimes expressed, both within the Bank and outside, that in so doing, the Bank is depriving itself of greater possibility for "leverage" with governments in the area of population policy generally).

Preferred Types Activity

The Bank has envisaged its population assistance primarily as large-scale support for the replication of approaches that have already demonstrated their usefulness. Increasingly, however, it has come to finance a wide range of experiment and innovation. (In Thailand, for example, it is furnishing the contraceptives for Dr. Mechai's startlingly unconventional programme of commercially-based distribution of contraceptives). On the demand side, in particular, the Bank is now financing activities that it would not have contemplated a few years before (seminars for M.P.s, feature films to promote the family planning "message", income-generating projects for women, youth projects, etc.). In Bangladesh, under the Second IDA Project, some $ 5.5 million is to be applied to the formation of Mothers' Clubs and co-operatives and — a particularly novel feature — a further $2 million has been set aside for funding innovative projects proposed by private agencies[18]. In Indonesia, the Bank has even on occasion come through with financing for certain experimental "support" projects, when the Government cannot find the money.

These ventures into innovation are still small-scale. Overall, the Bank tends to design its population projects with a view to convincing the Board of Executive Directors of their soundness as bankable propositions. Population officials in developing countries (although they sometimes refer to the population project financed by the Bank as "the Bank's project" rather than their own), recognise that the Bank, like other donors, has its own constraints, and generally have learned to adapt their population requests to what they know will show up well in the Project Justification.

Thus, Bank population loans have shown a high content of "hardware", i.e. the construction of physical facilities for service delivery and training, the equipment and furnishings necessary to make them operational, and vehicles. (In Bangladesh, for example, more than half of the Second IDA Project — $110 million total cost — will be spent on civil works, equipment and vehicles of various kinds). The Bank is sometimes criticised for this predilection for "hardware", as being a solution of facility. Certainly, lending for infrastructure is the Bank's traditional business. It is also something that

---

16. The Bank and the government agree on an overall strategy for the sector, and the Bank undertakes to finance a certain percentage of the expenditures incurred.

17. Critics of the Bank sometimes maintain that by insisting on "projects" which, albeit multiple, still only constitute a part of the government's total programme, the Bank risks creating inbalances between "its" project and the rest — particularly if the "rest" is less generously financed and well looked after.
"Whereas conventional Bank projects are usually intended to serve as catalysts for private investment, projects in a social sector depend much more on how well they are co-ordinated with other governmental activities in the same and related sectors". Barbara Crane and Jason Finkle. "Organisational Impediments to Development Assistance: The World Bank's Population Program". World Politics, July 1981.

18. The idea, originally proposed by the Population Officer on the Bank's Resident Mission, using savings under the first Project, has proved very successful. The officer concerned now sits on a specially appointed "Subvention Committee" to select suitable private agency projects — some of them as small as $1,000. Other donors are also contributing to the fund.

other population assistance donors are generally not keen to do, and the Bank feels that as "donor of last resort", it should give priority to those elements of a government's population programme for which it is difficult to find other takers. On the whole, the preference for "hardware" suits the developing countries too — as being more suitable for foreign borrowing than "software" activities such as technical assistance, research, training etc.

It should be noted also that the civil works element in a Bank population project is very different from the type of infrastructure habitually financed by the Bank. The buildings to be constructed usually consist of large numbers of small and relatively low-cost structures, widely-dispersed throughout the country, rather than major hospitals or advanced urban facilities. Sometimes it is the Bank that persuades the government to modify its traditional standards and priorities.

As the Bank's population projects are becoming increasingly diversified, the amount devoted to "hardware" of various kinds is being progressively reduced. In the first population loan, to Jamaica, hardware accounted for 95 per cent. The proportion in more recent loans is nearer 50-60 per cent.

In their place, the Bank is now prepared to include a variety of "software" activities (e.g. in Bangladesh, Women's projects account for quite an important part of the loan). "Software" activities, however, generally involve local cost expenditures, which the Bank, traditionally, has been reluctant to cover. In the case of social development projects, which obviously have greater local cost requirements, special justification had to be made for including them. The Bank has markedly relaxed its earlier rules in respect of local cost financing, and population projects, in fact, led the way. Subsequently, the Bank set a percentage for local costs for each country (based on its overall economic situation), to be applied across-the-board, whatever the sector. Prior to the establishment of this rule, there was considerable diversity as to the amount of local costs included in the Bank's earlier population loans. The First IDA Population Project in Egypt, for example, was to cover foreign exchange costs only, while that in India was to cover *all* the costs of the project, foreign exchange and local currency — an exceptional arrangement made on the grounds that the project was intended as an action research programme.

Overall, the Bank has very few a priori exclusions as to what types of activity it is prepared to include in its population loans. It will provide technical assistance either to develop a project or assist with implementation (normally specialist short-term assignments). It does not normally fund bio-medical research or basic data collection, as other aid agencies are usually prepared to do this, but will do so if requested. (It provided a computer to Indonesia). Similarly, it does not normally provide contraceptives as straight commodity assistance except as part of a wider Bank-financed activity — not as a matter of principle, but because it is usually more convenient for countries to get their supplies from US AID. However, it made an exception for the commercially-based distribution programme in Thailand, and would be prepared to do the same elsewhere. Increasingly, the Bank is adapting what it can and should do in its population loans to the needs of the particular country situation.

III. CONTRIBUTION TO SELF-RELIANCE

The Bank's population assistance is geared to providing facilities that should be both replicable and possible for governments to operate from their own resources (e.g. low-cost delivery systems for health and family planning services, population education courses in schools, etc.). The following paragraphs discuss some of the ways in which the Bank's population loans contribute to governments' ability to eventually run the programmes themselves.

Financial Capability

Recurrent costs

The Bank's lending rules normally preclude the financing of recurrent costs. However, in the case of population projects, reimbursable local currency expenditures were allowed to include incremental operating costs also. These may cover salaries of additional staff, training stipends, direct costs of research, operating costs of added vehicles etc. required by the government to implement the project. This concession, made initially for population projects, but subsequently extended to other sectors, immediately raised the question of what were properly *project* costs and what should be considered as normal running costs, to be met out of the government's regular operating budget.

The Bank has tended to take a very flexible line on this question, particularly in cases where the government's overall budgetary situation is tight. The idea is that by picking up these expenses at the start, it will encourage the government to eventually increase the budget allocation to the programme. (The Bank says that the government's health budget normally increases as a result of the Bank project). In Bangladesh, the IDA Project is covering the salaries of over 13,000 family planning field-workers ("Family Welfare Assistants"), together with the costs of their training or re-training. The normal Bank rule is to require the government to assume the responsibility for salaries etc. on a phased basis, and even in Bangladesh, the hard-pressed government budget is expected to take over a growing number of these salary costs each year. Even in cases where the government's budgetary situation is not particulary tight, the Bank has sometimes been prepared to pay for some border-line "recurrent" costs in order to get an activity moving. (In Malaysia, for example, it agreed to pay the salaries of teacher trainers and the production of teaching materials, if no other source of financing could be found). Often, however, the Bank's practice of making over-lapping "second" and even "third-generation" population loans makes it possible for it to continue to carry some of these recurrent costs as part of programme implementation expenditure.

In making its population loans, the Bank will usually try to make a rough estimate of the future operating costs of the activity and to assess their reasonableness for the government to carry, in relation to its overall budgetary resources. However, these calculations can at best be rough approximations only.

In some cases, the measures taken with a view to getting the project moving may well have the effect of increasing its subsequent operating costs. One example is the payment of financial incentives to field-workers ("performance premiums"). The Bank is not keen on incentive payments, but will provide them if asked. Another is the payment of salary supplements for key project posts. The Bank is in general very ready to pay these (in all sectors, not only in population), although it is sensitive to government policy on the matter. (In Egypt, it was the Government which requested the Bank to supplement the low salary scales of the Egyptian public service for the senior Population Project posts). Bank officials recognise, however, the long-term problems involved in distorting a government's regular pay structure.

Administrative and Managerial Capability

The Bank approaches lending for population projects in the knowledge that the administrative and managerial problems that they face at the recipient end are exceptionally difficult. The population programme as a whole often commands only a low level of government commitment, while to carry it out effectively requires an unusual degree of administrative organisation extending horizontally to many different services of government, and vertically down to the humblest field level. The Bank's appraisal reports for population projects normally include an assessment of the administrative and managerial capability of the relevant government services (covering the organizational structure, bureaucratic and financial procedures, manpower resources, training needs etc.), but, as Bank staff admit, these aspects of the project's environment are not usually examined with the degree of thoroughness that they require. Certainly, in no sector of its lending does the Bank make the same rigorous examination of a country's administrative capability as a potential borrower, as of its economic capability (although it has been giving more attention to this problem in recent years). In the case of population projects, many of the problems involved are so complex and deep-seated that Bank staff, under considerable internal pressures to produce a bankable project, are usually unwilling to protract still further the already lengthy process of project preparation[19]. Usually, they simply go ahead, using the experience gained to make better arrangements, where necessary, the second time round.

As the range of the Bank's population assistance has widened, the organisation of project implementation has become increasingly complicated. Today, the user departments have been extended way beyond the health ministry (or family planning board), and may embrace the departments of social affairs, education, information, labour, rural development etc. as well. Orchestrating these various power and interest groups adds a new dimension to the problems of implementation.

In its early population loans, the Bank tried to assure effective implementation of its projects by setting up special Project Implementation Units (PIUs) within the user department, as was current Bank practice in other sectors. Intended originally to manage the large civil works components of the projects (for which the health ministries, unused to construction projects of such magnitude, generally lacked the necessary experience and resources), these units, with staff paid by the Bank and with ample Bank funds at their disposal, came to occupy an anomalous position within the health ministry. (In the Philippines, the PIU grew to be more influential than the Ministry itself, until the Bank insisted, in its Second Population Loan, that it be cut back in size and powers). In all countries where a PIU was established, it caused bitter (and lingering) resentment, although the Bank has since abandoned the arrangement. On the practical side, however, it seems to have had its merits. The Bank says that in Indonesia, where the PIU has finally been dispersed under the Third Population Project, implementation has been considerably slowed down in consequence.

The Bank has since tried a variety of solutions intended to strengthen the existing machinery of government to undertake not only the implementation of the Bank project, but also the longer-term management of the national population programme. These too have sometimes run into problems. In some cases, Bank support for the family planning programme involved only the family planning "wing" of the health ministry, with the result that the health wing — now less well-endowed but longer-established — became resentful and refused its co-operation. Sometimes, the arrangements proposed involved radical changes in the civil service structure. Thus, in Bangladesh, following a Management Study, the Bank first recommended that the Government merge the Health and Family Planning Secretariats of the Ministry of Health into a single service, and introduce a wide measure of decentralisation, and subsequently, when difficulties arose, proposed different arrangements. The Bank is frequently criticised in developing countries, not for proposing radical solutions to administrative and management problems, but for expecting results too quickly. (In Kenya, for example, the Family Health and Welfare Centre, the unit responsible for the family planning programme, was only allowed three years to prove itself). Whatever the structural arrangements in any given case, however, the Bank recognises that the efficiency with which the project will be carried out will be determined, in the last resort, by the efficiency of the bureaucracy as a whole and by the government's commitment to the population programme.

---

19. In the multi-donor discussions for a second Health and Population Project for Kenya, it is some of the bilateral donors, not the Bank, who have been urging that some of the major administrative and management problems be tackled before the Agreement is finalised. (Specifically, a Management and a Transport Study are to be made).

Technical Assistance

i) Consultants

In some of its early population loans, the Bank sought to deal with the problem of managing a huge and complex project by giving the national project director a number of expatriate advisers to assist him. In India, Indonesia and Bangladesh, the Bank stationed a staff member as Population Adviser to oversee the implementation of the project as a whole. In many cases, there was also a consultant architect or engineer to supervise the civil works project (and to advise on standards, specifications, procurement etc). In addition, specialist advisers, with assignments of varying length, were provided as consultants for particular components of the project, such as population education, management, information, training, research, etc.

Foreign consultants, in addition to their technical expertise, have the advantage of sometimes being able to achieve the co-ordination and co-operation of different services of the government, where national officials may not have the power (or courage) to do so. However, the Bank's tendency to include consultants in its population projects has not been popular in the receiving countries. Bank consultants are expensive[20] – (more expensive than those of the UN), and are a charge on loan funds which the government must eventually repay. As local cadres gain in experience, governments increasingly resent the presence at their side of highly-paid foreign expertise. In addition, some have antagonised governments by the very rigour which they have brought to the job, while in some cases their inability to communicate in the local language has restricted their effectiveness at the field level.

Although the Bank is still sometimes criticised for weighing down its population projects with consultants, long-term advisers are no longer a prominent feature of more recent population loans.

Consultants working on Bank projects are technically the government's consultants and not the Bank's. The government chooses the consultant – usually from two or three candidates suggested by the Bank (though occasionally it may ask for someone it already knows), and it is the government who makes the contract with them for their services, on terms of reference worked out jointly, and on terms approved by the Bank.

Occasionally, the Bank has tried appointing a national of the country concerned as adviser to the Project Director. (The Bank and UNICEF are the only agencies to do this). While a national consultant has the merit of combining professional expertise with understanding of the country situation, it is sometimes objected that the practice should be restricted to technical matters, as on problems of general government administration, a consultant of the country may hesitate to report objectively. Opinions differ as to whether local consultants are a potential cause of dissention (because they command Bank-scale fees), or whether they represent an imaginative use of local talent.

For national staff appointed by the government to fill senior project posts, the Bank normally requires to see the terms of reference and qualifications – at least for posts created by and financed out of the project. (Initially, candidates were to be subject to "Bank approval", but this was dropped in face of government objection). In practice, the problem often is not that the Bank rejects the government's proposed candidates as unsatisfactory, but that the government does not or cannot produce the people to fill the posts. The loan agreement normally specifies that certain key posts must be filled within 90 days – a requirement that the government frequently is unable to meet – and if the person, once approved, leaves the post, there is little that the Bank can do, except press the government for action. (In Kenya, for example, the post of head of the Information and Education Division of the Programme was never filled for the whole life of the project, while that of head of the Family Planning Centre has been filled by a succession of different people).

---

20. In 1980, the Bank estimated that the total cost of a consultant, including housing and travel as well as fees, was some $5,000 per month.

ii) Training

Implementing the Bank's population projects represents a heavy strain on the government's manpower resources at all levels. (For example, in Indonesia, the Bank required the body responsible for the project, the National Family Planning Co-ordinating Board, to take on additional technical staff to handle the civil works component, consisting of "at least 1 construction co-ordinator, 2 engineers, 4 job captains, 2 draftsmen and supporting clerical staff"). It did not however at the same time specify the requirements for general administrative tasks, 'such as' procurement, accounting, auditing, record-keeping, etc. — skills chronically in short supply in developing countries.

Although in other sectors, the Bank frequently includes arrangements for training in these basic administrative skills as part of the project[21], it does not do so in its population loans. Considerable attention and resources are applied to the training of the technical skills that will be required (training of teachers in population education, training of paramedical personnel etc.). Training in administrative skills on the other hand (as necessary for programme management as for project implementation), the Bank, in common with other donors, generally leaves to the government to take care of.

Occasionally, the Bank will provide special training for top level personnel (e.g. study fellowships for senior programme managers). The Bank does not, however, seem to go in as much as some other donors for the practice of "grooming" senior officials for management tasks that they will subsequently undertake under the project.

iii) Maintenance

The Bank is also contributing to the goal of self-reliance by training developing countries to pay more heed to the question of maintenance. The Bank has probably institutionalised its attention to this perennial problem to a greater extent than any other donor. There is a special section within the Bank whose task is to check on the results of Bank projects five years or so after implementation has ended. These reviews ("Project Performance Audits") include the maintenance of buildings etc. While examinations cannot be undertaken into the condition and subsequent utilisation of every facility the Bank has ever financed (five population projects have been audited to date), they at least seek to make the borrower more maintenance-conscious.

In the case of population projects, building maintenance is particularly hard to ensure, since the facilities provided under the project tend to be very small and dispersed all over the country. (In India, the Bank Project provided for over 1,000 small buildings, and in the Philippines, for over 1,500). However, the projects often include notable attempts to deal with the problem. Thus in Egypt, the Bank engaged an internationally celebrated firm of architects to advise on the maintenance of the health facilities, and vehicles and equipment were later included in the mandate. The costs of maintenance and of special training courses in maintenance were included as part of the loan. In Tunisia, where the Bank has made its most recent health and population loan (1981), the project includes eight workshops for vehicle maintenance[22].

iv) Local production of contraceptive supplies and distribution systems

Another way in which the Bank sometimes contributes to self-reliance in population matters, is by assisting countries to produce, themselves, some of the contraceptive supplies they need. In Indonesia, for example, under its second population

---

21. In Indonesia, the Bank organises annual training courses on accounting and auditing for the staff of all the departments concerned with Bank projects in all sectors. The courses are given by the international firm of auditors retained by the Bank and are much appreciated. The Indonesian head of the Bank Population Project not only sends his staff to the courses but seeks the firm's advice on practical implementation problems.

22. The Bank guarantees spares for vehicles provided under its loans for five years: US AID's guarantee is for one year.

loan, it provided technical assistance fellowships and equipment for a study of the feasibility of providing the raw materials needed for local production of oral contraceptives, using indigenous plants, while the third included the construction and equipping of over a hundred warehouses in the Outer Islands for the storage and distribution of contraceptives and other medical supplies.

IV. PROGRAMMING ARRANGEMENTS

Project Preparation and the Loan Agreement

The World Bank lending process begins with country programming which, after regular review and consultation with the government regarding each country's economic situation, needs and performance, fixes an approximate total for Bank support over a given period (usually 5 years revolving), together with the purposes to which it might be applied. "Population", therefore, has to compete among other possible contenders as an appropriate sector for Bank lending to any particular country.

The country programming exercise is largely for internal purposes, but the indicative lending figure is communicated to the country concerned. When agreement has been reached on lending for a particular project, it does not carry with it an assurance of continuing Bank aid in that sector, although in practice, further loans may well follow. The amount of the loan is worked out in relation to the particular project components agreed upon. In this, the Bank differs from other donors, who begin by telling the government the amount and duration of the population assistance it may expect, and then go on to discussion as to the activities on which it should be spent.

From the initial proposal for a project idea, through project appraisal, to the presentation of project documents to the Bank's Board of Executive Directors takes a minimum of two years in the case of a new project, and some 18 months for a "second generation" one. An enormous amount of work is involved on both sides to collect and analyse the information which the Bank traditionally needs to present as justification for the project, and evidence of its essentially "bankable" character. Three separate steps are involved: "project identification", a short document which defines the scope of the project and the approaches to be employed; the project "request", a major document giving a highly detailed description of the background of the project, its purpose, components, inputs and anticipated benefits; and the "appraisal report", which is the Bank's analysis of the request and justification for the loan. The first and third are prepared by the Bank: the project request usually by the government. A year or more sometimes elapses between the various stages.

Bank staff say that project appraisal is particularly labour-intensive in the case of population projects, in part because of the "fluidity" of the sector and the lack of established methodologies, and in part because of the absence of specialist consultants (with experience of Bank rules and requirements) to help governments prepare project requests (as there would be, say, for a highway project). The appraisal process therefore involves repeated and usually sizeable Bank missions — particularly in the case of first projects or major loans: the preparation of the First Population Loan to Egypt is said to have involved some 18 missions over a period of three years. The strain on the government is formidable, both in respect of the time of senior officials — the level at which the Bank habitually operates — and in terms of data collection. The Bank sometimes gives an advance to enable the government to engage additional staff or outside consultants for this purpose — a "Project Preparation Facility", maximum $2 million. (For the preparation of the First Population Loan to Indonesia, for example, 10 people were engaged full-time for three months. For the second and third loans, the Government was able to do the job with its existing staff).

There is no doubt that preparing a project for the Bank offers valuable lessons in appraisal techniques etc., and developing country officials generally recognise this. The problem is that countries sometimes lack not only the staff but the basic data necessary to provide really meaningful information in response to the Bank's questions. For the

Second Bank Health and Population Loan in Kenya, for example, which will include improvement of rural health facilities, project preparation involves checking the condition of existing facilities throughout the country and feeding the information into a computer. The Kenya Project, incidentally, (admittedly a particularly difficult and complex operation) involved an investment of 6 man-years of Bank staff and consultant time over a period of over 2 1/2 years to prepare the project document, plus a further 10 months to do the appraisal[23]. On the other hand, the Second Population Loan to India took only 17 months between discussion of the project idea and going to the Board. For a first loan, however, just the final stage, from appraisal to presentation to the Board, normally takes at least 18 months.

The Bank has been much criticised for the time it takes to get a population project ready for action. However, it often takes no longer than some bilateral donors. It is not the length of time involved but rather the heavy input of work in project preparation that is irksome.

During the time between appraisal and going to the Board, loan negotiations take place between the Bank and the government. The draft loan agreement will be sent to the Board, together with the Bank's appraisal report and other documents. Once the Board has given its approval, the loan can be signed.

Before the project can start, the government normally has to meet certain preconditions laid down in the agreement (such as acquiring sites, engaging staff, preparing equipment lists etc.). These may either be conditions for the loan to become effective or for disbursements to begin. In some cases, these take time: in others, most of these things will have already been done before signature. (The better a project is prepared, the fewer conditions will normally be required). The First Population Loan to India had so many conditions that it took one year to become effective. The second loan to Indonesia, on the other hand, became effective exactly two months after approval by the Board. Although the Bank is tougher than any other donor about preconditions, this need not necessarily mean a delay in the project, if the necessary actions are meanwhile being taken.

The Bank's loan agreements are generally reputed to be extremely detailed (or "over-designed"). (In the First Population and Health Loan to Kenya, even bills of quantities were included in the Agreement). With experience, however, the Bank has become more flexible and is putting more of the detail into implementation documents rather than into the agreement itself. The Agreement for the Second Indian Population Loan ($96 million, and prepared, it will be recalled, in record time) did not describe the Project beyond stating its general purposes, viz: "about" (X) sub-centres to provide health services in rural areas; "about" (X) primary health centres; "training facilities for the Lucknow Population Centre", etc.

Changes in the Course of Implementation

In theory, money borrowed by a government under a loan agreement with the Bank becomes the property of the government, and therefore the purposes for which it is to be used can be changed if the government so requests. In practice, the Bank is as variable in its response to proposals for change as any other population assistance donor. Indeed, it is very often the *Bank* that suggests a change, in the course of its regular supervision visits, although formally the request is sent from the government to Washington.

---

23. The Bank recognises that in terms of preparatory effort, the Kenyan project will be its most costly health and population loan ever. At the time of the author's visit to Kenya in June 1981, there had been four drafts of the project request (a document of 200 pages) prepared each time in response to specific Bank requirements, followed by the appraisal report prepared by the Bank team. The Kenyan officials involved were divided between admiration at the Bank team's round-the-clock working stints and annoyance that they were expected to share them.

In principle, a change that involved a switch of funds as between project categories has to be submitted to the Board for approval. Most countries have found that the Bank normally agrees, if a good case can be made, but both the bureaucratic procedures involved and the fact of having to apply to Washington to say "May I ?" cause resentment. It is for this reason that the Bank has sometimes tended to limit its description of the work to be done under its population projects to very broad terms only, so as to minimise the difficulties of subsequent adjustment.

One area where the Bank is generally flexible about making adjustments is the implementation schedule. Bank population projects are almost chronically very slow in implementation, suggesting that the construction schedules initially set were unrealistic. Subsequent revisions (required if the delay has exceeded one year) more often than not prove to be equally unrealistic, partly because of the difficulty of scheduling the different project components, and sometimes because the Bank has failed to fully appreciate the complications of the local scene[24]. For buildings to be completed two or three years late is almost the norm. The remarkably relaxed attitude taken by the Bank, which seems sometimes prepared to extend construction schedules (and in consequence, disbursement schedules) almost ad infinitum, is a source of amazement to other donor agencies — and sometimes also of annoyance, when they are associated in co-financing arrangements.

Local Representation

For a time, the Bank had Population Officers on the staff of its Resident Missions in those countries where it had major population loans (India, Indonesia and Bangladesh). They were assigned the two-fold task of advising the Government on population matters generally and assisting in the implementation of the Bank loan. The practice has since been discontinued except for Bangladesh, where the Bank's Population Officer occupies an important local co-ordination function between the Bank, the Government and the six bilateral donors that participate in the IDA Population Project. Half of the cost of his post is paid out of the bilateral contributions to the Project.

The presence of a Bank Population Officer in Dacca has undoubtedly contributed to the generally sympathetic approach that the Bank has shown in Bangladesh towards the problems of project implementation and those of the Government in general. By no longer having such representatives in other countries, the Bank has in a sense tied its hands — both vis-à-vis the host country government and local representatives of other donor agencies. (The decision was made on the grounds that the size of the population loans in relation to the Bank's overall lending to the country did not warrant it, and the Mission post was reallocated to other functions). However, the Bank is a highly centralised agency, and even with a resident Population Officer, virtually all questions of substance have to be referred to Washington for decision. (In Bangladesh, even the small private agency projects to be financed by the Bank under the special fund set up for that purpose require Washington's approval — although normally the recommendation of the Population Officer is accepted).

V. IMPLEMENTATION PROCEDURES

Disbursement

The Bank's disbursement procedures are intended to ensure maximum financial discipline and management probity. Designed for large-scale infrastructure projects, they constitute a major administrative burden when applied to population projects

---

24. In one province of Indonesia, construction was twice held up because the local custom requires a religious ceremony to be held, first, before building can begin, and again, when the roof is put on. In each case, the appropriate ceremony could only be held on a certain auspicious date — many months later. The consequent 13-months inactivity (over an 18-month period) was noted by the Bank in its supervision reports with the laconic mention "Construction delays".

with their large numbers of separate construction and equipment jobs and "software" activities of many different kinds.

Written guidelines for the withdrawal of the proceeds of Bank loans and IDA credits are given to the government at the time the loan is signed (together with guidelines for procurement and the use of consultants). There will usually be some explanation as to how these are to be applied, at the time of negotiations. In some countries, however, this information does not get passed down from the senior echelons represented at the negotiating table to the operating-level staff who will have to work them[25]. The latter may get a first lesson in how to apply the procedures from the Bank's supervision team on the occasion of the first half-yearly mission, or subsequently, as difficulties occur. In other countries, however, this works well, and officials find the Bank's manuals followed by explanation and training by Bank staff particularly helpful.

The loan agreement will include a schedule for disbursement for each of the broad project categories. (As previously noted, in practice, this is far from iron-clad). No payments can be made under the loan until it has been declared effective, although the government can start work on the project, using its own funds, as from the date of signature. In addition to the special advance to assist with project preparation (subsequently incorporated in the amount of the loan), the Bank, exceptionally, allows certain pre-project payments for contractors to prepare engineering designs etc. ("mobilisation funds")[26]. These, however, are intended for major infrastructure works only, and are not likely to apply to population projects, where the work of project preparation is done by the staff of the Bank.

Once disbursements under the loan are begun, the actual procedures to be applied are not particularly complicated. They are, however, very precise, and the Bank is rigorous in its insistence on their correct application.

With the few exceptions for pre-project work mentioned above, the Bank, unlike other aid agencies, never makes payment in the form of advances. (The Government of Bangladesh asked it to do so in the case of the IDA Population Project, to which some of the bilaterals were contributing in this way, but the Bank refused). The Bank's method is either *reimbursement* or direct payment to the supplier (the latter according to a number of different procedures). In general, all local cost expenditures will be covered on a reimbursement basis (with the exception of payments for training fellowships etc., which are made direct to the individual). Foreign exchange costs are normally covered by direct payment to the supplier.

When the time comes for repayment of the loan, the borrower has to reimburse the Bank in the actual foreign currency used, except in the case of IDA credits, where the currency of repayment is decided at the time of the negotiations. In the case of local currency expenditures, however, the country will repay in its own currency.

The reimbursement procedure used for local currency expenditures under the project has generally been an enormous headache for both Bank and borrower. Until very recently, applications for reimbursement had to be sent to Washington on two pro forma sheets, showing the contract category and sub-category and the details of payment. These had to be signed by the designated senior officer of the project implementing unit and a senior official of the Ministry of Finance, and the forms accompanied by the supplier's invoice, evidence of payment and evidence of shipment. However, the Bank is now simplifying these arrangements, and making disbursement on certified

---

25. In one country, the Project Manager did not let his staff see any of the project documents, not even the Loan Agreement.

26. Completion of engineering designs may take as much as two years, during which time no other work can start and the loan is lying idle. Governments do not like this. Not only does it give the impression that disbursement is slow, but they have to pay a commitment fee of 3/4 of 1 per cent on the amount undisbursed. (The corresponding fee under German loan funds is 1/4 of 1 per cent). Further, where other donors (e.g. Germany, the Netherlands, Japan) agree to split the project into two separate loans, one for engineering design and one for construction, the Bank insists on keeping the two in one single package.

expenditure statements only, with the vouchers retained in the country for spot-check by the Bank.

The difficulty for the project staff consists in accumulating the necessary evidence. In Kenya, for example, the project officers had been unable to present satisfactorily any claims for reimbursement until the Bank supervision teams sat down with them and reconstructed the bills. In Egypt, some 40 per cent of the construction work had been completed before the Bank had received a single request for reimbursement. The problem would seem to lie not in the inherently difficult nature of the Bank's procedural requirements, but in the lack of accounting staff and professional experience available to the project, plus, often, a reluctance on the part of project managers to delegate responsibility. The often disappointingly low level of disbursement of Bank population loans does not, therefore, necessarily reflect a slow rate of implementation, but an initial failure to appreciate fully the administrative weaknesses at the receiving end.

Once appropriately documented requests for reimbursement have been approved by Washington, it takes only a week or so for payment actually to reach the country. Reimbursement is made not to the project implementing unit but to the Treasury, which will have made an advance to the project to cover its local costs (usually on a quarterly basis).

Procurement

Once a Bank loan is signed, not only the money, but the goods purchased with it are considered the property of the government. It is accordingly the government's responsibility to award and administer the contracts for the goods and services required for the project, although the Bank exercises very tight control over how and where it does it. In the case of goods of foreign manufacture, therefore, countries tend to prefer the arrangements of other aid donors, who themselves buy and ship the items required, thereby saving them a considerable amount of work, and usually proving quicker as well.

The Bank system is also more complicated than that of many other donors in respect of payment of import duty. Goods may or may not be duty-free according to the country. If the government insists that duty be paid, the Bank will not include the extra amount under the loan, but expects the user ministry to pay it. In some countries this has proved a major problem because the ministry concerned does not have the necessary funds, and the goods pile up on the docks. Some other donors, who provide aid on grant terms, consider the equipment provided under their aid projects as their own property, and it is accordingly exempt from payment of tax[27].

The guiding principle of World Bank procurement is international competitive bidding (ICB). Sometimes, however, alternative methods of procurement may be considered more efficient and appropriate. The Bank is generally very pragmatic about deciding when this is likely to be the case — depending on the country, the size of the contract, the likelihood of foreign interest in tendering for it, and the capability of local industry. One notable feature of Bank loans is that they are virtually untied as to the source of supply (specifically, supplies may come from Bank members, Switzerland and Taiwan). The Bank is accordingly more open than almost any other donor to financing goods and services produced in the recipient country. Indeed, if it feels that local suppliers and contractors can do the job, the Bank is prepared actively to encourage local procurement by allowing a price preference (15 per cent for local manufacturers and 7 per cent for civil works) over foreign firms. Under population loans, a large proportion of the contracts tend to go to local firms partly as a means of building up local capacity. Some of this is "self-help" construction which the Bank is prepared to finance without fussing about building standards — a notable example of how the Bank has in some respects moved towards flexibility in population projects.

---

27. In the case of the UN, for example, the goods enter duty-free but remain the property of the UN for 5 years (or until completion of the project). By this time, their depreciated value is considered as not requiring payment of import duty.

Under every loan, the decision as to the procurement method to be used for each major project component, after being discussed with the government, is written into the loan agreement. Whatever the method decided upon in any particular case, the government has to follow closely the appropriate Bank regulations and procedures. The Bank fully appreciates that this is a lot to ask of an often understaffed and inexperienced administration. Where there are problems, therefore, it follows up its written Procurement Guidelines by sending a team of procurement officers from Washington to explain to the project staff concerned how the procurement procedures are to be applied. Usually, however, prior help is needed in preparing the equipment lists and specifications, and the Bank, like many other donors, is prepared to provide consultant help for this purpose. (The Bank includes this as an item under the loan).

When international competitive bidding is the agreed procedure, the government calls for bids, duly notifying the international community[28]. In the case of population projects, where the individual items tend to be small, the Bank often requires that they be grouped into a single item, large enough to interest international bidders. While agreeing that this arrangement results in lower prices and less administrative work, countries say it sometimes ignores the differences in local requirements.

Most governments have national tender committees, and they are responsible for issuing and evaluating the bids. The degree of Bank involvement varies somewhat according to the country, but normally the Bank in Washington follows closely every stage of the tendering process, beginning with review of the specifications, and requiring to see also the text of the invitation to bid, the advertising procedures to be followed, and the dossier of the tender selected, together with the justification for the choice and the details of the contract. In most cases the Bank approves the government's choice of tender, but occasionally it has requested more information, and exceptionally, even asked for the bidding to be re-opened. The whole process (designed for major contracts) is inevitably lengthy, sometimes (in the opinion of the local officials) disproportionately so, when relatively small contracts are involved[29].

Where ICB is not required, the arrangement agreed upon may be for the government to call for local tendering (which does not exclude foreign firms), using its own procedures *as have been agreed by the Bank* (and written into the loan agreement). There will normally be a compromise between those of the government and the Bank. Another arrangement may be what the Bank calls "prudent shopping", whereby the government may place an order after receiving three local price quotations. The government and the Bank will have agreed in advance the level at which tendering is not considered to be necessary, or, if it is necessary, the level below which the evaluation of the bids and the contract documents do not have to be submitted to the Bank for prior approval. (In Indonesia and Bangladesh, for example, local purchases under $50,000 do not need prior approval, although the documents must be kept available for possible random post-hoc checking). In some cases, the Bank may allow the government to undertake construction or maintenance work, using its normal public works department services, provided the Bank is satisfied that they can do the job. For some types of procurement – chiefly standard equipment or miscellaneous goods – it may be found convenient to use UNICEF as a procurement agency.

The health and other government officials who work on Bank population projects frequently find the Bank procedures irksome in that Washington has to be consulted at so many points (viz. the health minister who complained that he could not "wait to get permission from the Bank every time he wished to buy a tap"). At the same time, they recognise that the Bank arrangements give them the responsibility for *choice* of

---

28. By variously informing the embassies of those member countries of the Bank likely to be interested, advertising in at least one newspaper of general circulation, in the UN periodical Development Forum, etc.

29. One $3 million contract for vehicles required 6 months just to prepare the tender documents, although the Bank staff helped. The whole process took one year to approve and it was 18 months before the first vehicles were due to arrive.

contractor and supplier to a greater extent than those of many other donors, as well as encouraging local contractors to do the job when they can.

Local firms, however, sometimes prove unable to do the job. This both disturbs construction schedules and the scheduling of equipment and furniture. Either the contractor is unable to deliver on time (e.g. the Kenya Prisons Service who was to make the furniture for the new health centres), or the order is placed too soon (to avoid cost escalation) and the buildings are not ready to receive them, or else too late, and completed buildings stand empty and unusable for several years. (The responsibility for synchronising the various project activities is normally that of the government). It may be noted that when bilateral donors have participated with the Bank, as in Bangladesh and Kenya, they have often been impelled to bring in more consultants than were originally planned, in order to help expedite and rationalise the progress of the work[30].

The Bank obviously has to make constant choices between the competing demands of efficiency, speed, encouragement of local industry, and accountability. Further, its own manpower resources preclude its scrutinising every equipment list and contract proposal with the degree of thoroughness that might be necessary. On the whole, however, governments recognise that they stand to gain in useful experience by following the Bank's sometimes difficult procedural requirements. In Kenya, for example, the Government decided to continue using the arrangements laid down by the Bank for local procurement, even after the implementation of the Bank project had been completed.

Monitoring and Reporting

The Bank, as might be expected, has particularly thorough procedures for keeping watch on the implementation of its projects. These consist of regular progress reports which monitor project performance, and broader supervision exercises which, in the case of population projects, tend to spill over into monitoring the government's population programme as a whole. The population sector is unique in this latter respect.

The schedule and form of the reports to be sent in by the borrower are worked out during the project negotiations. To the extent possible, the Bank tailors these to the government's own reporting procedures, but in most cases the Bank's requirements are considerably more demanding. Developing country officials frequently find difficulty in assembling regularly all the data required by the Bank to show the current state of physical execution of the project and corresponding expenditures. Where possible, therefore, the staff of the resident Bank mission in the country (where there is one) or visiting Bank missions help fill in the forms.

The information required is largely quantitative in nature, since the Bank's prime concern is to be kept fully up-to-date on the rate of disbursements. Consequently, it is not uncommon to find letters going from Washington to a Minister of Health enquiring why there have been no requests for reimbursement lately. In general, developing country governments do not greatly care for the Bank's habit of monitoring by correspondence — particularly where there is additionally a difficulty of language. They prefer donors to have a resident mission where problems can be dealt with less formally.

Fuller and more substantive information on the progress of implementation is provided by the on-the-spot reviews undertaken by the Bank's "end-use" supervision missions. Each project will normally receive at least two such missions a year, who stay for a period of about three weeks. The missions' main function is to check on the physical progress of the project (an obligation written into the loan agreement), but they have

---

30. In Bangladesh, the arrangements for construction work under the IDA Population Project involve a formidable hierarchy of supervision. Local construction firms, chosen by the Governement and approved by the Bank, are supervised by local consulting architects (similarly chosen), who are themselves under the overall supervision of the Public Works Unit of the Ministry of Health. A foreign consulting firm is responsible for supervising the whole construction project, subject to the recommendations of the Bank's own architect in the Department of Health, Population and Nutrition. By the end of 1980, the latter had made 27 trips to Bangladesh (starting from the time the programme began).

evolved into a form of technical assistance for implementation problems, providing advice not only on the technical aspects such as building standards, specifications etc., but also on administrative problems such as procurement, reimbursement procedures etc. Project officials in the recipient country generally welcome these missions, which often provide a useful means of catalysing the government into taking some necessary action, but they also find them extremely time-consuming. The Bank, however, maintains that these arrangements enable it to monitor its projects with greater thoroughness than can sometimes be done by resident aid missions. Although the reports of these missions are pro forma, they have built-in arrangements for feedback to the government and to project officers, sometimes formalised in letters to the government. They may be accompanied also by a brief specialist report on some particular component of the project.

Auditing

The Bank's rules require annual audit of project expenditures. For population projects, the large amount of local expenditures involved makes the need for regular accountability particularly important.

Most governments want their own audit departments to do the annual auditing required by the Bank. In some countries, the government's audit rules are stricter than those of the Bank, and the Bank accordingly accepts audit by the government's own auditors (e.g. in Thailand). However, in most countries, the government audit department is under-staffed and badly in arrears, and the Bank receives its audit two or three years late. Governments usually reject the obvious solution of having this work done by an outside firm of auditors, because they do not wish to include this additional cost. Since the Bank cannot do the audit of large numbers of projects from its own resources, the auditing of population projects remains a perpetual problem.

Different solutions have been tried. In Bangladesh, some of the Government's General Audit Staff were borrowed to strengthen the Finance Division of the Ministry of Health. The basic problem, however, is the overall shortage of skilled auditors and accounts officers in the government service — a weakness that is not normally tackled by project assistance in population or in any other sector.

Evaluation

The Bank has institutionalised a number of procedures for assessing the performance of its projects, both as regards the process of implementation and, to the extent possible, their results ("impact"). The first step is a "completion report" to be prepared (in principle within six months of the final disbursement) by the Bank's project staff concerned. In some cases, the borrower may be asked to do this. (So far, this has only happened once in the case of a population project, when the Government of Indonesia was invited to write the first draft of the report "as a learning experience"). The completion report reviews frankly and often critically the project's history and the course of its implementation. These reports are to be followed eventually by a further report, prepared by the Bank's Operations Evaluation Department (an independent department within the Bank), on the basis of the files, interviews with the Bank staff and some field enquiry. This second review (the "Project Performance Audit Report") attempts to assess the extent to which the project achieved its objectives and to analyse the lessons implied in its implementation experience both for the Bank and the borrowers. The analyses, being made by an outsider, often contain radical criticisms as well as recommendations for the future. The country concerned is given an opportunity to comment before the report is finalised.

In the case of population projects, only a few of these twofold assessments have been carried out, because population projects tend to be slow of disbursement and are often overtaken by the next loan before the first has been fully disbursed. In Kenya, the work of evaluating the first and preparing the second population project overlapped, and each team was able to benefit from the information provided by the other.

The Bank has not attempted to make any evaluation of its population work from the point of view of "impact". Because of the long-term nature of population activities, and of the variety of other factors that enter in, it has felt that the exercise would not be realistic.

Co-ordination with Other Donors

The Bank is accustomed to play a co-ordinating role in organising the foreign aid effort for particular countries through its Consortia and Consultative Groups. Although the Bank has the recognised co-ordinating role for international assistance for general development purposes, in the field of population assistance, it is often the UNFPA that assumes this function. While there has been no formal division of powers (as the Bank set out to establish with FAO by means of a special Memorandum of Understanding, back in 1973), an effective co-operation between the two has been achieved at the top policy level. Official meetings and more frequent informal personal contacts have ensured that each is kept informed of the other's broad approaches, and there have been common attempts to focus on general problems of population assistance. (Thus the first Co-ordination Meeting of Population Donor Agencies, sponsored by the Bank in 1977, was followed by a second, two years later, sponsored by UNFPA).

When it comes to aid to particular countries, co-ordinated Bank-UNFPA action is rare. The Bank makes a review of the population sector as part of its project appraisal, and UNFPA similarly makes what is essentially a sector review in order to identify areas for its own population assistance (Needs Assessment Reports for Population Assistance). In fact, however, each takes cognizance of the scope of the other's programmes, and the result is not only a surprising absence of overlap but some useful dovetailing of their respective contributions.

At the country level, the Bank is handicapped by having no resident population officer. In Indonesia, for example, there are now regular meetings of the principal population donors to discuss the Government's new nutrition programme, but the Bank is unable to participate. Bangladesh, on the other hand, is the scene of an unusual degree of donor co-operation. At first, the Government chaired regular meetings of the representatives of its population assistance donors. Subsequently, the Government ceased to attend (although it is always invited), but the representatives of the Bank, USAID and UNFPA go together to call on the Deputy Secretary of the Ministry of Health each month, after the meeting, and give him an oral account of the discussions.

Co-financing

The Bank encourages other donor agencies to associate themselves with it in some form of "co-financing" of population projects. These arrangements (in which population led the way) offer a number of advantages. They mobilise a larger amount of external funding for the project, and at the same time soften the loan aspect by providing some of the funding on "softer" terms than World Bank Loans or IDA credits. In very poor countries, the grant contributions of the co-financing partners may be used to make up or even to substitute for the government's own contribution to the project (e.g. Bangladesh). Co-financing has the further merit that by co-ordinating the different objectives and programme activities of different donor agencies, it spares the government the risk of receiving conflicting advice.

Co-financing may either take the form of "parallel" financing in which each donor finances a specific component of the project using its own rules and procedures, or may be genuinely "joint" financing, whereby Bank funds and those supplied by other donors are merged in joint support to the project. For example, in the IDA Population Project in Bangladesh, certain items are jointly financed in an agreed proportion by the Bank and the Government of Australia. In such cases, the usual arrangement is for the Bank to assume the management responsibility according to its rules (e.g. for procurement, disbursement, reporting etc.), simply keeping the bilateral donors informed[31].

Co-financing has, of course, its draw-backs. Donors do not necessarily see eye-to-eye with each other, with the Bank or with the government. They each have their own procedures and schedule for signing their respective agreements with the government, and the Bank's scheduling of its loan agreement has to take account of this. Although all donor agencies have great respect for the Bank's appraisal reports, they are none of them prepared to base their aid decision solely on the Bank's analysis of the situation. Each therefore insists on going to see for itself. Sometimes, the Bank is able to organise a joint appraisal, as was done during the discussions of a second population loan to Kenya, but this is by no means the rule.

Even when there has been a joint appraisal, donors may still have a different evaluation of the situation or a different approach. There is then some uncertainty as to whether they should communicate their particular misgivings or conditions directly to the government, or whether the Bank should act as spokesman, or even, whether all donors should hold up their respective aid contributions until all (and notably the Bank) are satisfied that the problems have been dealt with. In Kenya, despite the joint appraisal, some donors, tired of waiting for action on a joint project, went ahead with separate bits under parallel financing arrangements.

Although joint financing does not necessarily spare the recipient country an initial appraisal mission by each of the donors interested in contributing to the project, once the activity is under way it does avoid separate inspection missions. The normal arrangement is for the Bank to organise a joint donor review at some point part way through the life of the project, in which all the contributing donors participate, sometimes sending staff from capitals, or possibly outside consultants. This seems to work well as a one-time event. (The organisation involved precludes its being done frequently). In Bangladesh, for example, the Bank sends its regular supervision missions to examine the IDA Project, and the other donors are satisfied to receive copies of these reports as a means of keeping informed of progress. Sometimes the local aid representative of one of them may, in addition, visit the part of the project that it is financing, but this would not be a regular arrangement.

Overall, the experience of joint-financing for population projects would seem to be that it works to the advantage of all concerned, in cases where there is a reasonable degree of unanimity as to the scope of the activity and the capacity of the government to carry it out. In circumstances where this is lacking, other donors lose confidence and are reluctant to give the Bank effective co-ordinating authority.

---

31. Some donors do not fully accept this arrangement. For example, for purchases from the German contribution to the Project in Bangladesh, KFW requires that its procurement rules be followed.

THE WORLD BANK
AID FOR POPULATION ACTIVITIES

i) Total volume of population assistance through 1981 (US $ million)

Commitments: 510.4
Expenditures : 340.4

ii) Annual expenditures on population assistance, 1975-1981 (US $ million)

1975	20.34
1976	25.94
1977	27.73
1978	31.38
1979	44.74
1980	80.34
1981	77.26

iii) Expenditures on population assistance as a percentage of total expenditures.

1975	0.60
1976	0.68
1977	0.71
1978	0.72
1979	0.84
1980	1.26
1981	1.01
Total	0.89

BILATERAL DONORS
NORWAY[1]

I. INTRODUCTION

Norway stands out amoing the bilateral donors of aid for its special concern with population. In 1971, the Norwegian Parliament decided that about 10 per cent of Norwegian aid should be applied to population activities, thus making Norway the only DAC country to set an official population assistance target. In the succeeding ten years, this proportion has been usually achieved, and in some years even exceeded. Norway thus considerably outstrips other DAC countries in the share of its total aid to population.

It is important to note, however, that Norway sometimes groups together Family Planning and Health as a single aid category. For reporting purposes, it uses the term "population activities" to cover family planning, mother and child health care (including vaccination programmes for children), nutrition education and preventive health education — the rationale being that lowering infant mortality is an important factor in the reduction of family size. Whether a programme is considered as a "health" or a "family planning/population" programme, in principle, depends on which of the two components is predominant. Yet in its reporting to UNFPA, for example, Norway includes as "population assistance" its aid to health projects in Kenya and Botswana, where the main focus is on health but where some family planning services are included. In fact, therefore, the Norwegian aid authorities appear to use the terms "population activities" and "health and family planning" interchangeably.

Independently of these considerations, Norway has proved remarkably consistent in its *interpretation* of the purpose of "population activities". In this, it differs markedly from most other donors of aid, who, since the 1974 World Population Conference in Bucharest (and some of them still earlier), have been progressively widening the scope of their population assistance to include all aspects of demographic change (i.e. urbanisation, migration and high mortality as well as high fertility), and thence to cover any activity which may be thought to influence either the causes or the consequences of such change. Norway, on the other hand, while fully appreciating that different areas of the world need different approaches to solve their particular population problems, has chosen to concentrate its own support, today as in the past, on the classical "core" population activities of family planning and mother and child health care (MCH).

This does not mean that Norwegian aid ignores the potential impact of indirect approaches such as programmes for women and youth, community development, etc. on family planning motivation (although NORAD's special Policy Guideline, which gives priority to women as a separate target group for bilateral ODA, makes no specific mention of fertility limitation or family planning as one of its objectives). NORAD's support for such activities (which is increasing) is not, however, included under the heading of "population assistance". In Bangladesh, for example, it is supporting a number of Women's Community Centres, some of which will, in fact, include family planning services among their activities, but defines this programme as a "Women's Project" and not a "Population Project".

As a corollary of its "traditional", (or possibly "purist") approach to population problems, Norway is prepared to provide family planning as an independent aid activity. It does not go quite so far as to provide sector aid for family planning (or for health either), but it will provide aid for a family planning "programme". Its support for the

---

1. Statistical table, see page 101.

All India Post Partum Programme (for which Norway is the sole source of foreign aid), although classed as a "population programme", in effect comes close to being sector support for *family planning*.

The Norwegian Government gives all its bilateral assistance in the form of grants. As a matter of policy, it tries to divide its total aid more or less evenly as between bilateral and multilateral programmes. In recent years, some 42-45 per cent of Norwegian aid funds have been channelled through international organisations, a proportion much higher than those of most other DAC countries. In respect of population assistance, the proportion is higher still. In 1980, some two-thirds of Norway's aid for population took the form of contributions to or in conjunction with multilateral organisations. The principal recipients of these funds, totalling about $25 million, were UNFPA, UNICEF, IPPF and the WHO Research Programme on Human Reproduction[2]. The amount thus allocated specifically for population activities (representing 13 per cent of Norway's total multilateral aid) is the more notable when seen in relation to Norway's contributions to such major multi-purpose international development institutions as UNDP (approximately $50 million) and the World Bank/IDA (approximately $42 million).

In addition to making annual contributions to these various international organisations, the Government of Norway provides further support for certain multilateral programmes by means of joint-financing ("multi-bi") agreements. Under these arrangements, Norway offers funds-in-trust to various agencies for certain mutually-agreed activities.

Norway makes more extensive use of this form of aid financing than any other donor, and in the area of health and population, has entered into agreements with UNFPA and UNICEF[3]. UNFPA has used the Norwegian funds thus provided to finance Basic Needs Assessment Surveys in a number of developing countries and certain administrative costs. The funds provided to UNICEF and IPPF are usually applied to specific projects. (For further information see last section).

Norway's multilateral aid activities are the responsibility of the Royal Ministry of Foreign Affairs, which also has overall responsibility for the country's aid policy and programme priorities. The bilateral programme is administered by the Norwegian Agency for International Development (NORAD), which acts as executive agency for the Ministry.

For the purposes of the present study on donor aid procedures and practices, it is Norway's bilateral population programmes, supported by NORAD, that are of interest. In 1980, "Health and Family Planning" accounted for 10 per cent of Norway's bilateral assistance[4], a considerably higher proportion than that of any other DAC country.

Obstacles to Expanding Bilateral Population Assistance

It seems unlikely that the share of Norway's bilateral aid applied to population activities will increase to any significant extent in the near future. Norwegian aid officials consider the present level to be generally appropriate in terms of priorities, and practical in terms of implementation. Five years ago, there was felt to be a disappointing lack of demand for population assistance on the part of the developing countries. Today, the main problem is seen to be less that of demand than of absorptive capacity. NORAD officials point out that in most of the countries to which Norway is providing

---

2. Other population institutions in receipt of Norwegian funding are the International Committee on the Management of Population Programmes (ICOMP) and the International Union for the Scientific Study of Population (IUSSP).

3. Norway currently has co-financing agreements with seven UN Agencies, the World Bank and the African and Asian Development Banks.

4. This category of aid ranks third in importance in Norway's bilateral assistance after Transport, Communications and Water Supply (25 per cent) and Agriculture (15 per cent).

bilateral population assistance, the aid contribution already represents so large a proportion of the total foreign exchange cost of the national programme that it would be unbalanced to exceed it.

Another limiting factor is that Norway is today less involved in the health sector than in the past, even though NORAD recognises that health care programmes, particularly in Africa, frequently offer the only valid vehicle for family planning. It feels, however, that its aid may make a more useful contribution in other sectors, such as industrial or regional development. In Kenya, for example, where it previously provided aid for health facilities throughout the country, NORAD is now concentrating its aid on one major multi-sectoral regional development programme (in the remote Turkana District in the North). The Turkana Programme will include, among other activities, the provision of rural health facilities, and these will offer family planning services.

In other parts of the world, NORAD finds the same constraints affecting population programmes as other donor agencies have noted. These include faltering government commitment; shifting programme approaches (e.g. integration v. non-integration); the administrative and management weakness of many ministries of health; programme distortion by the setting of unrealistic performance targets[5], the moral issues inherent in systems of incentives and disincentives, etc., as well as the underlying problem of social and cultural traditions which are hostile to the whole idea of family size limitation. It also finds that it is difficult to bring family planning services within effective reach of the poorest and most vulnerable groups in the population — i.e. precisely those intended to be the main target for Norwegian aid efforts.

A further constraint to the expansion of population assistance in Norwegian bilateral aid programmes, as in those of some other DAC countries, is the geographical concentration of Norwegian aid[6]. Norway's bilateral aid is presently concentrated on nine programme "partners": Botswana, Kenya, Mozambique, Tanzania and Zambia, in Africa; and in Asia, Bangladesh, India, Pakistan and Sri Lanka. In some of these countries, Norwegian aid includes support for rural health facilities. In many of the African countries, however, these activities include little or no family planning.

Until the mid-70s, Norway extended assistance for family planning (and for certain other activities)[7] to countries outside of its programme group, on the grounds that "still only a minority of developing countries have effective programmes in this field, which is at the same time one of those to which Norway attaches prime importance[8]". Subsequently, however, these dispersed population activities have become less frequent, though they may still be benefiting from Norwegian aid indirectly through Norway's various joint financing agreements with institutions in the population field. (Only rarely does Norway contribute to joint-financing arrangements in the same countries as those with which it has entered into country programming agreements). Moreover, Norway's country programming arrangements mean that the taking on of new aid partners is a major political and administrative step, and "old" clients tend sometimes, in certain sectors, to be retained longer than is perhaps warranted.

Finally, bilateral aid for population activities is circumscribed by NORAD's interpretation of its own role as partner in development co-operation. Norway's whole approach to aid, while deeply committed, is deliberately unassertive. It thus tries to respond sympathetically to aid requests and proposals, but would not itself take the initiative and suggest activities for co-operation. In general, therefore, NORAD's population assistance is likely to remain limited to providing support for such specific activities as the government of the country concerned may decide that it wants.

---

5. The Norwegian Authorities were concerned at the emphasis on targets for sterilisation under the Indian programme at the time of the Emergency.
6. See section below on Country Programming.
7. Viz: Maritime transport; projects supported by non-governmental organisations; private industry; scholarships and fellowship schemes.
8. Parliamentary Report No. 29 "Norway's Economic Relations with Developing Countries", 1975.

II. APPROACH AND PRIORITIES

As the figures show, Norway has remained consistent in the priority it accords to population assistance. In keeping, however, with its "low-key" approach to development co-operation generally, its support for population activities, both vis-à-vis its aid partners and in international fora, has been characterised by quiet conviction rather than ideological fervour. There has been no attempt to proselytise.

As already noted, although, after Bucharest, most donor agencies, including some of those previously most closely identified with the supply side approach, were declaring that a "free-standing" family planning programme in developing countries was virtually useless[9], Norway seems to have largely resisted the "development approach" and remained unshaken in its belief in family planning per se. Although fully convinced of the desirability of encouraging other kinds of development activity as eventual "alternative ways in" to family planning acceptance, NORAD takes the view that it is for the requesting government to suggest them where it thinks them appropriate. Thus in Sri Lanka, the Government suggested including health and nutrition in a rural development programme supported by Norway[10], but did not suggest including family planning, and the Norwegian Authorities did not suggest it either. (On the other hand, along with training of community health workers, the "health" component provides for training in family planning for assistant medical practitioners).

NORAD officials recognise that more could be done to use Norwegian aid in other fields as a "carrier" for family planning (aid for rural development, co-operatives, etc.) but as a practical matter think that this is unlikely to happen. The obstacle lies partly in NORAD's reluctance to impose its own ideas as to project formulation and design, and partly in the Agency's organisational structure, which is set up on sectoral lines, and is thus not best suited to encourage the habit of multi-disciplinary thinking.

Norway's choice of both aid partners and specific aid programmes reflects its own strongly humanitarian bias[11]. Assistance for population activities is accordingly seen as one way of helping to improve the conditions of life for the most disadvantaged elements in the population.

Because of its policy of concentrating its aid efforts, Norway's assistance for population and health activities tends to be large-scale and of long duration. The smallest projects are in Tanzania ($3 million), Kenya ($3.5 million) and Pakistan ($4.6 million), the largest in India ($46 million - three successive Agreements) and Bangladesh ($29 million). Its commitment to the Indian Programme began in 1971, that to Bangladesh in 1975, (in both countries the latest Agreements are to run to 1983). In Kenya, Norway provided aid for health and population activities for some 15 years.

NORAD defines the difference between "programmes" and "projects" as a function partly of size ("programmes" are major, nationwide activities) and partly of the degree of aid agency involvement. In programme aid, the major management responsibility is assumed by the recipient country. The Indian Programme has accordingly been left to the Indian Authorities to run. NORAD is generally well satisfied with the results, but admits that it has been a relatively easy programme to administer – a consideration which prompted the initial aid decision! It therefore sees little immediate likelihood of providing aid for family planning "programmes" in other countries. NORAD, like SIDA,

---

9. At a meeting of heads of population assistance agencies and representatives of developing countries held at the OECD in Paris in May 1978, this point of view was put forward by most of the agencies present.

10. The Government of Sri Lanka, like the Union Government of India, assigned different areas of the country to different aid donors.

11. The principal criteria, as laid down by Parliament in 1977 are: degree of poverty; contribution to improving the condition of the poorest and most needy; government commitment to development and social justice; and human rights.

is finding that contrary to expectations, non-project aid is proving administratively *more* demanding rather than less[12].

The major part of Norway's aid for population goes to physical facilities and the training of personnel to staff them. In Bangladesh, for example, about 60 per cent of Norway's contribution to the IDA Population Project is for civil works. In Kenya, similarly, its aid for rural health has been applied largely to construction of new or repair of existing health facilities. This is a logical consequence of Norway's reluctance to get involved in the delicate area of population *policy* or even the design of population programmes. (Any "advisers" that it might provide in the population field are thus usually on specialist technical assignments).

While, as a matter of general aid policy, NORAD tends to favour commodity assistance, it has not applied this in the area of population. Despite its long-continuing support to family planning programmes in a number of countries, therefore, it has never been an important source of their contraceptive supplies.

III. CONTRIBUTION TO SELF-RELIANCE

NORAD officials define developing country "self-reliance" largely in terms of "knowledge" and "resources"[13]. Illustrating this in respect of population assistance, they refer to the Indian Programme, in which India is providing the knowledge, and Norwegian aid is contributing to resources, and to Bangladesh, where because the Population Programme is much more recent, aid is still needed to contribute to both.

Strengthening Administrative Capability: Consultants

Although not specifically mentioned in its definition of "self-reliance", the capacity of the recipient country government to administer and manage its aid programme is a problem to which NORAD has in fact been devoting increasingly close attention. For many years, NORAD considered the area of administration and management as the responsibility of the recipient country government. Thus its project appraisals would not normally include an assessment of the administrative resources and experience available for carrying the project out.

It was the experience of the IDA Population Project in Bangladesh that convinced NORAD of the importance for project implementation of the administrative and management capability of the recipient country. The project ran into serious difficulties of implementation, delays in disbursement and disappointing results overall, due in large measure to organisational problems and weaknesses of the administrative infrastructure concerned.

In Bangladesh, where not only the Population Programme but the civil service structure itself is of recent creation, the capacity of the administration to manage a new and ambitious Population Programme was of particular importance. Although not directly concerned with implementation, as the World Bank is managing the project on behalf of all the participating donors[14], in the second Project, NORAD has decided to step in directly to assist the implementation of the facilities that it is financing. It is therefore providing a Norwegian engineer to speed up construction of the planned rural health facilities and to supervise the quality of the work. The engineer is attached to the Public Works Department (which, understandably, has difficulty managing a project

---

12. NORAD told the Development Assistance Committee of the OECD that to handle non-project aid efficiently, it would need to strengthen its local aid representation and extend its evaluation work to cover non-project activities. It would also require a greater degree of attention to strengthening the administrative capacity of the recipient.
13. Definition given to the author in the course of interview of Norwegian aid officials in Oslo.
14. NORAD is contributing 40 per cent of the cost of a resident Population Officer provided by the Bank; his task is to act as liaison between the various donor agencies concerned and the Government of Bangladesh.

covering construction in some 1000 different sites, mainly rural, and where some of the building is done by private contractors and some by direct community effort), and the head of the service concerned is, nominally at least, his local counterpart. The main purpose of the assignment, however, is to expedite the work rather than build up the experience of the local officials.

When NORAD provides experts, it rarely insists that they be backed by local counterparts. The aid agreements usually state that counterparts are to be provided "if possible". In Kenya, however, the Agreement relating to the Thika School of Community Nursing made the nomination of Kenyan counterparts mandatory.

NORAD provides training (which may be given in third countries as well as in Norway and the recipient's own country) under its Technical Assistance Programme. Its training offers, however, are more likely to be general than applied to the "grooming" of selected local personnel for special responsibilities.

NORAD is prepared to pay local salaries — and salary supplements. In Bangladesh for example, it is paying the teachers in the Family Welfare Visitors Training Schools. (The concern is as much to ease the Government's budgetary difficulties as to attract staff to work on the activity that it is financing). Further, because of its interest in building up rural health facilities, NORAD is prepared to provide housing for local staff assigned to work in those areas.

In general, NORAD's approach to staffing matters is that these are essentially the concern of the recipient country. Although, as noted above, it is prepared to provide staff to assist in project implementation when necessary, it usually seeks to limit its own involvement to questions of administrative structure and to the top-echelon posts within it. Where technical assistance is to be provided, the host government submits the terms of reference and NORAD provides a choice of candidates. If the purpose is to give advice to NORAD on the other hand, the country cannot select the consultant, but still has the chance to approve the terms of reference. While, in theory, technical assistance personnel can be nationals of "third countries", in practice they rarely are, since recruitment is done in Oslo.

Recently, NORAD has set up a Personnel Fund in Kenya and Mozambique whereby those countries can make their own direct contracts with foreign experts as needed. This offer is particularly appreciated as an indication of Norway's genuine desire to save its partner country money that can be applied to more productive development purposes[15].

Local and Recurrent Costs

Norway has a generous attitude to the financing of local and recurrent costs[16]. In certain cases, it is prepared to finance activities that are 100 per cent local costs, as for example, for the Family Welfare Clinics in Pakistan. Indeed, the Norwegian Authorities state that they try to make no sharp distinction between a project's local and foreign exchange costs.

Where NORAD finances recurrent costs, it generally pays them all, as opposed to a certain percentage only, as do some donors. It also tends to be pragmatic about requiring the government to take over this responsibility on a phased basis. For example, neither for Kenya, where it is financing some training within the country, nor in Bangladesh, is any such arrangement provided for in the Agreement. In the Indian Population Programme where, initially, the Government of India financed part of the Programme itself, NORAD later agreed to finance the recurrent costs in order to ease the difficulties of the flow of funds from the Union to the State Governments. Under the third Agreement (1978-1983), however, NORAD is obliging the Government of India to take care of part of the recurrent costs of the Programme during the final three years.

---

15. Comments of Kenyan Ministry of Health officials.
16. It points out that its practice is more generous than that recommended in the DAC Guidelines on Local and Recurrent Cost Financing.

(At no time has NORAD financed the total cost of the Programme). In the rural health programme in Botswana, on the other hand, all recurrent costs were made the responsibility of the Government from the outset.

One interesting aspect of NORAD's approach to recurrent costs is the variety of activities that it sometimes finds itself financing. Thus in Bangladesh, it subsidises the training allowances paid by the Government. In India, Norwegian funds were used for making cash payments not only to the people undergoing sterilisation, but for a time, also, to the doctors performing the operations[17].

In the case of the Indian Population Programme, NORAD showed a particular awareness of the financial aspect of long-term "self-reliance" by making a calculation, at the outset, of the likely ratio between the capital cost of the Programme and subsequent costs. In most cases, however, NORAD (like many other donors) considers that it is the responsibility of the recipient country rather than the donor agency to make this sort of calculation, and does not seem to have done a similar exercise for its health and population projects in other countries.

IV. PROGRAMMING ARRANGEMENTS

Programming

Norwegian bilateral aid to its main partner countries is based on a 4-year programme cycle. Each country is given an indicative figure for a rolling 4-year period, and although this is not binding, most agreements for specific projects commit in advance the funds required for the whole life of the project. Although Parliament votes the aid budget annually, NORAD has never had any difficulty in meeting its commitment for an agreed activity.

Very large aid activities have to be approved individually by the Norwegian Parliament (the Indian and Bangladesh Projects, for example). Lesser, but still important projects require Cabinet approval.

To the extent possible, NORAD seeks to minimise the administrative burden involved for the partner country in preparing formal project requests. In Bangladesh, for example, it is prepared to accept a request submitted according to the format required by the Government of Bangladesh for inclusion in the next year's budget. NORAD is the only donor to do this.

The actual time taken between submission of a new project proposal and signing of the agreement naturally varies according to the size, complexity and state of preparedness of the request. If possible, NORAD likes to get expert opinion from outside before presenting a preliminary appraisal to its Board and to the Ministry of Foreign Affairs, and before deciding whether the project should be included in the next annual country programming consultations. For large projects, the time between Board approval and signature is approximately 10 months; smaller ones take about 3.

In the case of the extension of the All India Post Partum Programme to subdistrict level, three and a half years elapsed between presentation of the request by India during country programme negotiations held at the end of 1977 and signature of the Agreement in May 1981. NORAD did not send an appraisal mission to India until October 1978, nearly a year after receiving the request[18]. Another fifteen months passed before a second mission returned to India to finalise arrangements. It then took six months to prepare the 43-page project document, which was presented to the Government of India in November 1980, and a further six months until the Agreement

---

17. As a matter of general principle, NORAD disapproves of incentive payments to doctors performing sterilisation operations.

18. This mission, which spent one month in the country, was composed of one staff member from NORAD headquarters, a professor of obstetrics and gynaecology, a professor of social medicine and a district medical officer.

was signed. The Agreement involves support for a trial project for a two-year period (1981-1983). NORAD intends to await the results of the evaluation, to be carried out in 1983, before deciding whether or not to commit itself to a substantially larger programme. (This two-stage approach is becoming an increasingly frequent feature of Norway's development assistance).

Norway's aid agreements differ substantially in the degree of detail they include, according to the country, the activity, the aid relationship, previous experience, etc. The Agreement with Pakistan, for example, was extremely specific, to the point of defining how much each clinic should spend on electricity. Similarly, the Agreement for the Indian Post Partum Programme contained annexes setting out a very detailed breakdown of costs. Experience has shown, however, that it is unrealistic to expect the partner country to comply with requirements set out in such detail, notably when it comes to accounting (see below). In Kenya, the experience with implementing the Rural Health Agreement led NORAD to be much more flexible when it came to drawing up the later Agreement for the Turkana Project[19].

Norway does not normally lay down prior conditions to be fulfilled before its aid agreements can come into effect. There therefore need be no delay between signature and the actual flow of funds. (In the Turkana Project, for example, the first advance payment was made immediately upon signature of the Agreement). The agreements are also often vague about the government's obligations under the project, as already noted in connection with recurrent costs. The Botswana Rural Health Agreement (4 pages) provides only that the Government shall "be responsible for the administration, planning and implementation of the Programme", and shall "provide all recurrent costs... etc." Further, the aid agreements, if not exactly open-ended, are sometimes not too insistent about a cut-off date for completion, (reflecting NORAD's realism about the practical likelihood of completing projects according to the original schedule).

NORAD officials explain that they deliberately couch their aid agreements in broad terms, since the prime concern is to get something concrete accomplished; they consider that the details, and in particular, compliance with a pre-determined set of arrangements are of secondary importance. Given this approach, it is perhaps somewhat surprising to find that NORAD is relatively strict when it comes to requests for changes in a project in the course of implementation. Major changes must be submitted to the Board of NORAD, which meets once a month. If a substantive modification is involved, the proposal has to go to the Cabinet. Thus, the Cabinet had to pass, for example, on a request from the Government of Pakistan to extend the Project by one year and to modify the disbursement procedures and monitoring and reporting arrangements.

Resident Aid Missions

A certain amount of change can be agreed to informally by Norway's resident aid Missions. NORAD has posts in all the countries with which it has substantial long-term aid relations, and is seeking to strengthen them to the extent that staff resources will allow[20] and to give them a greater authority for decision-making. At the present time, NORAD's Missions are formally empowered to agree to changes involving up to approximately $12,000 equivalent, but in practice, individual Mission officers often interpret the rules flexibly.

NORAD local staff play a substantive role in the annual country consultations, in appraisal missions and in the mid-term and end-project reviews[21] which, under the terms of the agreements, are to be made of all Norway's major aid activities. They also

---

19. The Turkana Project covers activities in the areas of irrigation, forestry, fisheries, roads and health.

20. NORAD's total staff, which has been increasing in the past few years, now numbers some 200, including NORAD field missions. Four professional staff deal specifically with health and population activities.

21. Representatives of Norwegian universities or other research institutions usually participate in these reviews.

have an important monitoring role, in order to provide Oslo with more substantive information on the progress of Norwegian projects than is generally afforded by the statements received from the recipient.

V. IMPLEMENTATION PROCEDURES

Disbursements

NORAD variously finances its bilateral aid partners by advance payments and reimbursements. In some countries (India), it uses the system of advance payments only, and in some (Bangladesh), reimbursement only. In Kenya, where it initially used the reimbursement procedure, it subsequently changed to advances in order to speed up implementation.

In Bangladesh, NORAD is financing both the Women's Community Centre Project and the IDA Project on a reimbursement basis. The Government of Bangladesh would like NORAD to make its contribution to the latter by means of advances, as SIDA does, but the World Bank, as manager of the Project, prefers the participating bilateral donors to finance their respective activities under the Project by means of a consistent disbursement procedure[22].

Under reimbursement arrangements, NORAD requires not payment vouchers but audited statements of expenditure as a condition of each disbursement, to be followed by audited accounts. The NORAD mission, after examination, sends the statements to Oslo for payment to be made. This requirement of audited statements has often proved a major stumbling block. It has resulted in major delays in disbursement and difficulties in actual project operations, and has also been a source of irritation between donor and recipient. In Pakistan, the inability of the Government to produce the audited statements necessary for disbursements was one of the principal reasons for Norway's decision to suspend the Agreement.

The problem in Kenya (as in many other countries), is that the Ministry needs to have the actual vouchers relating to each purchase as a basis of issuing the audited statements to the donor. That the vouchers are difficult to locate, slow to be presented, or wrongly made out, and that the ministries are short of accountants and auditors to process them is only too common an experience.

NORAD has generally proved very understanding of such difficulties, and although there are limits to its forbearance, its inclination is to give flexibility a higher priority than strict accountability so as not to hold up the work. For example, NORAD has sometimes found that the government lacked the funds needed to make the initial payment. In Kenya, it has frequently helped the Ministry of Health get round this problem, either by giving an advance (when the formally agreed procedure was reimbursement), or by itself making direct payment to the supplier or contractor.

In respect of the statements needed for advance payments, NORAD tries to tailor its requirements to what the country is likely to be able to produce. Generally, the amount of information requested is kept to a minimum. In Kenya, for example, the statements (two per year) need contain no more than the expenditures made during the preceding period and a plan of disbursements for the coming one. In Botswana, the Agreement asked for more detail regarding the expenditures planned (number and location of buildings to be constructed, staff to be posted, etc.). The statements need not conform to any particular pattern (there is no form to be filled in). They must, however, be made in English.

NORAD has further shown itself to be very helpful in respect of some of the difficulties holding up disbursement that arise out of the internal regulations of the partner country. In Kenya, for example, the Turkana Project was unable to start because the

---

22. Under the IDA project, NORAD, like the other donors, releases funds when the Bank has received evidence of disbursement which it considers satisfactory. NORAD is not directly involved.

Government had failed to get it included in the Estimates in time. NORAD first proposed to get round this problem by making the Government an advance, and when this solution was refused by the Kenyan Treasury, resorted to direct purchase of some of the equipment required in order to get the project started.

Reporting, Accounting, Auditing

As indicated in the preceding section, although the Norwegian Government is of course concerned to know how its aid money is being spent, NORAD is taking an increasingly pragmatic approach to the reporting, accounting and auditing of its activities.

For most projects today, NORAD requires the accounts to be presented under two headings only: capital costs and operating costs, but even this sometimes presents difficulties. In India, although the Programme works well, the Health Authorities concerned were unable to produce any meaningful breakdown of the total expenditures within each State. Consequently, if NORAD is satisfied that the global figures it receives are roughly in line with those agreed, it does not question the matter further. NORAD officials admit that this approach can be justified when the level of performance is high, but may be disastrous in programmes where it is not (viz. Pakistan).

Audited accounts have to be presented to NORAD annually. NORAD's practice is to accept the government auditors of the country concerned. This is sometimes satisfactory, sometimes not. (In India, for example, NORAD recognises that it would take years to get a proper audit of so vast a programme. Since its vigilance is concerned with project content rather than form, it simply does without).

NORAD appreciates that for many of its partner countries, the practical problem in respect of the auditing requirement is not the level of professional competence, which is often high, but the shortage of accountants and auditors in the government service. In Kenya, for example, the Ministry of Health cannot afford to set aside one accountant solely for the Norwegian project (although this is provided for in the Agreement). The work is therefore done by the Ministry's accounting pool, with consequent delays while it waits its turn in the queue. The official auditing of the accounts, when these are finally prepared, is done by the Kenyan Ministry of Finance. NORAD finds this fully satisfactory, now that an arrangement has been worked out whereby the relevant extract of the Government's Annual Audit is sent to NORAD a few months before the complete Audit is published, thus meeting the Norwegian Government's time-limit of 18 months.

The Norwegian Government always has in the background the possibility of making its own audit from Oslo. Three auditors, responsible not to NORAD but to the Auditor-General's Department, are assigned to NORAD's activities, and sometimes visit projects. Their Report is submitted to Parliament. NORAD is generally satisfied with this system. The auditors find that they are able to get all the information they require from the countries concerned, and on the occasions when they have made criticisms of a programme, NORAD has usually already taken the appropriate corrective action.

Procurement

Norwegian aid has hitherto been mostly untied, as a matter of principle. (In 1981, Parliament reaffirmed its position regarding untied commodity assistance: Norwegian supplies may be preferred only when reasonably competitive in the international market as to price and quality).

Where foreign goods are to be supplied under a Norwegian-assisted programme, the procurement is usually done by the government of the country concerned, and NORAD will reimburse in foreign currency on an item-by-item basis.

When procurement is done by the government, the national authorities concerned call for tenders, review the bids and make their choice according to the procedures standard in the country. NORAD asks to be kept informed, and will sometimes ask to see the tender documents and bids before any decision is made. Where construction contracts are concerned, NORAD is supposed to approve the drawings before releasing the funds. Occasionally, NORAD has queried the choice of a supplier or contractor when receiving the request for reimbursement.

There are some disadvantages to government procurement, notably the country's own bureaucratic procedures, delays in getting goods from the dock to the project site, and the complications of customs duty. In Kenya, for example, the Government often prefers NORAD to do the purchasing on its behalf, as a way of circumventing its own requirement of tendering, and being generally speedier and more efficient[23]. Under the Turkana Agreement, accordingly, at the Government's request, NORAD has agreed to direct purchasing of local as well as imported goods and services. Although NORAD would be pleased to help build up procurement expertise in the recipient country, it thus finds itself increasingly taking on the role of direct supplier.

VI. CO-ORDINATION WITH OTHER POPULATION ASSISTANCE DONORS

Norway's bilateral aid for population is marked to an unusual degree by the desire of the Norwegian Government to co-ordinate its programme with those of other aid donors.

Nordic Group Co-ordination

As one of the Nordic Group, Norway participates in the established aid co-ordination arrangements between the three Scandinavian countries and Finland. This provides an institutional framework for co-ordination at the political level (an annual Ministerial meeting backed by Divisional level meetings three or four times a year), and keeps the four countries concerned informed of each other's major aid decisions. Sometimes this exchange of information may also include pending requests, but this is not automatic.

Co-ordination between the Scandinavian donors at the country level varies considerably according to the programme and the individual officers in post in the country concerned. In Tanzania, for example, all four countries which have been assisting the rural health programme supported a joint mission to evaluate it. In India, on the other hand, where the Nordic countries are each supporting different programmes, the Swedes, the Danes and the Norwegians were at one point each planning to send an independent appraisal mission at about the same time. (A measure of co-operation was achieved eventually, and the ODA and UNFPA subsequently joined in too). One reason why co-ordination between the Nordic donors is not closer is that they do not necessarily share the same approach to population programmes in the country concerned. These differences have been particularly marked in the case of India, but have occurred also in Pakistan, where SIDA withdrew some time before Norway decided to do so.

"Multi-bi" Financing Arrangements

As mentioned earlier, Norway participates in a large number of "multi-bi" financing arrangements with a wide range of multilateral aid organisations. Here too, the motivation was partly to enable Norway to make a bigger contribution to aid in the health and population sector than would be possible for NORAD alone to handle. These arrangements also offer the Norwegian Government a degree of political flexibility by enabling it to provide assistance to countries outside Norway's limited number of established aid "partners".

The first umbrella agreement covering Norwegian financing for multi-bi projects (called "noted projects" by UNICEF) in the health and population field was signed

---

23. Under Government of Kenya procedures, the Planning Office of the Ministry of Health prepares specifications, sends copies to NORAD (and possibly discusses them with the NORAD Mission), then sends them to the Ministerial Procurement Board, which sends them to the Central Tender Board, which then sets in motion the tendering procedures.

with UNICEF in 1971 (for training of nurse-midwives in Uttar Pradesh and Bihar in India). Similar arrangements followed with FAO, IMCO[24], ITC[25], UNFPA, UNESCO, ILO, the World Bank, the African Development Bank and the Asian Development Bank. The aid provided to UNFPA has been largely applied to the costs of Basic Needs Assessment Missions for Population Assistance. The projects jointly financed with UNFPA and UNICEF nearly all include a substantial family planning component. (A list is given in the annex to this chapter).

It is through its contribution to these projects, which is included in Norway's bilateral aid to population, that Norway is able to maintain so high a proportion of bilateral aid for population activities. With less than two staff members (Foreign Ministry), Norway is currently assisting approximately 100 multi-bi projects amounting to a total of some $40 million a year. The projects themselves (average: 3 years) are usually shorter-term than those financed by NORAD. They vary in size and (again markedly different from NORAD's practice) may be as small as a single consultancy.

NORAD itself is not involved in these activities at all — though it receives, for information, lists of the projects which have been agreed. The Norwegian Foreign Office, however, receives from the Agency concerned the draft Plan of Operation for approval, and does occasionally require some modifications. Once the Plan has been approved, the Agency has responsibility for managing the project, and receives from Norway a 13 per cent administrative overhead for the purpose.

The Norwegian Authorities recognise that there may be certain disadvantages in multi-bi arrangements. They tend to be slow to get moving: it takes an average of two and a half years, for example, between the first submission of a project proposal by the UNFPA and the first disbursement of funds by Norway — a situation which shows up as a pipeline problem for UNFPA, though not for Norway. Further, they pre-suppose a high degree of confidence in the executing agency, which handles the project entirely in its own way, according to its own aid procedures, and is required simply to submit to Norway an annual report and statement of account. The Norwegian Authorities feel generally that they would like to have more substantive information on the progress of the activities that they finance in this way. Only occasionally do they participate with the agency concerned in a joint evaluation exercise.

---

24. IMCO—Intergovernmental Maritime Consultative Organisation.
25. ITC—International Trade Centre.

NORWAY
AID FOR POPULATION ACTIVITIES

i) Total volume of population assistance expenditures through 1981, $219 million

ii) Annual expenditures on population assistance, 1975-1981 (US $ million)

1975	13.7
1976	21.8
1977	21.7
1978	32.0
1979	33.3
1980	34.7
1981	32.0

iii) Expenditures on population assistance as a percentage of total (net) ODA, 1975-1981.

1975	7.4
1976	10.0
1977	7.4
1978	9.0
1979	7.8
1980	7.1
1981	6.9

iv) Division of total expenditures on population assistance as between bilateral, multi-bilateral, multilateral and non-governmental organizations, 1975-1981.

	Bilateral		Multi-bilateral		Multilateral		Non-governmental Organizations		Total
	$ thousand	%	$ thousand	%	$ thousand	%	$ thousand	%	$ thousand
1975	5 340	39.0	—		6 431	47.0	1 907	14.0	13 678
1976	11 063	50.8	—		7 977	36.6	2 749	12.6	21 789
1977	6 787	31.3	852	3.9	11 132	51.4	2 912	13.4	21 683
1978	12 432	38.9	451	1.4	15 647	48.8	3 486	10.9	32 016
1979	10 132	30.4	2 252	6.8	17 081	51.3	3 833	11.5	33 298
1980	9 750	28.1	2 504	7.2	18 533	53.4	3 910	11.3	34 697
1981	9 758	30.5	2 056	6.4	16 855	52.6	3 363	10.5	32 032

ANNEX

SPECIFIC PURPOSE CONTRIBUTIONS FROM THE GOVERNMENT OF NORWAY SINCE 1976[1]

AfDF
Niger : Health Science School in Niamey.

FAO
Zambia : Nutrition Education.

IDA
Thailand : Population Project.
Tunisia : Population Project.

ILO
Indonesia: Strengthening of the Family Planning Programme for Enterprises.

UNFPA
Ethiopia: Support for Health/Family Planning Programmes through the National Literacy Campaign.
Jamaica: Primary Health Care and Family Planning.
Jamaica : Family Life Education in Schools.
Nepal : Training for the Community Health Integrated Project.
Seychelles : Family Life Education.
Sri Lanka: Strengthening Hospital-based Family Planning Services.

UNICEF
African Liberation Movements: Supplementary Assistance for Children and Mothers.
Bangladesh: Special Assistance Programme.
Burma: Services for Children (local drug production).
Chad: Special Assistance for Children and Mothers.
Gambia: Special Assistance Programme.
Lesotho: Basic Services for Children and Mothers.
Mauritania: Nutrition Rehabilitation.
Mozambique: Special Assistance for Children and Mothers.
Niger: Relief and Rehabilitation.
Senegal: Special Assistance Programme.
Seychelles: Services for Children.
Sudan: Rural Water Supply I (1973-1978).
Sudan: Primary Health Care.
Sudan: Rural Water Supply II (1978-1980).
Tanzania: Young Children Protection Programme.
Tanzania: Special Assistance Programme (Health Services).
Upper Volta: Rural Water Supply.

---

1. Information provided by Royal Ministry of Foreign Affairs, November 1979.

SWEDEN[1]

I. INTRODUCTION

Sweden occupies a special place in the history of population assistance in that it was the first — and for several years the only — donor agency to provide aid to a developing country government for a family planning programme. Since 1958, when SIDA (the Swedish International Development Authority) made an agreement with the Government of Sri Lanka to provide personnel and material to a family planning project, the population problem in its manifold aspects has continued to be one of the priority concerns of Swedish development co-operation.

Swedish aid has always had a particular interest in the social development of Third World countries. It therefore has a heavy bias towards the sectors of health, education and rural development, and towards the relief of poverty generally. Many of the activities supported by Sweden in these various areas could be considered as helping indirectly to deal with population problems through their effects on the causes or the consequences of high fertility, mortality, migratory movements, etc. Many Swedish aid officials consider them in this light. For statistical reporting purposes, however, Sweden does not consider any of these activities as constituting "population assistance". In fact, Sweden uses the term "population assistance" only for its contribution to the multilateral agencies which provide aid in this field. Under its bilateral programmes, its aid in the population sector is listed squarely as "family planning" — a category which usually includes also associated mother and child health care[2].

For the past decade, total Swedish aid for population, bilateral and multilateral, has represented some 4.5 per cent of total Swedish ODA. This percentage, in itself perhaps hardly remarkable compared to Swedish aid to some other sectors, is nonetheless the second highest for aid to population among DAC donor countries (after Norway).

Sweden early became a strong advocate of the desirability of providing population assistance through multilateral channels. It took an active part in the creation of the UNFPA in 1967, and has since directed an increasing share of its population assistance funding to support for UNFPA programmes and for those of the IPPF. By the end of the 1970s, more than two-thirds of Swedish aid for population assistance was provided in the form of contributions to these and other international organisations (WHO International Research Programme on Human Reproduction, the World Council of Churches, etc.). This proportion is the more significant in that in 1976, only four years earlier, bilateral programmes still accounted for slightly over half of total Swedish expenditures on population assistance.

The decision regarding the relative proportions of Swedish multilateral and bilateral assistance is made by Parliament when it approves the annual aid budget. For aid within any particular sector, this decision lies with the Ministry of Foreign Affairs, whose Office of International Development Co-operation administers the multilateral programmes. Bilateral programmes are handled by SIDA.

In addition to its bilateral programmes, SIDA provides some financing for family planning activities indirectly through its growing support to Swedish non-governmental organisations (humanitarian and religious groups, trade unions etc.), many of which

---

1. Statistical table, see page 117.
2. For the purposes, however, of annual reporting of aid flows to the DAC, which does use the term "population assistance", Sweden includes under this heading both its contributions to multilateral agencies, and its bilateral support for family planning programmes.

undertake development activities in Third World countries in the family planning and health fields. SIDA considers its support to these organisations as a valuable supplement to official aid, in view of their special ability to "test innovation, initiate experiments and support neglected groups"[3].

To complete the picture of the official bodies through which Sweden provides support for population activities, mention should be made also of the Swedish Agency for Research Co-operation with Developing Countries (SAREC). Set up on an experimental basis in 1975, and given permanent status four years later, SAREC funds research projects and researchers in developing countries in a remarkably wide range of development fields, which include aspects of population and population-related problems.

All Swedish aid for family planning programmes is given in the form of grants. Exceptionally, a minute amount — 2 per cent — of SIDA's programme is in the form of loans, but this is in special circumstances and on very generous terms.

The paragraphs that follow describe Sweden's bilateral programmes of population assistance and the way in which they are prepared and administered by SIDA on behalf of the Government of Sweden.

The Role of SIDA

As an aid agency, SIDA enjoys a number of unusual advantages. The first is that the aid programme overall commands strong public support in Sweden. As a consequence, Parliament would always approve the full amount of the Government's requests for aid funds (where there were dissenting voices, they were demanding larger appropriations than those actually requested!). It is only very recently (since 1982) that the Swedish aid programme, like that of every other donor country, has been affected by the economic recession, and as a consequence, subject to pressures from the Treasury — constraints from which until now it has been happily free.

The very positive attitude to development co-operation on the part of Swedish public opinion is also a source of strength within SIDA itself. SIDA's Board of Directors, chaired by the Director-General, is composed of representatives (13) of political parties, trade unions, co-operative groups etc., with two members from SIDA staff. Given these close contacts between SIDA and important groups of Swedish society, Parliament is prepared to leave SIDA a very free hand in respect of the content as well as the management of Swedish bilateral aid. Although the Swedish Parliament plays an important role in formulating principles and policies for development assistance, and decides on the budget, there is little direct Parliamentary involvement in the composition or geographic distribution of bilateral aid. Within the Government, political responsibility for the aid programme rests with the Office for International Development Co-operation. In practice, however, government decisions regarding bilateral assistance are normally based on proposals from SIDA.

SIDA, in fact, is more than an implementing agency. The Government has delegated to it considerable autonomy for programme administration and financing. Most decisions about projects and activities to be supported are nowadays taken by SIDA, not by the Government, which has speeded up the time needed to get projects approved by several months and saved administrative capacity for other tasks.

Obstacles to Expanding Bilateral Population Assistance

Although SIDA feels that it would like to do more in the general area of social development and "basic needs", it sees a number of obstacles to any important expansion of its bilateral assistance for family planning.

The first difficulty is inherent in the current Swedish approach which considers family planning to be part of primary health care, in line with the Alma Ata Declaration[4]. This may make it hard to find satisfactory new outlets for family planning

---

3. SIDA's Aid Through Non-governmental Organisations: SIDA Fact Sheet, November 1978.
4. Alma Ata Conference on Primary Health Care, organised by WHO and UNICEF, Sept. 1978.

programmes where developing countries lack a health service infrastructure or where, if the infrastructure does exist, the Government does not perceive the desirability of broadening its scope to include family planning.

In its relations with developing countries, Sweden used to take the line that it should not seek to impose its own views and approaches on the government. In recent years, however, this attitude has been changing, and SIDA's earlier inhibitions about "donor bias" have given way to a policy of what it calls "concerned participation", which would establish a dialogue between donor and recipient as to the appropriate course of action to be pursued.

A second obstacle to the expansion of bilateral programmes is the Swedish view that for population assistance, multilateral channels are generally more suitable than bilateral. As already noted, the proportion of bilateral aid in Swedish population assistance has recently been steadily diminishing in relation to contributions to multilateral programmes.

A third difficulty lies in the Swedish policy of geographical concentration of aid. In accordance with Parliament's guidelines, aid was for some years focussed on twenty (now seventeen) "programme countries", of which only twelve are currently receiving support for health and family planning activities. Further, of the twelve, only nine (Angola, Ethiopia, Kenya, Tanzania, Zambia, Bangladesh, India, Zimbabwe and Viet Nam) have programmes of any significant size. (Health and/or family planning assistance to Portugal, Sri Lanka and Tunisia was phased out in 1981).

In the early years of its population assistance, when Sweden was virtually the sole donor in the field, SIDA made an exception to its policy of geographical concentration and was glad to provide population assistance to any country which asked for it, and where it felt it was likely to make a useful contribution. It accordingly supported population activities in some twenty-five developing countries. Gradually, however, it has been reducing these activities, and today SIDA provides no bilateral assistance outside of the programme countries.

A fourth obstacle to expanding bilateral aid for family planning is that within the programme countries, unless it is already one of the areas receiving Swedish aid, it is difficult to shift support from one area to another. Under the Swedish system of country programming, new sectors can only be introduced at the request of the recipient government as old activities phase out. In practice, activities are slow to do this. Once SIDA has begun support for a particular sector in one of its programme countries, it is likely to continue for a considerable time. New sectors desiring Swedish support may, therefore, be faced with a long wait.

Obstacles to the Effectiveness of Population Assistance

SIDA has noted a number of practical problems in implementing its family planning programmes, some of which are common to other social development sectors, others more specific to family planning.

One of the most common noted by SIDA officials is over-hasty project preparation, a shortcoming for which they recognise donor and recipients are equally to blame. (Sri Lanka was cited as a case where good project preparation had paid off). Another problem, for which SIDA recognises it is itself mainly responsible, is the failure to estimate realistically the length of time needed to do the many different things involved in setting a project up — e.g. acquiring sites for buildings, selecting and training staff, training trainers, etc. (Under the India Population Project, it took three years for the State of Karnataka to acquire the sites for the 2000 health sub-centres planned and to start the building work, whereas in Lucknow, this stage had been adequately planned for in advance). Further, when projects finally reach the implementation stage, new problems tend to arise because of unsatisfactory staffing, particularly in rural areas.

These are, of course, general problems of aid implementation, but in addition, SIDA finds that there are a number of special problems due to the intrinsic nature of family planning programmes. One is that family planning programmes are particularly prone to target-setting (both in demographic terms and performance), and the targets set are often unrealistic. As a consequence, family planning programmes not only demand a more rigorous system of monitoring than it is feasible to provide, but when the targets are not met, the failure is damaging to both donor and recipient expectations and to the morale of project staff. SIDA is also fearful that emphasis on targets may lead to coercion of the individual client.

Another practical problem affecting family planning programmes is that many kinds of contraceptive practice require medical back-up. In developing countries, the relevant services are in many cases simply not available. Although the development of health care services (including family planning) is one of the priorities of Swedish assistance, as a practical matter, the absence of acceptable medical services often effectively limits the variety of family planning methods which can be offered.

Finally, SIDA stresses the peculiar importance in family planning programmes of the *opinions,* both public and private, of the people concerned. Because of the personal and intimate nature of family planning, day-to-day project implementation is very closely affected by people's *attitudes* and *fears.* (Thus in India, after the intensive sterilisation campaigns under Emergency, people in some areas felt that *all* injections were for purposes of sterilisation — even those against smallpox!) To be effective, therefore, family planning projects require a much more close and continuous collaboration between project management and the public in the country concerned than is necessary in other sectors of aid.

II. APPROACH AND CRITERIA

Changing Approaches to Population Problems

There is no doubt that the population problem and family planning programmes no longer occupy the same importance in Swedish development co-operation policies as they did in the 1960s. In 1968, in "Swedish Development Aid", SIDA described population as an area of "vital importance in the present world situation". Ten years later, the Swedish Government still held that "population questions remain a central problem" and that it was "important that Sweden continue to render extensive and long-term support efforts in this field"[5]. Yet in 1980, "Sweden's Policy for International Development Co-operation"[6] does not mention population at all. The issues which are seen as of special relevance to the 80s have now become (reflecting the preparation for the new International Development Strategy) resource transfer and structural adjustment, plus such special problems as energy, the environment and the situation of women in developing countries.

Within Sweden today, there is a distinct current of opinion which considers that the population problem has been "over-sold" in developing countries. Sweden has wholeheartedly endorsed the views which the developing countries expressed so forcibly at the World Population Conference at Bucharest (and with which it was actively associated). It therefore maintains that every country has the sovereign right to develop its own population policy (i.e. free from foreign interference).

Still adhering closely to the Bucharest philosophy, Sweden today takes the position that population problems can only be treated as part of the overall process of development. Thus "population" ceases to be a separate issue, susceptible of special treatment. Where countries feel that they have certain specific population problems (whether high fertility, or high rates of mortality and morbidity, unsatisfactory geographical distribution, etc.), the response can only be through a "development" approach. This said, Sweden is still prepared to provide help to those countries wishing to reduce their population growth rate, but no longer by means of family planning programmes alone. For some time now, Swedish assistance for family planning has been linked with the provision of health care. Indeed, in current Swedish thinking, a family planning

---

5. Excerpt from Proposition 1978/79, Appendix 6. Foreign Office.
6. Extracts from the Budget and Finance Bill for Fiscal Year 1980/81.

programme in isolation is not only likely to be ineffective but is also socially and morally wrong. SIDA does not, therefore, support any "independent" family planning activities.

This broad interpretation of "population" problems and how to deal with them is only partially reflected in the internal structure of the Swedish aid agency. SIDA operates through country desks, plus four substantive sector desks: Health (which includes Population and Nutrition), Industry, Agriculture and Education. A certain amount of broad discussion takes place before SIDA teams depart for the country programming exercise, which is done annually. Although, at the project level, different teams go out to examine specific project ideas, they normally consider their implications for other sectors. A large water project, for example, would be automatically examined from the health aspects (as was the Botswana Water Project). Similarly, programmes to meet basic human needs (notably rural development programmes) would be examined from the point of view of their likely impact on health, population and nutrition.

The insertion of family planning (or health) objectives among those of other development activities seems likely to occur in Swedish aid programmes only if the host country takes the initiative. Thus a Swedish-supported adult literacy project in Tanzania used Health Education as the subject of teaching — at the instance of the Tanzanian Ministry of Health. However, in an adult literacy project in India for which it is supplying the material, SIDA did not suggest inserting a health and family planning component.

Criteria for Population Assistance

SIDA describes its function as an aid donor as largely supervisory, confining its involvement to planning and evaluation, and leaving implementation to the country concerned. The Swedish Government assumes that the recipient government knows its own business best, and indeed it has stated that one of its criteria for selecting its aid partners is their "ability to undertake a development policy compatible with Swedish aid policies which can be implemented with a great measure of mutual confidence and trust".

Implicit in the above statement is the condition that the countries themselves must be pursuing economic, social and *political* goals with which Sweden is broadly in sympathy. The countries which Sweden supports are generally the poorer developing countries, those that have recently achieved their liberation from colonial or repressive regimes, and those whose goals are economic and social equality.

Within these countries, SIDA will not, of course, necessarily agree to assist whatever activity the government might propose. There are a number of strong negative criteria. One, as already mentioned, is a growing distaste for any programme concerned with fertility limitation to the exclusion of broader health and welfare objectives. (A few years ago, after long consideration, SIDA decided that the Indian Government's current approach to the country's population problems was no longer sufficiently in tune with its own "development" approach as to warrant further Swedish aid in that sector). Another is against the use of coercion, notably in the case of sterilisation programmes. Voluntary sterilisation is acceptable as part of a broader health project, but not as the main family limitation method[7]. Sweden would insist that any programme it financed should have an acceptable balance, not only as between health and family planning components, but also as between various family planning methods, with the individual client being allowed to choose between them.

Once a programme satisfies these criteria, SIDA has certain preferences as to the particular types of activity it considers most suitable for Swedish assistance. Thus it prefers "software" (education, motivation, training, etc.) to the provision of infrastructure and equipment. It does not normally finance demographic surveys, statistical

---

7. Along with other aid donors, Sweden has expressed some concern lest the Bangladesh Government's emphasis on sterilisation in the National Population Programme should lead to an element of coercion.

research, etc., since there are other donors who like to do so[8]. And whereas, in the past, a considerable part of Swedish family planning assistance was provided in the form of commodities (contraceptive supplies), the need for this kind of aid has declined, as a result of the massive supply programme of US AID and the increasing ability of developing countries, helped by Sweden and other donors, to produce or package their own contraceptive materials. (SIDA previously, if so requested, would supply Depo Provera among other types of contraceptive, but now no longer does so, on the grounds that developing countries lack the facilities necessary for medical follow-up).

There is also a growing trend in favour of sector support. SIDA now has sector support agreements with ten countries, some six of which include health. (As family planning is not considered a sector on its own, there is no question of Swedish support for the "population sector" but, in most of these countries, the health sector programmes include a certain amount of family planning activities. Swedish sector support, the terms of which vary according to circumstances, is generally an advantage to the recipient country in terms of greater flexibility and fewer implementation requirements than conventional project agreements. SIDA staff tend to like it too, compared to projects, which are often slow to disburse, complicated to administer, and unpredictable as to the order in which the different elements will actually be implemented.

As regards the scope of the family planning programmes that SIDA is prepared to assist, there are no upper financial limits, beyond what the government of the recipient country is considered willing and able to handle. (Very large projects have to be submitted for Parliamentary approval, but a family planning activity is unlikely to come into this category, which is intended for projects requiring a big capital investment). SIDA is, however, showing an increasing reluctance to undertake very small activities, which are felt to constitute a disproportionate administrative burden on its staff resources. It would not therefore support requests for individual fellowships, study visits, etc. unless they were an integral part of a wider Swedish-supported programme. It is for administrative reasons, for example, that SIDA says it has decided to cease its support to a number of small international projects (e.g. the Family Life Education Project in the West Indies) and population institutions (notably, the IUSSP[9], ICOMP[10] and the International Children's Bureau). However, a further reason would seem to be a growing feeling within SIDA that it does not get enough substantive information about the actual programmes of these various bodies — a complaint that it is being heard to make with increasing frequency with respect to all the international institutions, large and small, to which it has been accustomed to provide funding.

III. CONTRIBUTION TO "SELF RELIANCE"

SIDA points to its assistance to Sri Lanka as a classical case of aid being applied to strengthen a country's capability, financial, administrative and technical, to carry out its own population programmes. In Sri Lanka, it was the experience of the two pilot family planning projects begun with Swedish aid that encouraged the Government to start a programme of its own. Sweden continued to assist the programme of the Sri Lanka Government for many years, and when it felt it could safely begin phasing out its aid, provided technical assistance in certain administrative functions (e.g. in purchasing procedures to enable the Government to buy contraceptive supplies previously provided by Sweden) to help the Government prepare to take over.

Local and Recurrent Costs

In providing financial assistance, SIDA's view is that it can be most helpful by giving its contribution to the recipient government to use as it sees fit, with as few

---

8. Among them, multilateral agencies to which Sweden contributes.
9. International Union for the Scientific Study of Population.
10. International Committee on the Management of Population Programmes.

strings attached as possible, hence the growing preference for sector support[11]. Similarly, the Swedish contribution to the IDA Population Project in Bangladesh, in which it is participating with five other donor countries, is not ear-marked for a specific component or set of components, but is added to the account of the Bangladesh Government to make up its agreed contribution to the Project. The Government of Bangladesh has found this arrangement highly convenient. It has been able to draw upon these (convertible currency) funds, which can be used for *any* purpose under the Project, as a ready interim source of finance when contributions from other donors (which are tied to specific activities) have been slow to arrive. Originally, SIDA expected that disbursements from the Swedish fund would be made bi-annually, but in fact, they have followed the actual requirements of the Project[12]. Not surprisingly, the Bangladesh Government wishes other donors would agree to similar arrangements.

As a consequence of giving its aid in this spirit, Sweden sometimes finds itself financing activities that other donors might not be so willing to do. Examples are activities that involve entirely local costs, such as training of health workers and construction of housing for health service personnel, whether expatriate or national. This latter form of assistance is particularly appreciated by developing country governments, who recognise how greatly it contributes to the effectiveness of project implementation[13]. (It is in any case a normal practice of the Swedish Government, which builds staff housing in order to encourage doctors to go and work in the remoter areas of northern Sweden).

In the matter of *recurrent costs*, SIDA has become increasingly generous since it became clear in the late 1970s that support for "basic needs" programmes would necessarily have to include a large element of recurrent costs. Today, SIDA is prepared - to a certain extent - to pay local salaries, salary supplements to staff working in rural areas, or the cost of a new post, whether filled by an expatriate or a local officer, if it is considered important for the project.

SIDA recognises that this sympathetic approach runs up against some problems. One is inflation in the host country, which may lead to a disproportionate amount of financing being applied to recurrent expenditures. Another is the failure of both government and donor to work out at the design stage the project's long-term implications in terms of running costs. This is one reason why SIDA's involvement often tends to be both greater and of longer duration than anticipated. It also means that the goal of financial "self-reliance" for the partner country is likely to become increasingly difficult to achieve.

Strengthening Administrative and Managerial Capability: Consultants and Training

As regards measures to build up a country's administrative capability to carry out population programmes, SIDA for some time preferred not to interfere, and to have confidence in the host country government. In recent years, however, it has been getting more actively concerned in this aspect of aid implementation, making suggestions where necessary for the creation of new administrative machinery or for changes in the administrative structure.

In respect of managerial capability, the problem is compounded by the difficulty of objective assessment. While SIDA tries to include some appreciation of managerial capability in its project appraisal, it feels that intervention to strengthen managerial capability is best left to areas of specific *technical* competence. Thus in Tanzania and

---

11. Paradoxically, Sweden's continuing interest in developments in the particular sector it is assisting, exercised through its local aid mission, could lead to a degree of involvement in the country's development *policies*, which it would normally eschew in its project assistance.

12. Bangladesh officials report that this arrangement sometimes results in the Swedish contribution being "overspent" as a consequence less of delays in disbursement on the part of other donors than of unsatisfactory planning on the part of the Government.

13. This point was stressed very strongly by the representatives from a number of developing countries who attended a meeting at the OECD in Paris in April 1979, which discussed the procedural obstacles to aid implementation.

Kenya, for example, it has provided architects for the Health Ministry. SIDA admits, though, that such assistance is usually proffered post hoc, after the annual sector reviews have revealed that performance is lagging, and particular problems or deficiencies have been identified.

On the whole, Sweden does not provide many consultants in the family planning field, although there are more in health — particularly in Africa. (In Tanzania, SIDA used to supply doctors to the district hospitals so that local doctors could be released for further training). The cost of consultants is part of the project cost (and is thereby known to the partner government), and countries are normally given a choice of candidates.

Consultants financed by SIDA can come from third countries, but in practice this does not occur very often because of the administrative complexities (taxation arrangements, social security, etc.). To get around these, SIDA has tried the device of putting special "Consultancy Funds" at the disposal of developing countries, who can then do the actual hiring themselves (the funds being part of the overall country "frame"). The largest such fund — Sw.Kr.30 m. (US$ 5.5 million) — was set up to enable Mozambique to cover its needs for personnel in all sectors and from any country.

One practical problem with this arrangement is that the consultants themselves are often reluctant to be hired directly by developing country governments. SIDA therefore increasingly uses consultancy firms (Swedish and foreign) to do the recruiting. In Viet Nam, for example, over 300 expatriates (most of them Swedish) have been engaged in this way, of whom some 50 are working in the two Swedish-supported hospitals. SIDA is on the whole satisfied with the calibre of the expertise that it can provide under these various arrangements, but finds that the overheads involved make this a costly form of aid. It is seeking to restrict the consultant element in its aid programmes, partly for reasons of cost, and partly in response to a growing sentiment in the developing countries that, except for highly specialised expertise, local talent can do as well as expensive expatriates.

Ideally, SIDA hopes that its consultants in developing countries will be backed by local counterparts, but it is realistic about the difficulty of meeting this requirement in practice. It finds that the best chance of securing satisfactory counterpart backing — and thereby of making the best use of consultants to strengthen national capability in the long term — is to provide assistance for an on-going government programme, rather than for some new activity which the government may consider as external to its own priorities.

An increasingly important element of Swedish aid for health and family planning is being applied to training activities, notably at the sub-professional levels, i.e. rural medical aides, nurse midwives, nurses, etc. This reflects Sweden's particular interest in helping countries reach the WHO objective of "health care for all by the year 2000", and leads it to sometimes finance construction work, if this is required (e.g. in Tanzania, where it is building nursing schools, student hostels etc.). SIDA is generally less disposed to provide advanced training at post-graduate level, but at the other end of the scale, is sometimes prepared to include training in non-related technical skills at a very modest, practical level.

SIDA's interest in developing the potential of para-medical and auxiliary health personnel to deliver health and family planning services, particularly in rural areas, has led it to sponsor training programmes outside the context of particular country projects. It has accordingly organised training in London in association with the British Institute for Teaching Aids at Low Cost[14] and the Appropriate Health Resources and Technology Action Group[15].

So far, SIDA has not made any specific efforts to follow up on the results of the various training programmes that it is supporting. It considers that it is rather for the recipient country itself to do so.

---

14. Associated with the Great Ormond Street Children's Hospital in London.
15. Associate of the Intermediate Technology Group.

IV. PROGRAMMING ARRANGEMENTS

Country Programming

Although most Swedish aid is based on three-year rolling agreements, the Swedish Government today has the possibility of entering into long-term agreements to provide aid for a particular activity, with firm financial commitments covering the whole implementation period.

Under its country programming arrangements, an overall "frame" for each country is agreed between the government concerned and SIDA, and approved by the Swedish Parliament. On occasion Parliament will raise or reduce the amount proposed (in the case of Viet Nam, it reduced it). Parliament's annual appropriations for a country may not be exceeded, but any unutilised amounts may be carried over to the following year. Although the rolling agreements cover three years only, SIDA has never had to pull out of its commitment to a country. It provided family planning assistance to Sri Lanka and Ethiopia, for example, until well after the date originally fixed for withdrawal.

Although only the first year of the rolling agreement (the "budget year") is a firm obligation, the amounts discussed for the two following years are now considered as minimum figures, to be renegotiated before the expiry of the agreement period. This gives the country an effective degree of assurance covering three years. Further, although the country frame is not broken down into sectoral allocations, it may include a number of specific agreements on aid to particular projects or sectors with firm commitments for the whole life of the activity, subject only to the proviso that the yearly amounts expressed in the various agreements do not add up to more than the total amount available for any particular year (country frame plus possible appropriations carried over from the previous year).

In a number of countries, family planning programmes have benefited from continued Swedish support for periods of many years. Thus Sweden assisted the programme in Sri Lanka from 1958 to 1981. In India, its support began in 1968 and continued until 1980. Its aid in Pakistan would probably also have been provided on a long-term basis but for the situation which led Sweden, together with Pakistan's other donors, to withdraw their support from the Government's programme[16].

Sweden's aid cycle with its programme countries is a continuous process. Each year, discussions take place with SIDA on the country's proposals for allocating the amount to be made available during the budget year and the provisional amounts indicated for the two following years, as between on-going projects, planned projects and new proposals. This regular dialogue between SIDA and the government makes it possible for new activities to be considered at any time. If a new activity is proposed within the context of the country Agreement, it could be approved by the Review Group at the time of the annual programme discussions.

In Zambia, for example, Nutrition was identified as a sub-sector of Rural Health, which Sweden was already supporting under a sector "Umbrella Agreement", and which had been approved in principle by SIDA before any specific project was proposed. When the new activity proposed is within the financial limits already agreed upon, it can be approved at once. Further, if the total amount under the Agreement is not yet fully committed, a new project can start at once, upon receipt of SIDA's approval. SIDA might or might not decide that a new mission should be sent to examine the proposal — it would depend on the circumstances of the request and, in particular, how well it fitted into the existing Agreement. In India, for example, where SIDA has an Umbrella Agreement covering aid to the Health sector, the Government requested additional funds for a water project. This being a new element, the request had to be submitted to SIDA's Management Committee and to the Board (which meets once a month). Approval would thus take about three months.

In the past, the processing of major aid requests has taken about two years from the time of initial discussions between SIDA and the government concerned to the

---

16. In 1971.

signing of the agreement. For example, Sweden's biggest health project, the Indian Health Sector Support Project (Sw.Kr.125 million or US$22 million), was first discussed in December 1975, the official request was submitted in the Spring of 1977, and the Agreement was signed in April 1978, becoming effective almost immediately thereafter. Other large projects have similar timing.

SIDA is trying to speed up approval of new activities by progressively lightening its requirements with respect to background documentation to be supplied with project requests. If it is satisfied as to the government's commitment (for SIDA, the principal criterion), it is sometimes prepared to undertake itself the work of collecting the necessary background data, formulating the proposal, and even preparing the project request.

SIDA Field Offices

Much of the above work will fall to SIDA's field offices ("Development Co-operation Offices") which in recent years have been expanded in number and given substantially increased authority. They have discretion to reallocate funds between different activities, increase or decrease the financial resources allocated to each, and even prolong the agreement governing a particular activity, provided the essential content is not changed[17]. Any such decisions are simply recorded post facto in the quarterly report which the field offices are required to make to Stockholm on all activities.

The field offices play a particularly responsible role in respect of sector aid. They participate, together with the host government and officials from Stockholm, in the Annual Sector Review, after which they have complete responsibility for handling the funds. They are also expected to follow closely developments in the sector as a whole and the evolution of government policies, so as to be able to reassure Stockholm that its sector support will continue to be applied to purposes with which it is in sympathy.

SIDA says that these arrangements have brought "decision-making about Swedish aid and responsibility for programme implementation closer to the scene in the developing country, where the relevant information is available". For the recipient country, they have the advantage of flexibility and speed of implementation. They also reduce the number of missions sent out from the Agency Headquarters. It is only at the project appraisal stage that SIDA sends large-scale and lengthy missions (e.g. one month in India to examine the proposal for health sector support; five weeks in Kenya to examine follow-up to the health sector support). Otherwise, it will simply send a staff member from Stockholm and possibly an outside consultant to join the field office staff in the Annual Sector Review or the World Bank Review Group missions. Occasionally, SIDA will send a small specialist mission for a short visit to look at a specific activity within a sector (e.g. in Kenya in 1979 to look at maternal and child health and family planning activities).

V. IMPLEMENTATION PROCEDURES

Disbursement and Reporting

Ideally, Sweden would like its aid recipients to be able to consider Swedish aid funds as part of the government's own resources, their use subject only to the rules and regulations of the country concerned. In practice, this is not entirely realistic, since in Sweden, like anywhere else, Parliament and the public like to know something of the results of the aid they have given and, in the last resort, there are government auditors

---

17. In Kenya, for example, it agreed to pay the salaries of both some local and expatriate personnel engaged to work for the Ministry of Health on the project, although this had not been provided for in the initial Agreement.

who require a reasonable rendering of accounts. It is primarily for this reason, but perhaps also in part because it is felt that it is hardly fair to put all the burden of implementation onto the recipient, that Sweden has recently evolved the concept of "concerned participation", which enables it to play a more active role in the aid process.

Swedish aid funding is made available in the form of advances — either bi-annual or, more usually, quarterly — on the basis of requests supported by such reports on the progress of implementation as "the Government of Sweden shall reasonably request". The form of report is normally that which the government of the country requires for its own purposes — which SIDA feels is the only way the system is likely to work at all.

If payments are to be made half-yearly, the report does not necessarily have to cover a half-year period, but can cover three months only. Even with this latitude, reports tend to be two or three quarters behind. Sometimes, if no report has been received, but requests for disbursement are due, the SIDA field mission will undertake an inspection of the situation, in order to avoid slowing down the disbursement process.

Sometimes, if there is a particularly bad gap in the flow of reports, SIDA has withheld disbursements, simply as a means of obliging the recipient to put in a report as required by the Agreement. It did so in Tanzania, for example, with the co-operation of the Ministry concerned. (SIDA is prepared to accept reports in Swahili, if necessary). SIDA's interest in the reports it receives naturally varies according to circumstances. (If there has been a coup d'état, it will obviously wish to follow events much more closely). In normal circumstances, however, it takes a very relaxed view with regard to reporting — a practice which it recognises may sometimes encourage its recipient countries in bad management practices.

For the recipient country, the disbursement arrangements under Swedish aid are particularly convenient because they spare it the difficult and time-consuming business of collecting vouchers and receipts, and the requirements in terms of supporting statements could hardly be less onerous. In some cases, SIDA will also reimburse the government for project work undertaken before the Agreement was signed. Not surprisingly, developing countries are often heard to wish that their other aid donors would apply similar arrangements.

On receipt of a disbursement order from SIDA, the State Foreign Exchange Branch transfers the funds to the recipient government's Central Bank. From there, the flow of finance to individual projects varies from country to country. Generally, however, the Central Bank puts the portion allocated to local costs at the disposal of the Ministry concerned and retains the portion earmarked for foreign purchases.

Although the possibility of checking on disbursements and the actual use of funds is laid down in Swedish agreements, SIDA has generally chosen not to take advantage of it, for it considers monitoring to be the responsibility of the recipient government (the whole aid relationship being founded on the premise of mutual confidence). Recently, however, the Swedish Government has been feeling that it would like to have more substantive information as to the real progress of the activities it is assisting, not for purposes of financial monitoring, but as a means of satisfying interest on the part of Parliament and public opinion in the Swedish aid programme overall. In 1980, it accordingly modified its reporting requirements. It is now asking for reports to be submitted every six months instead of quarterly, in the hope that it will thus receive fewer reports but more real information. Even now, the information requirements are less than rigorous: the pro forma sheet asks only for the overall amount spent as against the amount received, the reasons for any discrepancy between the two, and any major difficulties encountered or anticipated. Further, if activity on the project has been slower than expected, and the project does not need more funds for a time, there is no obligation to submit a report at all.

In countries where Sweden is participating in the IDA's Joint Population Projects (e.g. Bangladesh), its reporting requirements are satisfied by receiving from the World Bank's Resident Mission in the country a copy of the Bank's regular progress reports. These terse statements of the amount of work achieved as against the project schedule are sent to all participating bilateral donors (through their respective field missions or embassies), who supplement them by occasional field visits and reports of their own. SIDA also participates in the annual Project Review Group led by the World Bank, but leaves inspection and supervision entirely to the latter.

SIDA similarly leaves auditing of project accounts to the country concerned. (It considers that it has no legal right to examine accounts administered by a recipient country government). By being so undemanding in the matter of financial reporting, SIDA recognises that it is sometimes difficult to know whether it is striking the proper balance between flexibility and accountability.

However, its guiding principle is that the requirements of implementing Swedish aid should not impose on the administration of a developing country demands that might be burdensome even for the government of a developed country. Sweden is therefore content to accept the minimum of reporting and of accounting control that the *country itself* needs to have for efficient project implementation.

Procurement

Goods provided by Sweden under project aid are not tied to supply from Sweden. (The contraceptive supplies provided under Swedish aid, for example, are products of West Germany, the United Kingdom, Japan, and other Western countries). The import support programmes are tied to some extent, but the Swedish Government considers its aid programme overall relatively free from pressures to design projects especially tailored to Swedish exports.

The Swedish Government recognises that tying of aid decreases flexibility. Sometimes, for example, a recipient country has asked it to reduce the amount of import support provided for under the Agreement in favour of increased sector support, but where import support is tied, such transfer is difficult. At the present time, there is a tendency to move away from import support in favour of forms of aid likely to reach the poorer groups of the population more directly. Thus in India, a gradual decrease in the relative share of aid for import support has made it possible to allocate more funds to projects of a social nature.

Sweden will normally do the procurement itself when the recipient country is particularly isolated, has inadequate experience, etc. (Some SIDA officials think that they may have gone too far in this direction). Where the country can do the procurement itself (e.g. India), SIDA is glad to let it do so and use its own arrangements. (SIDA does not ask to see the specifications). International competitive bidding is, however, normally required wherever this is practicable. In some countries, e.g. Viet Nam, where the Government had no experience of purchasing outside of the Socialist countries, Sweden sent advisors to show what was available on the world market and how to set about ordering it.

Evaluation and Follow-Up

During the past five years, SIDA has done relatively little in the way of ex post evaluation (which it terms "evaluation as a fine art"). The emphasis has rather been on evaluation of on-going activities as a means of providing guidance to both donor and recipient for future operations. Such evaluations have been carried out more often in respect of sector assistance than individual aid projects. SIDA is, however, formulating a long-term plan for ex post evaluation of all major projects and programmes.

In the field of health and family planning, SIDA has carried out annual reviews of its programme support in the following countries: Angola, Ethiopia, Kenya, Tanzania, Zambia and India. It has also evaluated project performance in Bangladesh, Sri Lanka, Guinea Bissau and Portugal.

In each case, nationals of the country concerned have participated in the evaluation work and sector reviews, thereby ensuring some degree of feed-back to the government department concerned.

VI. CO-ORDINATION WITH OTHER POPULATION ASSISTANCE DONORS

Joint Financing Arrangements

As a member of the Nordic Group, Sweden has had experience of participating in joint financing arrangements since the beginning of the 1960s, when the Scandinavian countries and Finland began to set up a number of Joint Nordic Projects in Africa. Inspired by political considerations, such arrangements have proved administratively very complicated[18], and SIDA staff accordingly do not encourage the creation of new ones. There have been no joint Nordic projects in the family planning field. Sweden has, however, participated in co-financing of population projects with the World Bank. The projects concerned (in India and Bangladesh) are major long-term population activities, and the nature of the participation arrangements differs in each case.

In India, Sweden in 1973 agreed to contribute a grant of $10.6 million to complement an IDA credit of $21.2 million. The Government of India was to pay all regular operating costs, and all project expenditures were to be split between IDA and SIDA by a two-to-one ratio. Management of the project was to be the responsibility of the IDA (the "executing agency"). SIDA later felt that this arrangement put it somewhat in the position of a "sleeping partner". Also, the fact that only two donor agencies were involved might constitute a potential invitation to the recipient country government to try to use one partner to influence the other.

In Bangladesh, where Sweden contributed Kr. 15 million (US$ 3.4 million) to the first IDA Population Project (1975), and Kr. 36 million (US$ 6.4 million) to the second (1980)[19], the co-financing arrangements, described earlier in this chapter, put Sweden in the position of being a rather closer partner of the recipient country government than of the other participating donors. Here, also, it is the World Bank that has the responsibility for managing the Project, an arrangement which SIDA has found to work well.

SIDA recognises the advantage of joint financing arrangements to the recipient country, in terms of easing the administrative burden of different donor requirements, and possibly, also, increasing the total volume of funding. It is, however, just a little wary of associating with the World Bank on ideological grounds, lest the Bank put a greater emphasis on family planning and fertility control than is consistent with Sweden's own approach. Its decision not do join with the Bank in the Second IDA Project in India was made for this reason.

Generally, SIDA prefers co-financing arrangements with the Bank which include several bilateral donors, in that the participating agencies together are in a better position vis-à-vis the Bank, the major partner. It feels, too, that the presence of several donors is an advantage to the recipient country, since their differing criteria and approaches make it more likely that there will be a positive response from at least one donor to an unexpected or novel request. There is, of course, a potential disadvantage — that the participating donor agencies might make common cause in opposition to the recipient country, but this situation does not seem to have arisen.

When SIDA participates in joint financing arrangements with the Bank, it makes a bilateral agreement with the country concerned, referring to the IDA project to which its contribution will be applied. Although it is content to leave to the Bank the active management of the activity, it continues to apply its own approach of "concerned participation", and follows the progress of implementation by means of its informal contacts with the Bank representative and those of the other participating agencies, as well, of course, as with officials of the recipient country. (In Bangladesh, SIDA feels that the Bank is showing the same flexibility and openness to innovation that it itself likes to apply).

---

18. Even after the initial practice of joint management was abandoned in favour of entrusting this responsibility to one of the participating agencies only.

19. Total cost $45 million and $110 million respectively.

Exchange of Information

SIDA's attitude to exchange of information with other donors is to a considerable extent a function of its small size as an aid agency. Some SIDA officials feel that as a practical matter SIDA cannot effectively absorb a significantly greater volume of information than it is already getting. This applies both to written material and to meetings with representatives of other agencies, notably at headquarters level. Exchanges of information at field level are felt to be much more useful, and on the whole, are getting better all the time. This is partly because the agencies involved are fewer in number and are directly interested, and partly because, with its well-staffed field missions, SIDA now has the resources to do a good job of collecting information. There does not seem to be any problem with respect to the willingness of other donor agencies to exchange relevant information — with the notable exception of the Socialist countries (in Viet Nam, the Russians built a maternity home barely 150 yards away from a children's hospital financed by Sweden). Nonetheless, as a general rule, SIDA does not feel that it would serve any useful purpose to have an exchange of information among donors regarding new requests still under consideration. It maintains that it is for the government of the country concerned to select potential donors and channel its requests in the way that it considers most appropriate.

However rich the flow of information from other donors, SIDA would still want to form its own first-hand opinion of any aid request that it receives. It would make use of appraisal or other reports of other agencies that might be available (e.g. UNFPA Basic Needs Assessments, World Bank reports, etc.) as background information, but would wish to send its own appraisal mission as a basis for any eventual aid decision. Once the aid decision is taken, SIDA likes to participate in joint donor missions when possible, in order both to economise on its own staff resources and to lessen the strain of consecutive donor missions for the recipient country.

SWEDEN
AID FOR POPULATION ACTIVITIES

i) Total volume of population assistance expenditures through 1981, $295 million

ii) Annual expenditures on population assistance, 1975-1981 (US $ million)

1975	26.7
1976	32.6
1977	35.7
1978	31.6
1979	34.4
1980	35.9
1981	30.4

iii) Expenditures on population assistance as a percentage of total (net) ODA, 1975-1981.

1975	4.7
1976	5.4
1977	4.6
1978	4.0
1979	3.5
1980	3.7
1981	3.3

iv) Division of total expenditures on population assistance as between bilateral, multi-bilateral, multilateral and non-governmental organizations' programmes, 1975-1981.

	Bilateral		Multi-bilateral		Multilateral		Non-governmental Organisations		Total
	$ thousand	%	$ thousand	%	$ thousand	%	$ thousand	%	$ thousand
1975	4 750	17.8	0	0	14 942	56.1	6 960	26.1	26 652
1976	6 911	21.2	563	1.7	17 066	52.4	8 058	24.7	32 598
1977	9 983	28.0	0	0	18 325	51.3	7 377	20.7	35 685
1978	4 272	13.5	0	0	19 707	62.4	7 622	24.1	31 601
1979	4 620	13.4	607	1.8	21 076	61.3	8 064	23.5	34 367
1980	4 987	13.9	598	1.7	21 566	60.1	8 733	24.3	35 884
1981	3 568	11.7	229	0.7	18 982	62.4	7 658	25.2	30 437

THE UNITED KINGDOM [1]

I. INTRODUCTION

The British Government has been including aid for population activities as part of its development assistance since the mid-1960s, when it first provided some modest support for family planning under its bilateral aid. A grant from the Ministry of Overseas Development (now the Overseas Development Administration)[2], first to the IPPF, and then to the newly-created UNFPA, followed shortly after. The Government has since remained firmly persuaded of the importance of the population "problem" and the need for population assistance, and has taken a number of measures designed to strengthen U.K. capability to help developing countries in this area. In volume terms, aid for population grew during the 1970s to reach approximately 1 per cent per year of the total U.K. aid programme. It has remained at about that level since.

Prompted essentially by concern about the effects of excessive population growth on economic and social development, U.K. aid for population, as that of most other donors, began as support for family planning. (The notion, popularised by the World Population Plan of Action, that family planning was a "basic human right" provided an additional rationale). Soon, however, the Government came to take a broader view of the problem of population growth in developing countries, and to extend the scope of its population assistance accordingly. After a full review of the U.K.'s population aid policy in 1973, the new approach was announced the following year (World Population Year), but *before* the World Population Conference at Bucharest gave to the concept of "beyond family planning" its subsequent international acclaim. In the succeeding years, the British policy of focussing special efforts on aid for the poorest countries and the most disadvantaged groups of the population[3], served to further underline the importance of population assistance in general and of the broad "development" approach in particular[4]. Activities designed to relieve poverty, and "population assistance" in fact came sometimes to coalesce.

The major part of U.K. aid for population (currently $17.7 million) is given through multilateral channels. The actual proportion has varied from two thirds to four fifths (1980), mainly through contributions to UNFPA, IPPF and to the WHO Special Programme of Research Development and Training in Human Reproduction to which the U.K. is the second biggest contributor. When the British Government wishes to increase its aid for population activities, the multilateral organisations with their constantly expanding programmes offer the readiest opportunities. Expansion of bilateral population assistance, on the other hand, has proved slower and more difficult. (In the 1970s, after the Government had announced its readiness to broaden the scope

---

1. Statistical table, see page 131.
2. The Ministry for Overseas Development (ODM) was set up as a separate Ministry in 1964. Since then it has twice (in 1970 and 1979) been dissolved and its functions transferred to the Foreign and Commonwealth Office where they have been carried out by the Overseas Development Administration (ODA) under the direction of a Minister for Overseas Development.
3. "The Changing Emphasis of British Aid Policies: More Help to the Poorest", White Paper HMSO, 1975.
4. Thus, a discussion paper on population, resources and pollution, published by the Government in 1976, concluded: "On a global scale, the most urgent and important problem is the limitation of population growth... Aid is needed first to relieve poverty and raise living standards, and to help *create a social framework which is conducive to the practice of fertility regulation.* It is also needed to provide staff, training, supplies and equipment for comprehensive population programmes". "Future World Trends", Cabinet Office, HMSO, 1976 (Author's italics).

of its bilateral aid for population, it was disappointed that there was not a more immediate response).

Bilateral aid for population has been found to suffer from a number of constraints that perhaps do not apply to aid in other sectors. Some are internal; viz, the small size of ODA's population staff, the difficulty of getting the rest of ODA (who tend to equate "population" with family planning), to consider population as a valid area of development assistance, etc. Population projects also tend to run into special difficulties at the receiving end, notably the less-than-total commitment of some developing country governments, plus a number of practical problems of management (weak health ministries, the competitiveness of their health and family planning "wings", the reluctance of doctors and nurses to work in rural areas, etc.). Similar problems have made it difficult to include population activities in U.K. aid in other development sectors, although in principle, it is ODA's policy to look for occasions of doing so[5]. Moreover, ODA's essentially responsive attitude towards its aid partners probably means that if the requesting government does not itself propose an integrated approach, ODA would not take the initiative and push it. Only in the area of informal education has a degree of fusion been achieved. (The U.K. has projects in Ecuador, India and Papua New Guinea, which use informal education as a vehicle for population communication and information).

Nonetheless, ODA has done its best to make its bilateral aid for population as accessible to developing countries as its aid regulations will permit. A large part of its population assistance is provided on grant terms — a concession not designed specifically for aid for population, but for the "poorest countries"[6] (whatever the aid sector) — but which nevertheless benefits population, since many of the beneficiaries of population assistance are among this group. Under normal U.K. aid arrangements, although technical co-operation is provided on grant terms, capital aid is provided in the form of loans, except for the poorest countries. In addition, all countries can receive a small amount of supplies and equipment on grant terms (up to £100,000) — a concession that applies only to population assistance.

Another concession for population projects concerns support for the work of private (British) voluntary organisations. ODA is prepared to fund 100 per cent of the cost of their population projects in developing countries, as against a 50:50 rule for projects in other sectors.

Although both bilateral and multilateral aid to population suffered from the cut-back in the British aid programme overall, which followed the economic recession of 1979, population assistance has continued to figure as one of the important concerns of British aid policy. (It may be noted in this connection that "population" has its own aid lobby in the U.K. in the form of an across-party Parliamentary Group on Population and Development). When in 1979, the Government declared that it would henceforth be constrained to give greater weight in the allocation of its aid to "political, industrial and commercial considerations", it added that "every effort would be made to maintain the level of assistance to population commensurate with other priorities of the programme[7].

Two years later, at the UN Conference on the Least Developed Countries, the Minister for Overseas Development announced the allocation of an additional £1.5 million for population programmes, by increased support for multilateral organisations. ("We recognize the important role which population programmes play in economic and social development. We consider that in the short term the most effective way of

---

5. Following the Colombo Conference of Parliamentarians, the Minister for Overseas Development (March 1980) directed that a "population component be encouraged wherever possible in new development projects financed by ODA".

6. Defined as countries with GNP per capita of $320 p.a. or less in 1978, plus all other countries defined as "least developed" by the UN.

7. Report of Population Activities, Overseas Development Paper No. 21, June 1980. (Reference to Ministerial Statement of aid policy made to the House of Commons, February 1980).

assisting population programmes is to increase our contributions to international agencies active in this field"). As things have turned out, however, expenditures on U.K. bilateral aid for population have increased also, thanks to an exceptional (and exceptionally large) population project in India. This is, however, a special case, being financed out of part of the local currency funds made available under the Retrospective Terms Adjustment[8]. There have not so far been any other major new bilateral population projects, though ODA has been examining various possibilities (notably Pakistan).

II. APPROACH AND PRIORITIES

Although the greater part of British population assistance has naturally been concerned primarily with family planning and mother and child health care, ODA is prepared to support any activity that it feels "can reasonably be regarded as population assistance" (it takes as guidance the five broad programme categories of the UNFPA)[9]. It will thus consider any sound population request that conforms to the overall policy of the government concerned, that is legal and that does not imply coercion.

The broadening of its approach to population programmes is well illustrated by the U.K.'s Population Projects in India. The first Project, made in 1969 (£3 million over 4 years), was concerned solely with providing the means of limiting fertility, i.e. it covered the construction and equipping of facilities at sub-district hospitals and primary health centres for voluntary female sterilisation and medical termination of pregnancy. The second Project (finalised in 1979), although limited to one State only (Orissa), is very much broader in scope. Amounting to the equivalent of £10.8 million over 5 years[10], and consisting, as explained above, entirely of local currency, it includes technical assistance as well as construction and equipment, and covers not only family planning, but a wide range of health and social development activities, such as water supply, project management and evaluation, media improvement (for health education), pilot schemes (in female literacy, improved nutrition, for example) and research into various practical community problems such as latrines, weaning foods, etc.

Among the possible range of activities that might be considered as constituting "population assistance", the British Government has a particular interest in demographic data collection and demographic research and training, areas in which it feels that U.K. institutions and expertise give it a comparative advantage. ODA offers courses in demography and population studies in various U.K. universities and specialist bodies[11]. It also contributes to a number of UN regional institutions engaged in population research, viz, the Cairo Demographic Centre, the Centro Latino Americano de Demografia (CELADE) and the Economic and Social Commission for Asia and the Pacific (ESCAP). The U.K. has also shown a special interest in the work of the World Fertility Survey (WFS). It made a contribution to the WFS Conference held in London in 1980, and at the request of the governments concerned, financed under its bilateral assistance, half of the governments' contribution to the work of the Survey in Kenya, the Sudan and the

---

8. Whereby donors agreed to waive the outstanding debts of very poor countries. The British Government agreed to use the amount due to it from India to cover the local costs of new development projects: one-third of the amount in any one year is to be applied to poverty-related projects. (The total amount is considerable. India had at one time received as much as £100 million p.a. in capital aid from Britain, representing about one-seventh of the total British aid programme).
9. Basic data collection; population dynamics; population policy; population education and information, and "family planning".
10. The Orissa Project is 2 1/2 times the size of the U.K.'s second largest population project (Egypt).
11. For example, the London School of Hygiene and Tropical Medicine; the David Owen Centre at University College, Cardiff, and the London School of Economics.

Yemen Arab Republic. In 1982, it provided core assistance to the WFS to the tune of £250,000.

ODA applies very few "a priori" negative criteria to its population assistance. It does not provide sector aid for population or health activities, but neither does it do so in other sectors. It does not usually supply any large amount of contraceptives, but has occasionally included some under its programme aid to a country (e.g. Thailand). It can also supply Depo Provera, if a country asks for it and is informed of the conditions pertaining to its use in the U.K. (It provided some to Indonesia, who could not get it under its programme with US AID). ODA is also prepared, if a government so requests, to support a family planning programme which includes abortion, provided it is not the sole method of fertility limitation offered.

Unlike some other bilateral donors in the field of population, ODA has no particular inhibitions about getting involved in the formulation of population policies and programmes. U.K. experts ("technical co-operation officers"), at the request of the governments concerned, have, inter alia, drawn up a pilot family welfare project for the Sudan, made a survey of family planning needs and recommended population strategies for Sri Lanka, etc.[12]. ODA's professional population staff, in the course of their overseas visits, also offer advice to governments.

Overall, ODA has become increasingly flexible as to what it is prepared to include under its population assistance. For example, whereas at one time it would not provide housing even for British experts, its projects today not infrequently include construction of residential accommodation for local staff in rural areas, together with that of the health facilities in which they are to serve. (Under the Indian Project, for example, ODA is paying for houses to be built for Assistant Nurse Midwives and other health workers[13].

Geographical Criteria and Size

The major part of British aid (approximately 80 per cent) is directed to Commonwealth countries and to the poorest countries, many of which are also members of the Commonwealth. In the case of population assistance, although the U.K. is prepared to consider requests from any country with which it has an aid agreement, the most important projects tend to be in Commonwealth countries. The one major population project outside of the Commonwealth is in Egypt (£4.8 million, where the U.K. has a parallel financing arrangement with the World Bank for the latter's second Mother and Child Health and Family Planning Project. In Kenya and Bangladesh, the U.K. is also participating in population projects jointly financed with the World Bank, but as one of a group of several bilateral donors.

Taken as a whole, the U.K.'s bilateral population assistance may be seen as consisting of a small number of major and continuing projects and a much larger number of small and generally short-term ones. The small and frequently ad hoc population activities that the ODA assists in a variety of countries are of interest, precisely because they *are* small. As a matter of policy, ODA not only considers that nothing is *too* small, but sees a particular usefulness in providing finance to small countries and/or for small activities that may find it difficult to attract the interest of other, and larger, population donors.

These small requests derive in part from the somewhat personalised style of ODA's population operations. The specialist advisors on ODA's staff (in population as in a number of other development sectors), by their visits to developing countries, have close and continuing personal contacts in governmental and professional circles. They can thus informally discuss and sometimes stimulate requests for U.K. aid. In the population field, these contacts have in many cases resulted in requests for U.K.

---

12. The latter survey included an enquiry into the potential for voluntary organisation of community services for health and family planning.

13. Being Untouchables, they are not permitted to live in other people's homes.

support for a single modest activity (sometimes technical co-operation only — the services of a consultant or a training programme), which serves as preparation for a much more important project activity later. Sometimes assistance for the subsequent project is requested from some other, bigger donor agency (most often UNFPA). Thus the U.K. provided the services of a geographical adviser to help Tanzania prepare the 1978 census: the census itself was later funded by UNFPA. In other cases, ODA assists the follow-up activity also, as in Ecuador, where, having sent a U.K. adviser and equipment to prepare a pilot population communication and education project, it went on to support the resultant project also. One of the reasons for ODA's interest in the pilot projects put forward by voluntary bodies in the population field is that it sees in them possible precursors of eventual larger-scale new project approaches. (A typical example is a Women's Project undertaken by Oxfam in Bombay). ODA considers that these sometimes very modest "one-off" population activities can often make an effective contribution out of all proportion to the initial financial outlay involved.

III. CONTRIBUTION TO SELF-RELIANCE

On the technical side, ODA often feels that it can make a direct contribution to building up developing countries' capability to deal with their respective population problems, by training staff, promoting local manufacture of contraceptives, and as noted above, by supporting pilot activities. In the matter of financial and administrative capability, it recognises that U.K. aid usually represents only a small part of a country's population programme, and that its contribution to building up eventual self-reliance has therefore to be seen in that context.

Financial Capability

Since the U.K. traditionally has preferred capital aid projects (which offer important "hardware" components to be supplied by British manufacturers), it has tended to be wary of taking on local cost expenditures, which it considers, in principle, should be the government's responsibility. However, it appreciates that developing country governments cannot be expected to cover all the local expenditures involved, particularly in the case of social development projects, with their usually high local cost components. It has therefore come to take a more flexible approach, based on "established need". Population projects have accordingly benefited from this flexibility. Thus when some years back, it was found that the local cost element of the Egyptian Population Project to be financed by the U.K. amounted to 43 per cent, special Treasury agreement had to be obtained. Subsequently, the arrangement has been to fix a proportion of local to foreign exchange costs for each country, according to its economic situation, to be applied across-the-board in all aid sectors. In special circumstances, however, ODA may be prepared to go beyond this. In Kenya, for example, the agreed proportion is 50:50, but the U.K. is supporting one development project that is almost entirely local cost. Certain technical co-operation activities which ODA is financing in the population field similarly consist almost entirely of local costs.

In respect of recurrent costs, the U.K. takes a much tougher line, although it has accepted the DAC Guidelines on Local and Recurrent Cost Financing. While it does not entirely rule them out in the case of population and other social development activities, its view is that recurrent costs should properly be the responsibility of the government concerned, and that it would be unwise to take on what might prove to be an open-ended commitment. Thus it is usually opposed to covering local salaries[14], and on

---

14. In the Orissa Project (entirely local cost), the U.K. is paying all local salaries as well as other recurrent expenditures for 5 years: the Agreement, however, provides for the Government to assume this responsibility on a phased basis.

principle, to paying salary supplements or incentive payments to local staff[15]. (When asked to do so for the field-workers conducting the World Fertility Survey in the Sudan and Yemen, ODA refused).

Administrative and Managerial Capability

Although ODA's project appraisal exercises include the question of the administrative and managerial capability of the recipient institutions concerned, this aspect of a project has not normally been treated with the rigour that it is now felt to require. One factor has been a certain reluctance on the part of some ODA officials to convey to a developing country their personal assessment of its administrative and managerial capability — particularly in the case of Commonwealth countries, sometimes prone to suspect lingering colonial attitudes. Where weaknesses have been identified, therefore, the most usual way of dealing with them has been by some form of technical co-operation, i.e. either by sending a British expert and/or by training of local manpower, which has always represented an important element of U.K. aid. (Whereas technical co-operation personnel supplied under U.K. aid have to be British nationals, training programmes can be arranged in other developing countries, as well as in the U.K. and the host country itself)[16].

In recent years, the slow progress of some of its major population projects has made it clear to ODA that a more radical approach is needed to the problem of strengthening the administrative institutions and management capability of the recipient country. The new approach is seen clearly in the arrangements made for the management of the Orissa Project, where the broad and varied range of activities imply major problems of co-ordination (and where the scale of the U.K. contribution gave the ODA a locus for proposing radical measures to deal with them). The Project accordingly includes a management survey to be made by the Indian Institute of Management in Calcutta, advice on management communications systems from the finance officers of the State of Karnataka, the creation of a special "Project Cell", and the appointment of a Project Liaison Officer to provide unified project management covering all the different ministries involved (as well as the Ministry of Health) at the district, state and central government levels.

Maintenance

Another way in which the U.K. may be considered as trying to help developing countries along the path of eventual self-sufficiency is by building up their skills in maintenance. An interesting start has been made in Egypt, where ODA is assisting the Ministry of Health with training in the maintenance of vehicles, and has also helped set up a training school for the repair and maintenance of medical equipment.

IV. PROGRAMMING ARRANGEMENTS

Although Parliament votes the U.K. aid budget annually, the Governement is able to make umbrella agreements with individual countries on a multi-year basis. These are usually for three years but may be for up to five, and the sectors to be assisted may or may not be fully identified at the time the agreement is signed. Within the frame of the

---

15. On the other hand, the British Government is still paying salary supplements to large numbers of U.K. nationals serving in government posts in developing countries, mainly in anglophone Africa (the Overseas Service Aid Scheme — over 400 in Kenya alone).

16. Training programmes are sometimes running into some unexpected problems these days. In Bangladesh, for example, nursing tutors, badly needed for the population programme, having completed their training, promptly left for Saudi Arabia, lured by the high salaries offered. The proposal by ODA to replace them by technical co-operation personnel was declined by the Bangladesh Government.

umbrella agreements, individual agreements are then worked out for specific projects, which provide for disbursement over a given period of time. Since, however, project implementation not uncommonly proves slower than initially planned, the project agreements may be successively extended several times.

Although aid allocations cannot normally be carried over from one year to the next, in practice this does not necessarily constitute a serious constraint. ODA frequently takes on new activities in the course of the financial year, to use up the slack caused by under-spending on already agreed projects. (The new activities have, of course, to fit the priority sectors covered by the country agreement. Also, the possibility of extending the project period means that the funds allocated to a particular project are not "lost"). In the First Bangladesh Population Project, where implementation proved particularly slow, the disbursement period of the U.K. - financed components had to be extended several times[17].

The time taken for approval of new requests naturally varies with the importance of the project, the administrative capability of the requesting government, and also the availability of ODA staff to undertake appraisal missions. ODA applies to its capital aid projects the sophisticated appraisal methodologies set out in its Guide to Project Appraisal in Developing Countries, but has to take a less formalistic approach to projects in the field of population, as in other social development sectors, where it is not possible to establish future rates of return etc. in financial and economic terms. Nonetheless, the appraisal of ODA's major population projects has required numerous missions (the Orissa Project involved three ODA missions, plus a seminar to get expert views from outside), and in countries where ODA is engaged in joint financing with the World Bank, it has always sent its own appraisal missions before making the project decision[18].

There is a standard U.K. format for the preparation of capital aid projects and guidelines for technical co-operation projects. Requests for population assistance are expected to follow these as for any other sector. However, in the case of smaller projects, the process of approval is likely to be considerably shortened, thanks to ODA's personalised operating style, since many of them will have already been discussed informally with the Population Advisor or other visiting ODA official. (Indeed, there have been cases where a consultant for a technical co-operation assignment has been lined up before the formal request for his services was even received).

Once a project has been approved and the agreement signed, if the request had passed through ODA's Project and Evaluation Committee, requests for any major changes or cost over-runs have similarly to be submitted to the Committee for approval. There is, however, no difficulty about changing from capital aid to technical co-operation (within an agreed country total). Indeed, this is encouraged, as giving ODA flexibility in meeting new requests.

Requests for modification of projects in the course of implementation have to be referred to London, although ODA has been progressively introducing a greater measure of decentralisation into its aid administration[19]. In countries where the U.K. has a

---

17. The U.K. High Commission became very concerned about the large proportion of the U.K. allocation that was still unspent after several years, at a time when aid requests elsewhere were having to be turned down for lack of funds. The money eventually, with the agreement of the Government of Bangladesh and the World Bank, was used for the expansion of other facilities under the Project.

18. Major projects (over £1.5 million, £2 million for India) have to be submitted to ODA's Projects Committee for approval. The documentation will normally be communicated to the government concerned, which will in many cases have participated in its preparation.

19. ODA has 5 Development Divisions: Caribbean; Southern Africa; East Africa; South-East Asia, and now a Pacific Division, based on Fiji. Initially largely advisory, the Development Divisions have power to appraise and approve projects (in co-operation with the British Embassy or High Commission concerned) up to a total of, now, £1 million. Their primary concern is with capital projects. They do not normally advise on population projects, because they do not include Health and Population Advisers on their staff.

substantial aid programme, ODA has seconded aid staff to work with the diplomatic mission. However, although they follow the progress of U.K.-financed projects in the country, the primary role of the mission staff is to act as informed liaison with London. Even quite minor matters, therefore, have to be referred to London for decision. This is sometimes a cause of irritation to developing country officials, and possibly one of the reasons why they sometimes rate the U.K. as one of the more "difficult" of donor agencies.

V. IMPLEMENTATION ARRANGEMENTS

Disbursement Arrangements

The basic rules applying to the administration of U.K. aid are set forth in a Manual of Procedures and Practices. Certain negotiable arrangements, however, are covered in an exchange of letters which accompanies the "umbrella" aid agreement. Disbursement procedures are among this latter category, but in practice do not vary greatly from country to country. They provide for foreign exchange costs (covering U.K. goods and services) to be paid by London direct to the supplier: local currency costs are normally financed on a reimbursement basis. In the case of very poor countries, ODA may, exceptionally, be prepared to make advance payments (it has done so for Nepal), but this is very unusual. Reimbursement could in principle cover project expenditures made by the government prior to the signing of the agreement — but this too would be very unusual.

Reimbursement is normally made quarterly[20] against presentation of certified expenditure statements. Grouped by sector and by district, these have to be submitted to the British Embassy or High Commission for forwarding to London. An annual audited statement, listing reimbursement of local currency costs, project by project, is required at the end of the recipient's financial year.

ODA does not require the quarterly expenditure statements to be accompanied by the actual payment vouchers. Nonetheless, developing country governments frequently find it difficult to collect up the evidence of disbursement that they need to issue the certified statements, particularly when a large number of separate project activities are involved in many different parts of the country. In the case of the IDA Project in Bangladesh, for example, ODA was able to make the first reimbursement, since when the Government was unable to submit any further accounts for several years, and in consequence no further disbursements could be made[21]. Meanwhile, work on the project was continuing, with Government money, as normal under reimbursement procedures. (This not only gave rise to a "pipeline" problem, as regards aid disbursements, but since prices had been rising substantially throughout the period of construction, the delay in presenting the bills meant that the donors financing the project did not know how much the work had actually cost). A similar situation arose in Kenya, where the construction work had been largely completed, but no claims for reimbursement had been submitted. ODA eventually asked the Government to submit bills *monthly,* which albeit an administrative headache for the Kenyan officials concerned, would avoid a pile-up of accumulated bills.

---

20. ODA's disbursement arrangements are easier in respect of institutional recipients, to which it provides "core support". For example, the International Institute for Research into the Control of Diarrhoeal Diseases receives a single annual advance from the U.K. which is released on a "proof of need" basis.

21. Although the World Bank has management responsibility for the Project, each participating donor agency applies its own aid procedures to the project components that it is financing.

Procurement

Since one of the intentions of the British aid programme is to encourage British industry, much of U.K. assistance is tied to supply of British goods and services, freighted in British carriers[22]. However, where a project includes substantial local currency expenditures, as is the case with population projects, goods and services (including transport) produced by the recipient country itself may also be eligible.

To qualify for aid-financing, the supplier firm must be not only resident in the country, but must be majority-owned and managed by either nationals or British. This rule applies also to local firms supplying materials and equipment for construction work financed out of U.K. aid. Before a local building contractor places an order for the supplies and equipment he needs for a job, therefore, the eligibility of the potential supplier has also to be vetted (normally by the Development Division or post) to ensure that he too conforms to the U.K.'s procurement criteria[23].

The recipient country government can apply its own procedures for contracting and local procurement. If competitive bidding is involved, local firms can bid on an equal footing with off-shore producers, but the U.K. does not offer any preference for local production[24]. Before calling for bids, the government has to get London's approval of the specifications, and the contract with the successful bidder must also be sent to London for approval.

In practice, the technical qualification requirements often work against small local firms in favour of (larger) British ones. This is the case not only in respect of equipment but also for construction contracts. In Kenya, for example, where there are a number of important British construction firms, some of the contracts for building rural health facilities were awarded to them because the generally smaller Kenyan firms did not have the resources to undertake construction jobs in distant parts of the country. While this has sometimes caused some resentment in Kenyan circles[25], it is unfortunately a common aid experience to find construction of health facilities in rural areas held up sometimes for several years, because the small local firms who had been awarded the contracts had neither the physical nor financial resources to complete the job.

Where possible, ODA likes to apply British building standards to the facilities that it is financing. In the case of Commonwealth countries, many of which still follow British practice, this may not pose any problem. (In Kenya, for example, the U.K. was able to accept the designs for new rural health centres prepared by the Government's (Scandinavian) consultant, because he had based them on old British designs). In some cases, however, the U.K. is considered difficult in the matter of design standards. (In one instance, it held up approval for three years because it considered the designs proposed were too lavish – although other donors had approved them). However, it should be mentioned that in Kenya, the U.K. is also financing the up-grading of rural health centres by self-help labour from the local communities – where, clearly, traditional building standards cannot be applied.

For procurement of goods of U.K. origin, ODA uses the services of the Crown

---

22. ODA maintains that its aid is not wholly tied, in that British manufacturers may include components of foreign origin. (Some donors have been known to reject purchases which have important foreign-made components). Technically, there is a procedure for waiver of the U.K.'s tying rules – they would have to be approved by the Department of Trade and Industry – but it would be exceptional.

23. In one country, where the U.K. was financing the construction of rural health centres, it was discovered that a nationally-owned firm which had been approved as eligible to provide the local contractor with some building supplies, had a non-national managing director. Although the supply contract had already been made, ODA made the construction firm cancel the order.

24. The World Bank, for example, does.

25. The Kenyans claim that the British firms tend to use imported (British) equipment also – which is both more expensive and a cause of delay.

Agents[26]. They either, themselves, find the most convenient source of supply, or send price quotations and delivery dates for the government to make its own choice. Commonwealth countries are in any case accustomed to using the Crown Agents, and a number of other countries also find them a convenient procurement channel — for their own imports as well as for U.K.-financed goods. Sometimes developing country officials complain that purchase through the Crown Agents is expensive (their commission may add up to 15 per cent of the cost — depending on the size of the purchase), or that delivery is slow (even sometimes for off-the-shelf items). Since, however, similar complaints are sometimes heard about UNICEF procurement also, some of the problems may be inherent in overseas procurement done through any intermediary agency.

Reporting and Auditing

ODA has itself recognised that its past arrangements for project monitoring have generally been somewhat "unstructured". The requirements in the matter of written reports are set out at the time the agreement is signed. They usually provide for progress reports to be submitted quarterly, and there is no set format for presentation. In some countries, the ministry of health officials concerned have found the U.K. to be admirably pragmatic in respect of reporting ("The U.K. does not bother about written reports"); in others, quite the contrary (e.g. in Kenya, where ODA eventually concluded that the only way to get any information as to what was happening was to require a report every month). In common with other donors, ODA finds that the written reports that it gets from the country are not usually adequate to provide any really substantive information on the progress of the activities that it is financing.

Reports from the recipient are however supplemented, at least in the case of the more important population projects, by on-the-spot monitoring undertaken, variously, by ODA officials or professional advisers from London, the aid staff on the High Commission or Embassy or, possibly, technical co-operation consultants[27]. There is no set timing for these visits, but ODA's Population Advisers have usually gone on at least one lengthy circuit each year to discuss possible new projects and review the progress of on-going ones.

Where ODA is jointly financing a population project with the World Bank (as in Bangladesh), it leaves the management responsibility more or less to the Bank. That is to say, like the other participating donors, it forgoes its own customary reporting requirements, and settles for copies of the Bank's (somewhat laconic) internal six-monthly supervision reports. These are supplemented by occasional visits to the site of the U.K.-financed components by the aid staff on the High Commission. The latter also participated in the joint donor review organised by the Bank mid-way through the project. In Egypt, on the other hand, where the U.K. is participating with the Bank under parallel financing arrangements, ODA's normal aid procedures are applied — for reporting as for other implementation arrangements.

For population projects undertaken by voluntary agencies, ODA requires six-monthly progress reports. In addition, audited accounts are required annually and on project completion.

In the case of its major population activity, the Orissa Project, the arrangements made for monitoring are unusually elaborate, and are intended to provide both ODA and the Indian Authorities with regular substantive information as to the way this (essentially pilot) undertaking is working out. These accordingly provide for the preparation of a base-line study (prior to the start of implementation), the participation of

---

26. They also undertake a number of other day-to-day administrative functions on behalf of ODA, such as arrangements for payment, insurance, shipping, etc. For example, it is the Crown Agents who open an account on behalf of the recipient government in which funds are held pending disbursement.

27. Monitoring the progress of ODA projects is one of the duties of the Regional Development Divisions, but as previously mentioned, they do not normally cover population projects.

the London School of Hygiene and Tropical Medicine in the monitoring of the project data, and the holding of a Tripartite Review (Government of India, State Government of Orissa and ODA) after two years.

Recently (1980), ODA has introduced new and more systematic arrangements for the monitoring of its projects, following the issue of the DAC Guidelines for Improving Aid Implementation. Recipient governments are required to submit progress reports, usually quarterly (although the convenience of the government is also taken into account). Not only the information to be provided, but also the officer who shall be responsible for providing it, are specified in advance in a monitoring plan (which includes also a time-table of monitoring visits)[28]. However, if British personnel are working on the project, it is usually they who are given the reporting responsibility.

For auditing purposes, recipients are required to submit annual statements showing actual expenditures on reimbursable costs incurred in the host country, countersigned by the appropriate audit authority of the country. These have to be sent in no later than twelve months after the end of each financial year.

VI. CO-ORDINATION WITH OTHER DONORS

ODA staff are generally of the opinion that present arrangements for exchange of information between donors in the population field provide a satisfactory basis for both decision-making and operations. A great deal is done through what they call "the old boy net" (a corollary of ODA's personalised style). Ample opportunities for discussing population programmes, actual and potential, as well as broader policy issues are provided through meetings with the staff of other agencies when they pass through London on their way to visit their respective population projects, as well as through informal contacts afforded by international population meetings. (ODA is, of course, a participant at the meetings of the World Bank's Consultative Groups, and has been known to be very out-spoken on some occasions, when aid to a country's population programme has been a special item on the agenda).

These various informal arrangements can cover discussion of a project at all stages, including sometimes project *proposals* that are still under consideration. Occasionally, a project may even be discussed at the design stage — as when ODA has sought the advice of WHO on the technical aspects of a project. Indeed, ODA staff maintain that there is probably more exchange of information between donors in the field of population than in other aid sectors, where shortage of good projects has sometimes led to a certain spirit of competitiveness.

Exchange of information as between donors at the country level is, of course, largely determined by the attitude of the recipient government concerned. In India, where the Government is quite happy about the arrangement, the donors providing population assistance exchange their respective reports, including sometimes internal mission reports and new project proposals.

ODA would not, however, make any project decisions solely on the basis of appraisal reports prepared by another donor. (The Treasury would be unlikely to agree to the tax-payers' money being spent on an activity for which the British Government had not itself identified the project and made its own independent appraisal). For example, when donors decided that the time was ripe to consider resuming population assistance to Pakistan, ODA followed up the Population Needs Assessment Mission of the UNFPA by sending its own consultant to advise on suitable areas for possible U.K. support.

---

28. The frequency of visits will depend on the size and complexity of the project, the effectiveness of the local institutions and the prospects of getting regular progress reports. The time-table may be modified as the project proceeds.

So far no regular arrangements exist for doubling up appraisal missions with other population assistance donors, although ODA recognises that this would be desirable in principle. Joint missions have occasionally been organised under the aegis of the World Bank[29] (in Kenya, Bangladesh) but very largely on an ad hoc basis.

ODA, despite varying experiences to date as regards the effectiveness of implementation, is generally in favour of joint financing of population projects. It recognises that joint financing does not necessarily entail any significant diminution of the administrative burden on its own staff (particularly if ODA is to do its own project appraisal and apply its own aid procedures), but considers that the arrangement is nonetheless to be welcomed as providing an opportunity for substantive co-operation between donors at the actual operating level.

---

29. The Bank itself admits that the organisation of a multi-donor mission is an onerous business.

UNITED KINGDOM
AID FOR POPULATION ACTIVITIES

i) Total volume of population assistance through 1981 (US $ million)
   Commitments   135 401
   Expenditures   102 422

ii) Annual expenditures on population assistance, 1975-1981 (US $ thousand)

1975	6 756
1976	7 270
1977	10 866
1978	14 104
1979	19 490
1980	17 653
1981	13 127

iii) Expenditures on population assistance as a percentage of total (net) ODA, 1975-1981

1975	0.75
1976	0.82
1977	0.98
1978	0.96
1979	0.90
1980	0.95
1981	0.60

iv) Division of total expenditures on population assistance as between bilateral, multilateral, and non-governmental organizations' programmes

(US$ thousand)

	Bilateral			Multilateral			Non-governmental Organisations			Total	
	Commitments	Expenditures	%	Commitments	Expenditures	%	Commitments	Expenditures	%	Commitments	Expenditures
1975	3 126	91	1.3	5 766	3 999	59.2	3 333	2 666	39.5	12 225	6 756
1976	111	303	4.2	5 636	3 929	54.0	3 056	3 038	41.8	8 803	7 270
1977	2 054	1 085	10.0	8 038	6 217	57.2	3 564	3 564	32.8	13 656	10 866
1978	1 454	4 265	30.3	10 749	6 478	45.9	4 430	3 361	23.8	16 633	14 104
1979	1 256	2 817	14.5	7 426	11 617	59.6	5 092	5 056	25.9	13 774	19 490
1980	24 852	3 583	20.3	6 048	8 141	46.1	5 434	5 929	33.6	36 334	17 653
1981	422	2 082	15.9	6 794	5 735	43.7	5 145	5 310	40.4	12 361	13 127

US AID[1]

I. INTRODUCTION

The United States Government, through the U.S. Agency for International Development (US AID), the agency under the State Department responsible for foreign aid[2], is the source of more than half of the international funding made available each year for population assistance. AID is by far the biggest bilateral source of population assistance to developing countries. Moreover, a large number of the institutional donors, both international and U.S.-based, who provide aid for population activities are themselves generously funded by the AID. By 1982, the U.S. Government had devoted a cumulative total of over $2 billion to population assistance.

Since the mid-1960s, when the U.S. Government first decided that it was essential for developing countries to curb their high rates of population growth, "population" has been one of the important priorities of the U.S. aid programme. Beginning as part of the broader attack of the War on Hunger, the object of U.S. population assistance has always been, squarely, the limitation of fertility, and the principal means, the provision of voluntary family planning services. U.S. "population assistance" also includes various other activities considered helpful for this purpose — such as persuading governments of the need to check population growth, and couples of the desirability of limiting their family size, improving the quality of family planning services and methods, etc. Specifically, AID population funds have been applied to six categories of activity: demographic data collection and analysis; population policy development; biomedical and social science research; family planning service delivery systems; communications (information, education, and motivation); and manpower and institutional development. The heart of U.S. population assistance, however, remains family planning.

Thanks to growing interest in population assistance on the part of the U.S. Congress, by the late 1960s, "population" was receiving a special allocation in the U.S. foreign aid budget. Subsequently, the aid budget has been structured into five main functional categories[3], and "population" has been grouped, sometimes with "health"[4], and sometimes with "human resources", but either way with a sizeable sub-total plainly ear-marked for population activities. For the past several years, population has accounted for some 2-3 per cent of total ODA[5], a proportion that has remained remarkably constant despite changing aid policies and political attitudes in America.

Some 60 per cent of AID's population assistance is given in the form of contributions to multilateral agencies and private bodies (U.S. and international) active in population work. It provides one-quarter of the total budget of UNFPA, more than one-quarter of that of IPPF, and is the major source of funding of the Pathfinder Fund,

---

1. Statistical table, see page 154.
2. US AID is a semi-autonomous part of the State Department, but reporting to the White House; US AID's Administrator is the President's chief advisor on foreign assistance.
3. Agriculture, food and nutrition; population planning; health; education and human resources; selected development activities.
4. There are certain accounting rules for the proportion of "health" activities that can be included in U.S. aid projects financed out of "population" funds. However, the Government has generally been flexible about this, according to the circumstances and the relative demand for "population" or "health" funds. In some African countries, where AID feels it can only hope to win an interest in family planning by providing health care, it is prepared to consider health services as a "population" activity.
5. Total ODA includes U.S. contributions to the U.N., the World Bank, the regional development banks, etc., as well as the programmes funded by US AID.

the Population Council and numerous other specialist institutions. AID is particularly active in support of private voluntary organisations in the family planning field: indeed close to one-third of the total population account is devoted to this purpose.

The 40 per cent or so of AID's population budget which is applied to bilateral programmes is the highest percentage of bilateral population assistance among DAC donors. In fact, however, less than half of this amount is applied to direct bilateral programmes. The rest goes to what AID calls "global" population activities, such as the World Fertility Survey and the Contraceptive Prevalence Survey, or "regional" activities (for example, films about teenage pregnancy, intended primarily for the Caribbean region).

After a somewhat hesitant beginning in what was a totally new field, AID's population programme grew in both resources and confidence. By the early 1970s, expenditures were over $100 million a year. Today, although population is still recognised as an essential part of U.S. development assistance, AID officials do not feel it likely that U.S. assistance to population will increase substantially — at least for the present. One reason is that the U.S. Congress tends to look warily at the programmes of the international agencies, which are less responsive to its views than AID's bilateral programmes. At the same time, experience has shown that the possibilities for bilateral population assistance are limited by a variety of constraints, not all of which were fully appreciated at the outset — most notably, the particular sensitivity of the population issue, which not only prevents some governments from accepting the necessity for a population policy, but even if they nominally have a policy, makes for less than full commitment. Similarly, the "target" populations often fail to perceive of family planning (essentially a "preventive" programme) as one of their priority needs. Population programmes have been found, also, to suffer a number of practical constraints. One is the health orientation given to family planning in many countries, which associates it with often weak ministries of government and inadequate service infrastructure, and may at the same time obscure the need to search for alternative approaches. Another problem is that, involving often a person-to-person service, population programmes tend often to be particularly difficult to implement — both for the recipient country and for AID itself.

To assist it in the implementation of its population programmes, AID makes extensive use of (private) intermediary institutions. A distinguishing feature of U.S. assistance in all sectors of activity, this practice is particularly useful in the area of population, in that it offers an alternative in cases where it might be difficult or less effective for AID to act directly[6]. In this way, AID has been able to undertake some small population activities in countries (notably in Latin America) where the government does not perceive there is a population problem, but the private sector does. Even in the absence, therefore, of a government-to-government programme covering population assistance, AID has been able to encourage private sector interest in the hope that it will constitute the groundwork for eventual official acceptance of the need of a population programme (for example, by sending opinion leaders on "consciousness-raising" study visits to other developing countries)[7]. Even in countries where there is a regular AID-funded population programme, there are sometimes circumstances where action by an intermediary has a better chance of acceptance or may be more efficient. (In Indonesia, for example, a number of U.S. private institutions have provided training in sterilization techniques).

Most U.S. aid for population has been provided in grant form, although since 1970, AID has been obliged to provide part of its assistance in all sectors in the form

---

6. Although the use of intermediaries is not in any way intended as camouflage (and there is no doubt as to who the real "donor" is), there are sometimes considerable advantages in presenting an activity as that of the private sector agency concerned, rather than with a "made-in-USA" label.

7. The arrangements are made by private firms which AID/Washington maintains on contract.

of loans. In fact, there have been very few loans for population. Loans terms, for instance, have sometimes been used to fund the contraceptives supplied to countries which have been long-term beneficiaries of population assistance from AID (i.e. the most mature parts of well-established programmes). Very poor countries continue to receive population assistance entirely in the form of grants. Indeed, population as a sector stands out as being primarily grant-funded. To date, countries in receipt of an AID loan for a population project are Indonesia (since 1977), the Philippines (since 1980), and Thailand (since 1982). Interest rates on these loans range from 2 to 3 per cent.

II. APPROACH AND CRITERIA

Population Assistance Philosophy; the Role of Congress

For many years, AID's approach to population assistance was based on the premise that there existed in developing countries a vast unsatisfied demand for family planning. The U.S. policy was accordingly to deliver massive amounts of contraceptive supplies to selected Third World countries and to train local personnel to provide contraceptive services, in the conviction that ready supply would generate effective (and previously unperceived) demand. This "supply-side" approach dominated U.S. population assistance from the mid-1960s for virtually a decade, and was pursued with unshakeable determination and aggressive "salesmanship" within developing countries and the international community alike. After the World Population Conference at Bucharest, however, and the shock of the Third World's angry repudiation of family planning as the principal form of population assistance, the U.S., together with other aid donors, was obliged to reconsider the basic premises of its population assistance. Although it has maintained the levels of its contraceptive assistance, U.S. aid for population has increasingly come to reflect a concern for the "demand side" also.

In the subsequent re-orientation of the U.S. population assistance programmes, the initiative has been taken as much by Congress as by AID itself. One notable feature of the U.S. aid programme as a whole is that it is particularly vulnerable to the climate of opinion prevailing in Congress at any given time. The process of obtaining Congressional authorisation for the aid programme for the next fiscal year obliges AID each year to defend not only the broad sectors proposed for assistance, but also each individual project of any significant size, in a series of public "hearings" before Congress[8]. Given its sensitive nature, population assistance has, not surprisingly, been particularly subject to shifting attitudes in Congress, reflecting changes in the leading personalities concerned, as well as changing currents in U.S. public opinion.

In the mid-1970s, the line taken by Congress was to endorse the "development" approach and thereby add new dimensions to U.S. population assistance. It requested AID to give "particular attention to the inter-relationship between population growth and development and overall improvement in living standards in developing countries, and to the impact of all programmes, projects and activities on population growth"[9]. It also urged that "population planning programmes" should be co-ordinated with other programmes aimed at reducing the economic and social motivation for large families.

Although corresponding instructions were sent as guidance to AID Missions in developing countries, AID recognised from the outset that it would not be easy, in

---

8. This results eventually in an Authorisation Bill which approves the programme. A further piece of legislation (the Appropriation Bill) has then to be passed to make the funding available – habitually for a lower total than that originally requested.

9. These broad instructions, worked out together with AID in 1975, were not finally formalised until 1977 (Section 104 (d) of the Foreign Assistance Act). Headed, "Integration of Assistance Programmes", the Section notes particularly the relevance for reducing the desire for large families of programmes in the areas of "nutrition, disease control, maternal and child health services, improvement in the status and employment of women, agricultural production, rural development", etc...

practice, either to translate the concept of "impact" into actual project terms or to achieve a significant measure of integration of population with other development activities[10]. However, at about the same time, Congress was also calling upon AID to give its assistance a greater *poverty* orientation, and, to a considerable extent, activities designed to relieve poverty and those thought likely to affect the determinants of fertility were found to coincide. In the period since Bucharest, Congress has declared a number of new priorities for U.S. development assistance (improvement in the status of women[11]; basic human needs; primary health care, etc.). All of these can be taken as supporting the new approach to population assistance whereby AID is urged to use its imagination and look for new ways of combining family planning information and service programmes with broader development activities.

Overall, the response has not been, as some may have feared, to overlay AID's population assistance with economic and social development programmes to the detriment of its basic family planning activities. The policy emphasis of U.S. population assistance has swung back and forth several times over the years between the straight "supply side" and broader development approaches[12]. Nonetheless, AID has continued to provide developing countries with direct family planning and related services (including health care). At the same time, its population programmes have come to incorporate various development activities also, as particular countries' circumstances (and the ideas of the responsible AID officials) have indicated. (Examples are village development in Egypt, nutrition programmes in Indonesia, health programmes in Africa). There have even been some cases where AID population assistance has supported projects which have not included any family planning activities initially, although the implicit assumption has always been that they will not be far behind.

Positive Approach to Aid Requests

A characteristic of the U.S. aid posture is that it does not feel constrained to sit back and wait for developing countries to submit requests. In the case of population assistance, this active approach was effective in a number of countries in getting a population programme launched, (although not always with wholly felicitous results)[13]. Today, with the experience of several years of co-operation between the local AID Mission and government officials, it enables AID to take the initiative when it wants to test out some new idea or strategy and work up a new project in a country for the purpose.

Geographical Criteria and Size

The U.S. Government provides development assistance to a total of some 80 countries, although in widely varying amounts. It does not apply any strict economic criteria, in the sense of minimum income per capita, but it is the intent of Congress that U.S. development assistance be directed primarily to the poorer developing countries. (In 1978, Congress, reconfirming an earlier directive in this sense, called for "U.S. aid programmes to be directed in support of countries which pursue strategies designed to

---

10. A number of new questions were added to the already formidable list of factors to be checked when submitting new project requests to Washington, but as AID officials were themselves aware, this could easily become more routine than substance.

11. Also the subject of special legislation – the "Percy Amendment", 1975.

12. The late 1970s saw a spirited fight within the Agency between the respective proponents of these two approaches. At a meeting held at the OECD in Paris, at which both donor agencies and developing countries considered population assistance in the post-Bucharest era, the U.S. representatives went so far as to claim that a "free-standing" family planning programme (previously the very cornerstone of U.S. population assistance) was unlikely to achieve effective results – a seeming repudiation of the main emphasis of U.S. population assistance during the previous 10 years.

13. AID officials are very mindful of some of the earlier errors of exuberance, particularly in African countries.

meet basic human needs and achieve self-sustained growth and equity")[14]. The result has been a shift in favour of the relatively poorer countries and towards what AID describes as "smaller-scale, people-oriented projects".

Applying these criteria to population assistance, a number of countries are now considered to be "graduate" countries, i.e. to have already reached the point of take-off in overall economic terms and/or in the maturity of the national population programme (e.g. S. Korea, Colombia, Mexico, Tunisia, Brazil). However, AID is prepared to be flexible if it considers that the national programme needs continued U.S. support for its effective consolidation (e.g. Tunisia).

Political considerations also enter in, some countries being excluded for political reasons (e.g. India in the late 1960s), and others encouraged. In all, about 40 countries are currently in receipt of bilateral population assistance from AID. These include a number of Asian countries with important national population programmes which are supported by other bilateral and multilateral assistance donors as well as by AID, and others which receive aid from multilateral sources, but where AID is the only bilateral donor. In addition, some Latin American countries receive small amounts of money direct from AID/Washington for population activities undertaken by intermediary agencies on its behalf.

As a practical matter, AID has a natural preference for large population projects — since all projects, whether big or small, involve the same bureaucratic processes of preparation and monitoring. (There are about 100 professional population staff in AID Washington and in posts overseas — not enough to handle effectively a substantial increase in the work-load). Where some small activity is felt to be particularly useful, however, AID is prepared to finance it, either as part of some larger project, or grouped with other small activities in the same general area or, if need be, on its own, probably through the use of intermediaries.

Positive and Negative Criteria

AID's first criterion for its population assistance is that the programmes it is asked to support should involve no element of coercion. It will support programmes of sterilisation — provided that the service is offered on a purely voluntary basis. Abortion, on the other hand, is totally excluded — reflecting the strong anti-abortion lobby within the United States. Both these two exclusions are in response to directives from the U.S. Congress.

AID programmes as a general rule do not include a great deal of support for infrastructure. This is partly because in the context of the Congressional emphasis on the relief of poverty, it is sometimes more difficult to present works and buildings as direct help to the rural poor than other forms of aid. Nonetheless, AID's population assistance does include construction of physical facilities (clinics, health centres etc.), where they are considered integral to the programme.

A great deal of U.S. population assistance has been provided in the form of commodities, and AID continues to be the principal source of the contraceptives used by many developing countries, not only in the national family planning programme but often in that of the (private) Family Planning Association as well. (It provides 90 per cent of all the contraceptives used in Bangladesh, and in Brazil and Mexico, where it does not have a population programme, it supplies oral pills through a private organisation, Family Planning International Assistance). Although this form of aid is not always tied to a specific time-frame, AID hopes that, where possible, countries will eventually come to produce their own supplies. It also wishes to be satisfied as to the soundness of the programme in which they are to be used. Moreover, it is AID's practice not to supply to developing countries pharmaceuticals that are not allowed to be freely prescribed in the United States. Thus AID still does not provide Depo Provera, despite

---

14. Statement submitted by US AID to the Development Assistance Committee, 1981.

the advice of a special Ad Hoc Consultative Panel in 1980, which recommended that it was suitable for use in the aid programme.

As a matter of general policy, AID prefers the contraceptives that it supplies (as well as the family planning services that it supports) to be provided to the client without charge. In the Philippines, for example, it made this a condition of the Agreement. However, if the government has a contrary view, AID is prepared to work out some compromise arrangement. (In Pakistan, for example, there was a small charge). Where there is a user fee, the proceeds should in principle be put in a special account to be used for designated purposes. This often, however, proves difficult, and AID does not insist.

Unlike most bilateral donors, AID does not exclude from its population assistance the sensitive area of policy development. On the contrary, it actively seeks opportunities to provide guidance to governments in the formulation of their national population policies and strategies. (It helped with the section on Population in Nepal's latest Five Year Plan, for example). Thus, in the hope of being able to convince African governments of the necessity of population planning, AID supports a variety of research and other activities intended to point up the development implications of their respective demographic profiles and growth rates. These activities, mostly undertaken with central funding from AID/Washington, are generally carried out by private U.S. research institutions, but sometimes have the participation of the planning ministry or other relevant bodies of the government concerned.

Although AID provides some non-project assistance, particularly where countries have limited absorptive capacity for project assistance, it has not, to date, done so for population or the health sector. It does, however, provide some countries with commodity assistance which includes the needs of the health ministry.

III. CONTRIBUTION TO SELF-RELIANCE

Strengthening Financial Capability; Recurrent Costs; Salaries

Some AID population officials define "self-reliance" in population matters very directly as the ability of a country to take over an increasing share of the national programme effort[15]. Certainly, AID support for a population programme is never intended to be continued indefinitely, and aid agreements usually specify a progressive increase in the government's contribution. The ideal is that countries should in time achieve "graduate" status, and either no longer require U.S. population assistance, or else be able to receive it on loan terms.

In principle, AID does not agree to fund any project that is not likely to be eventually self-sustainable. In practice, however, this criterion is very much a counsel of perfection. Governments give a commitment to take over the running costs of a project on a phased basis, and then find that they are unable to do so, while AID for its part does not necessarily try to design its projects in such a way that it will be feasible for the government to do so. (One government claims that it turned down a design for rural dispensaries prepared by a U.S. consultant architect on the grounds that they were "fancy enough to be hospitals" and that it would be impossible to provide the staff to run them). Although this may be an extreme case, AID does not make it a rule to regularly include in its work of project preparation a calculation of the future operating costs to be assumed by the government, either in relation to the initial investment cost or to the government's anticipated budgetary revenues overall.

Population projects, almost from the outset, are likely to include a large proportion of recurrent costs. As a matter of general aid policy, AID does not like to

---

15. Statements made to the author in response to interview questions in AID/Washington and Missions overseas.

provide support for recurrent costs, but recognises that in the case of population programmes, it is necessary to take a longer view. Where possible, it tries to make the government assume responsibility for at least 25 per cent. Where this is not possible, it does not insist. Indeed, in some cases, it has agreed to finance population activities that are virtually entirely recurrent costs (the Menouffia Project in Egypt, for example).

Much of these costs consist of the salaries of local staff. AID is prepared to cover these, if necessary, sometimes on a large scale. (In the Philippines, it has provided the salaries for over 3 000 field-workers and their supervisors, with an Agreement providing for the Central and Provincial Governments to take them over on a phased basis). A more tricky matter is the payment of supplements to normal government salary scales. AID is, in principle, opposed to any such payments which distort the regular government salary structure. Thus it will not pay incentives for work in rural areas, nor does it approve of salary supplements for government officials appointed to key project posts. The government's argument in such cases is that officials are not likely to assume heavy new responsibilities without being suitably rewarded — a point that some other donors are prepared to accept. In Egypt, where the World Bank has dealt with the problem by giving "consultant" status to some of the senior staff working on its population project, AID has agreed, exceptionally, to give to lower-level staff some incremental payments for additional duties, and to pay honoraria to higher level staff employed outside of the Health Ministry[16].

Despite its general dislike of salary supplements, AID has been prepared, where it seemed necessary, to pay them to doctors who do family planning work in addition to their normal medical duties. In the Philippines, for example, it contributed a 20 per cent salary supplement for doctors in hospitals and rural health centres who did family planning work. (When the supplement was eventually removed, there was such a drastic drop in family planning services that the Government was obliged to reinstate it).

The question of incentive or "reimbursement" payments for sterilisation operations is still more difficult (although AID has tried to establish a clear policy in this area). In the early days of its population assistance, AID paid doctors in India a fee for sterilisation on a case basis (it was prepared to do so world-wide). Subsequently, to preclude any possible implication of coercion, it changed to a system whereby payment was made not to the doctor but to the health institution, on the basis of the number of operations performed. (AID advanced funds to the Ministry of Health to enable it to reimburse the hospital for the expenses incurred). Incentives to the individual client, however, are against AID rules. However, AID has responded flexibly when special circumstances required it. In Bangladesh, for example, when the Government requested help with its sterilisation programme, AID agreed to reimburse doctors, provide the individual acceptor with "medical apparel" (i.e. a new saree) and cover the cost of travel expenses to the operation centre.

Strengthening Administrative Capacity

The need to pay special attention to the administrative capacity of the potential aid recipient was underlined by Congress when it bid AID concentrate more of its aid on the poorer developing countries. Since these are the countries which receive a large part of the U.S. population effort, and are also those where administrative and management resources are likely to be weakest, AID is obliged to look closely at the capability of the institutions who will have the responsibility for carrying out its population projects[17].

---

16. Senior staff working on the World Bank Project are full-time; those on AID's Project are engaged part-time on other Ministry responsibilities.

17. Some AID staff admit that in the early days, in the eagerness to get a new population programme moving, they sometimes failed to check first on whether the existing structural and administrative resources were adequate to the task. In such cases, however, AID was usually only one of several aid donors to have acted thus precipitously.

Today, an assessment of the capability of the relevant host country institutions is one of the standard questions to be answered by AID Missions when presenting a new project. The teams charged with the preparation of detailed project design now include an assessment of the administrative capability of the government in the particular sector concerned. A notable example was the preparation of the AID population project in newly-independent Bangladesh, where the Government was proposing to embark on an enormous Health and Family Planning Programme (totalling over $1 billion at one point). AID, feeling that the administration lacked experienced staff at all levels, and seeing little chance that the health centres which it was planning to build could be effectively staffed and operated, sent out a management training specialist. He interviewed some 300 people in the Planning Commission, the Health Ministry, and the Health and Family Planning Directorate at both central and district levels, against a staff plan, with a view to identifying the gaps and selecting individuals for training.

AID, which prides itself on its flexibility and "innovation-mindedness", not surprisingly finds that it can exert a greater influence on the development of administrative capability in countries where the government is strongly committed to the population programme, and where the AID input is substantial. Even under these conditions, however, there may well be differences of opinion as to how good management can best be achieved.

One of AID's most successful experiences in this area has been its population programme in Indonesia. The Government's Family Planning Programme, the new independent institution set up to handle it (the BKKBN)[18], and AID support, all began at about the same time and grew in experience together. AID, without being directly prescriptive, has been instrumental in building up the effective capacity of BKKBN in a number of ways — including helping it to simplify its linkages with other departments of government. It has also made a particularly useful contribution by providing technical and financial help for the establishment of a management information and service statistics system. Intended to enable BKKBN to control the logistics of its contraceptive distribution and to report on the progress of family planning acceptances in the areas covered by the Programme, the system was adopted by the Ministry of Health as a basis of its national statistical reporting[19].

Training

What AID calls "participant training" has always been a major feature of its population assistance. It covers top-level policy-makers and programme officials down to workers at the field level. Arrangements are very varied and, as far as possible, country-specific. Third-country training is now common at all levels, and even training in the U.S. does not necessarily have a specifically "American" cast. (AID has persuaded the University of Chicago, for example, to give Public Health courses in French).

Much of this training has a professional rather than a general management slant, since the prime concern has been to train staff for the specific needs of the population programme. In Indonesia, for example, AID has provided as much as $600,000 a year for advanced training, covering the development of two specially-created Master Degree courses in Indonesian universities (for training of health professionals), as well as PhD courses in various U.S. universities[20]. Most of the senior staff of the BKKBN have thus been "groomed" for their jobs by receiving advanced professional training under AID

---

18. The National Family Planning Co-ordinating Board.
19. Not all AID's experiences have been so felicitous. In Kenya and Egypt, for example, AID's Population Projects have been constrained by the structural arrangements and administrative procedures of the responsible government departments.
20. The Ford Foundation assists by helping select candidates and in paying their travel expenses to the U.S.

auspices. At the middle level, further training financed by AID is sometimes offered as a reward for performance.

AID can feel satisfied with the results of its training effort under the Indonesian Programme in that the staff are back on the job — not always the case in developing country administrations, characterised by high staff turnover. The loss to the country is of course the greater if the training given is highly programme-specific and not relevant to other areas of the administration.

In some cases, AID's population assistance has included training in certain *supporting* administrative skills, such as workshops for family planning logistics (for several Asian countries), reporting and recording (Indonesia), administration and logistics (Senegal). Although, in common with most other donors, the emphasis of AID's training effort has been on the various technical skills required for population programmes, these initiatives show that AID is becoming increasingly aware of the need to strengthen also the administrative side of implementation capacity.

One aspect of training for population work to which AID has always devoted considerable effort is at the grass-roots level — the personnel who will be required to actually deliver the family planning service to the consumer[21]. A particularly interesting training experiment at this level was conducted in Bangladesh, where an intensive programme for the training of thana (district) level health workers was completed by a 3-week training course in Indonesia, under the auspices of the BKKBN. The plan involved sending some 500 workers over a period of three years. The strain implied for BKKBN staff was admittedly considerable (beginning with problems of language), but AID hopes to build up their training capacity on a permanent institutionalised basis, with pre-prepared courses and a tuition fee. The whole plan is considered as something of a breakthrough, in that it was the first time that middle and lower-level staff had been given the chance to see how programmes managers operate in other developing countries. (A further AID initiative to draw on the Indonesian experience has been to send a large group of mullahs from Bangladesh — with the idea of educating them by contact with their Islamic brethren who are supportive of family planning).

AID is not able to follow up systematically on the results of all its training programmes. Where continued programme co-operation with a country has enabled it to see the results of its training efforts, these have sometimes proved disappointing. In some instances, the government has failed to deploy the personnel as intended, or, as has happened in a number of Asian countries, trained nurses, doctors and hospital administrators have been lured away by the high salaries offered by the countries of the Middle East. Generally, AID today is trying to exert a tighter control over the use made of its training. (In a health project in the Philippines, for example, AID has included provision for follow-up of trainees to see to what extent they are actually applying the skills learnt).

Consultants

Consultant services still constitute an important element in AID population projects, both in terms of cost and administrative input. Wherever possible, AID sees its consultant services not only as providing the specialist expertise needed for project implementation, but also as a means of helping build up national capacity in the area concerned. Further, not all consultant support is necessarily at the senior professional and administrative levels, as AID well recognises the crucial role of middle-level management for effective programme administration.

---

21. The AID Administrator in his presentation before the Appropriations Committee (May 1982) declared "We believe that the U.S. has a responsibility to help strengthen the institutional capacity of LDCs to deliver basic services and implement development programmes themselves, using local infrastructures and the private sector to the maximum extent possible. For this reason, the U.S. has invested heavily in training of service providers as well as the personnel that manage service programmes".

AID encourages the use of local consultants and will sometimes finance the services of a local consulting firm to work together with a U.S. firm to gain experience[22]. The provision of local counterparts may be made a condition of the agreement, but in practice, AID is realistic enough to recognise that it can only receive such counterpart support as the government in any particular case is willing or able to provide.

AID does not normally engage nationals of the country concerned in a consultant capacity. If, therefore, there is some individual whom it would like for a particular project responsibility, it can do no more than indicate this to the government, and hope that the government will be prepared to make his services available. Sometimes, the implementation of AID's population projects has been badly hampered by the inability of the government to make available the full-time services of experienced officials on a consistent basis.

When providing expatriate consultants, AID as far as possible gives the recipient government a choice of candidates. In some cases, a government has rejected the candidatures proposed (particularly if it feels that nationals have the experience required), but more often, for reasons of cost. Consultant services provided by AID vary in cost according to the system of recruitment, but they often work out very expensive, and as such, are a source of resentment in countries where even senior civil service salaries are very low[23]. The per diem living allowances to be paid to consultants (which are frequently revised by Washington), and which are paid out of the project, also make for invidious comparisons with local salaries.

AID has a variety of methods available to it for the recruitment of consultants, whether of individuals or a team. One — "competitive contract procurement" — requires the advertising of the post in the U.S. business press ("Commerce and Business Daily"). AID recognises that this system has probably raised the quality of the expertise provided, but adds appreciably to the administative input and thence to the time involved (some posts have remained unfilled for two years). One complicating factor is that under this process, AID is bound by legislation obliging the U.S. Government to give preference in hiring to members of minority groups — a consideration which is likely to be of little interest to the developing country, but which can effectively prevent AID from going directly to a firm it considers qualified for the job. If recruitment is for a team, the complications and attendant delays are likely to be greater. AID having studied the bids, sends a short list to the government, who makes its selection on technical grounds, and then the financial negotiations begin. This has sometimes led the government to reject the winning bid on grounds of cost (even where AID might have been prepared to pay the price), and the negotiation process has to be started again with the next ranking firm. (One multi-million dollar project was held up for some two years pending negotiation of a $2 million contract). AID therefore prefers, where the government has the necessary capability, the system of "host country contracting", whereby the government examines the responses to the advertising and establishes its own short list of candidates.

Where AID does the contracting itself, it can avoid some of these difficulties by doing its recruitment indirectly through (U.S.) firms with which it maintains "umbrella" contracts to provide expertise as may be required. This arrangement frees it from the obligation of minority hiring (already satisfied in the initial choice of contractor), and enables it also to recruit third country nationals (e.g. it sent Filipino doctors to Bangladesh to teach sterilisation techniques). (AID prides itself on this flexibility:

---

22. For example, the AID-financed Urban Housing Project in Egypt includes contracts with two Egyptian consulting firms to work with the U.S. firms responsible, respectively, for the construction and the social planning aspects ("Health Sector Assessment"). The Project Agreement provides further that the U.S. construction firm must employ more than 50 per cent Egyptian engineers and architects.

23. For example, in 1980, AID calculated that the services of a consultant sent to a country for 36 days, hired through a contractor, worked out at about $18,000 including travel costs and per diem, the salary element accounting for slightly under $4,000. (The monthly salary of the director of a research institute or university professor in the country concerned is about $400).

"We go where the talent is")[24]. This process has the advantage of speed (it can get a consultant out into the field within 10 days of receiving the request), but recruiting through a profit-making body adds to the cost. AID also has an arrangement of this kind, however, with a number of non-profit professional associations, and this works very well. The associations are funded centrally, from Washington.

A further varient of contract arrangements enables the host country to make its own choice of consultant from names supplied to it by some U.S. organisation with which AID has an agreement for this purpose (e.g. the American Public Health Association). The country makes its request direct to the Association. Since the latter is non-profit, the cost to the government is reasonable, and since the contract is financed by AID/Washington, no costs are involved to the U.S. mission.

Contract arrangements tend to be a common (and complicating) feature of U.S. assistance. (The Egyptian Urban Health Project, as has been mentioned, involved four). In the case of personal service contracts, the legal arrangement, strictly speaking, is between the contractor and the recipient country government, but the actual contracts have to follow AID regulations (including U.S. per diem rates), and AID thus gets intimately involved in the whole proceedings. AID field Missions include officers whose sole task is to assist LDCs to interpret and negotiate the contracts to be made for the implementation of AID projects.

AID admits that it finds recruitment of consultants the most difficult part of project administration (the "people part"). Even quite simple consultant contracts generally take a year to finalise, while for a firm of contractors, two years is about the norm[25].

IV. PROGRAMMING

Project Agreements

AID's programming arrangements under bilateral assistance can be either rigid or flexible, according to the way any particular project agreement is drawn up. The system allows for both.

The arrangements begin with AID Washington making a provisional allocation of aid funds as between recipient countries (according to indications of need, commitment to development and other considerations), and passing the indicative figures to the field Missions for them to prepare country programmes. Each Mission accordingly prepares a broad 5-year development strategy for the country[26], based on its judgement of the country's economic and social progress, development policies, capacity for new investment etc., and proposing the allocation of U.S. support as between different sectors, problem areas and projects, (including the division as between project and non-project aid). The "strategy" is in effect a rolling programme, updated every year. The proposals are reviewed by AID/Washington as the basis for its annual submission to Congress. Once the budget has been approved, each Mission will be given its country total for the year.

These arrangements allow for only limited programming flexibility regarding the order of magnitude and pattern of U.S. support in each country. First, the field Missions have to draw up the country programme each year 16 months in advance of its receiving approval by Congress. When it approves the annual budget submission, Congress is at the same time giving its approval for each individual project. Consequently, no changes may be made of any significance without a further submission to Congress. If at the end

---

24. In practice, AID does not use third country experts often, because of the complication of security clearance.
25. There are, of course, other cases where AID has been able to move fast — for example where the requesting country has a particular individual that it would like for the job.
26. Country Development Strategy Statement.

of the year, there are unspent funds which have already been committed to projects, Congress may authorise their carry-over for the following year, but this is not automatic.

Although the country programme is for a rolling 5-year period, Congress gives AID authorisation to commit funds for one year only. (However, it is now quite common to put the whole amount in for the first year). Actual projects normally extend over several years, but AID's commitment to support them can only be given "subject to the availability of funds". In practice, this has not constituted any real problem. Developing country governments recognise that AID, like themselves, is bound by certain legislative constraints, and on the basis of many years' experience of co-operation, they have confidence that funding will in due course be provided in the amounts agreed. This arrangement is not firm enough, however, to enable the country to do long-term development programming in the assurance of a known amount of future U.S. input, other than for continuing support for already agreed activities.

Within the country aid total, AID will make a project agreement with the government for the provision of aid for population activities. It is at this stage that AID initiates a rigorous process of project development. The initial project idea is likely to come from the Mission, following informal discussions with the government authorities concerned. The Mission will send to Washington a brief description of the proposal ("Project Identification Document"), and if Washington approves it, the detailed work of project preparation will begin. In the past, this task was primarily the responsibility of the Mission staff. Being highly labour-intensive, it is now often done with the assistance of specialist consulting firms contracted by AID for the purpose.(Developing countries are generally less than enthusiastic about this practice, as the cost of the consultant contract comes out of the project). The appraisal exercise finally results in an exhaustive "Project Paper", which normally defines the project very carefully, as well as giving an estimation of costs and benefits, listing the conditions to be met, the inputs of each partner, the goods and services to be provided, the implementation schedule etc.[27].

The host government is intimately involved in the preparation of this document. Sometimes it is sent to Washington, together with the government's comments, something that is much appreciated as enabling the country to feel that the project as finally drawn up represents *its* ideas at least as much as those of the donor agency. What is much less appreciated, however, is the length of time that this process normally requires. The usual time is some 18 months, though it can be less, depending on the length of AID's involvement in the country's population programme, the strength of the AID Mission, the government's commitment, the availability of data etc. (AID Jakarta, for example, prides itself on the speed with which it can draft a new Project Paper, get it approved and sign the first obligating document). AID is also able to move quickly in cases of special urgency. (A health project in Burma was got ready and funds obligated in under 9 months). Second generation projects can also be processed quickly by means of Project Paper Amendments (done in under 3 months for Thailand). Repeats are not automatically speedy, however. (For the third Population Project in the Philippines, Washington asked for additional information, and the whole process took over a year).

The same process of project preparation has to be applied irrespective of the size of the project. (When AID wanted to train quickly a few nurses and doctors for Rwanda, where the Government had recently reversed its pro-natalist policy, it was obliged to start off by sending to Washington the standard PID, although the total cost involved was only $100,000).

AID's programming system nonetheless can allow for considerable flexibility in practice. The Project Paper (for internal AID use) is as already mentioned a very voluminous document, with numerous annexes, financial schedules etc. It forms the basis

---

27. As noted earlier, the Project Paper will also include some assessment of the recipient's administrative ability to carry out the project. The checklist of questions to be addressed is extremely comprehensive.

for the eventual Project Agreement, which sets out the terms and conditions under which assistance is to be provided. However, as regards the definition of the purposes for which the funds are to be applied, project agreements differ very greatly. They may be very specific, giving a precise definition of activities. (They also may or may not include a clause providing for the possibility of eventual change). Some countries therefore find AID's project agreements very rigid, because major changes in project implementation are subject to a signed amendment. On the other hand, the project agreement may serve simply as a general umbrella agreement for the purpose of committing funds for population activities, and within which project details can be worked out later. (In Egypt, for example, there are five sub-agreements, each with a different implementing institution). It is a particular feature of AID assistance that it can agree to make a sum of money available to a country to support its population programme *without necessarily having firm ideas as to all the specific purposes for which it is to be used.* While some of it may be for activities that are already on-going or ready to go, it is quite likely that discussions with the government may continue for some time as to the use of the remainder. This clearly offers the possibility of responding to new situations as they arise, since there is no necessity to get all the money sewn up for specific purposes all at once.

It is, for example, possible to fund a modest new innovative activity quickly (and without going through any of these bureaucratic hoops), provided it can be accommodated within something that AID is already doing. Project categories, while being country- and project-specific (they tend to be Mission-specific too), are likely to be at the same time very broadly defined. For example, for the new AID population/family planning project in Indonesia, categories currently planned are: "village family planning, primarily in West Java and 12 other provinces outside Java and Bali; urban family planning; manpower development and management; voluntary sterilization and small research and development activities". It is usually not difficult, therefore, to find the money for some small new project idea within an existing agreement. In Africa, under a new regional project, it is now possible for Missions to support activities up to $500,000 for a period of three years, using an abbreviated project review process.

Two other features of flexibility in AID's programming arrangements may also be noted. One is that it is prepared to make sub-agreements for particular population projects direct with provincial governments (it has done so in Egypt and Indonesia with the agreement of the central government concerned). Another is its very liberal scheduling of loan arrangements. For example, in Indonesia, where AID has made a $60 million loan for contraceptive supplies, the Government does not want the whole loan at once — which would oblige it to pay interest on the whole amount. AID has accordingly agreed to sign a new Loan Amendment for each new consignment of supplies.

The project agreement lays down various actions that the government is expected to take to get the project started. Ninety days are generally allowed for these to be done, but the "conditions precedent to disbursement" are not intended as formal requirements. Legally, the money can start to flow as soon as the agreement has been signed. In practice, the start of effective work on the project (and of disbursement by AID) may in fact await the government's having undertaken some essential preliminary action.

Field Missions and Project Modification

AID field Missions play a major role at all stages of the U.S. aid programme (the size of the Mission, the level of professional competence of the staff and the degree of responsibility that they exercise will, of course, vary with the country and the importance of the AID programme). In 1980, AID was maintaining an average of one staff member in the field for every two at Headquarters in Washington. Since then, the ratio has been somewhat reduced, but AID still maintains a strong field representation in order to apply its "highly rigorous and time-consuming approach to project identification, preparation, supervision and evaluation"[28].

The strength and degree of formal authority vested in the AID Missions tend to vary somewhat in response to changing attitudes in Washington and budgetary resources. With the move towards more "basic needs" type projects, which are heavily administration-intensive, the Missions were increased both in personnel and in responsibility. Overall, AID finds that a significant delegation of authority to its field Missions is a very effective way of operating its aid programme, and that large Missions, although expensive, are more than justified in terms of cost-effectiveness.

The responsibilities of the US AID Missions go beyond the identification of projects and assistance in their implementation. In countries of Latin America, for example, where there is no national population programme, the Health Officer on the AID Mission is expected to try to bring to the attention of the government the undesirable effects that excessive population growth has on its development efforts, and, if possible, to help develop a population strategy.

In countries where AID has a population programme, the population officers on the Mission staff are usually selected for their special competence in this field. In some cases, they have also been able to build up considerable experience in the particular country situation, by remaining for several tours of duty in the same post. In Indonesia, the senior population staff remained in post for seven years. They were also able to speak the local language, which enabled them to make effective contacts with middle-level officials and in the provinces. The Mission accepted formal communications from the field written in Indonesian — even project requests, which it would then translate into English to meet AID's own requirements.

AID Missions have delegated authority to approve projects up to an amount of $20,000,000, (provided they are part of projects already approved by Congress). In addition, Washington has central funds which the Mission can tap for local activities which form part of some larger regional or sectoral programme. The extent to which Missions make financial and other implementation decisions on their own initiative varies considerably, according to the style of the individual Mission Director, and in the case of population projects, the influence of the population staff. If he chooses, the Mission Director can have a considerable margin for discretion. He can agree to quite substantial changes in a project in the course of implementation, provided that the new activity proposed can be accommodated within the framework of the existing project agreement. In Bangladesh, for example, the Mission, on its own initiative, agreed to use the large unspent allocation for consultants in the Population Project to finance third country training. (The substantial new training programme was subsequently written into AID's next Population Project as an on-going activity). Another example was the decision of the Mission in Egypt to pick up a large project for the Commercially-based Distribution of Contraceptives, previously funded by the IPPF. Where, however, a change would mean a shift of funds to another aid sector, approval has to be sought from Washington[29].

The Mission also has wide discretion to extend the implementation schedule of a project. The initial time-frame for implementation and disbursement will have been worked out in consultation between AID and the recipient. Normally, projects are not expected to extend beyond 5 years, but quite often they do. (One project in Nepal lasted for 10). AID recognises that its initial disbursement schedules are sometimes impossible to realise (if only because of the delay in getting the key men out onto the

---

28. Statement made by AID to the Development Assistance Committee, 1980. At that time, AID was employing 1,500 Americans and 1,900 foreign nationals in 60 US AID Missions in developing countries.

29. In Bangladesh, for example, it was found that only 1 of the 25 rural health centres planned could be built: the Mission wanted to use the funds for other purposes, but had to request the approval of Washington.

job). The implementation schedule can therefore be adjusted by the Mission by up to one year, with Washington simply kept informed.

The very close and continuing involvement in the national population programme made possible by AID's highly labour-intensive style of project management is for the most part welcomed by the host country. It allows for informal discussion of new ideas and initiatives (and the ready provision of funds to try them out), and for the presentation to Washington of project ideas that have genuinely originated at the country end. It also, of course, enormously facilitates the application of AID's very complicated administrative procedures. Most developing countries complain that AID's bureaucratic procedures are very heavy, but often add that "the *people* in the AID Mission enable us to work with them". (It depends on the Mission. Some Mission staff tend to be sticklers for the rules: others are more "performance-minded").

This difference in style is also evident in the Mission's relations with non governmental organisations which undertake population projects in the country, using AID funds granted from Washington. The Pathfinder Fund, for example, is able to carry out populations projects in some countries, simply keeping the local AID Mission informed. In other countries, the Mission tries to use Pathfinder as virtually an agent of the AID, expecting it to conform entirely to AID's own population criteria and approaches for bilateral assistance.

One by-product of a large and continuing AID Mission is that, in time, it can help to strengthen administrative capacity in the host country, not only through explaining the rules of procurement, record-keeping, etc. to the officials working on particular AID-assisted projects, but more widely throughout the government service. (In Indonesia, for example, AID Mission staff give lectures in evaluation techniques to a wide range of Indonesian civil servants). Another advantage is that it probably spares the country the strain of frequent visits from Headquarters staff during the course of project implementation (i.e. once the stage of appraisal missions is over). Many of the visits from Washington tend to be at the request of the Mission, and consist often of specialist staff to consult on particular problems, rather than of general administrators who will require to be briefed by the government officials concerned.

Sometimes, of course, host government officials find the very active interest shown in the progress of the population programme by the AID Mission somewhat excessive. (In one country, where AID was funding research into population-related subjects, the Mission insisted on participating in the seminars held to review the substance of the work, instead of simply providing the funding and leaving this responsibility to the national research authority responsible for the project). Further, the fact that Mission staff can take off at any time and visit projects in any part of the country may, in certain circumstances, be a matter for irritation or concern rather than satisfaction, from the point of view of the local officials concerned.

V. IMPLEMENTATION PROCEDURES

AID has to operate the U.S. aid programme within the legislative constraints set by Congress and the still greater number of regulatory procedures that apply to all agencies of the U.S. Government. The latter are not always appropriate in the context of aid programmes in developing countries, and the Foreign Assistance Act allows them to be waived in particular cases. Indeed, AID claims that despite the thicket of bureaucratic regulations through which it must operate, the possibility of waiver, together with its large and well-informed field Missions, means that, in effect, the rules can nearly always be adapted to meet the needs of the particular local situation.

Specific procedures governing the implementation of the project are set out separately in a Project Implementation Letter (PIL) or series of Letters, signed by both sides. These cover the arrangements for disbursement, procurement, reporting, auditing, etc. Each PIL has been worked out in consultation with the host country officials concerned, and the operating procedures that it describes, therefore, will normally have been the subject of prior discussion as to their practical feasibility[30]. Each separate activity is likely to have its own PIL. (In Indonesia, where AID supports population programmes in 20 provinces, there is a separate PIL per province).

Disbursement Arrangements

A certain amount of AID disbursement takes the form of direct payment to suppliers — notably for bulk purchase orders and service type contracts, which are paid in foreign currency. (This is convenient for the recipient country, which does not get involved at all, either administratively or financially). For local currency expenditures, the preferred method is to reimburse the recipient for payments that it has already made using its own funds. Earlier, AID used to finance its projects largely by means of advances, with a big tranche paid over before the project began, and the rest, after a joint review, progress report and presentation of the accounts. (The Village Family Planning Project in Sumatra thus received 85 per cent to start off). Although the recipient government naturally liked this arrangement, it was viewed less favourably in Washington, which prefers to keep its money in the U.S. Treasury as long as possible. Today, AID usually makes a more modest initial payment (the proportion is variable — Washington would prefer it not to exceed one-quarter), and provides the rest in instalments, usually quarterly, as reimbursement for expenditures made. For activities that do not need an advance (e.g. seminars, training), the Mission pays the bills direct.

There is still, however, room for a lot of flexibility. If the implementing unit badly needs money to get the project started, AID may still pay a large first tranche as an advance. If funds should run out part way through the quarter, AID may agree to make an interim payment as an advance on the reimbursement payment for the next quarter. Should the project not have sufficient funds to manage with the reimbursement system, AID will obligingly make advance payments on a regular basis.

It should be noted, however, that AID is not invariably prepared to tailor its procedures to its clients' wishes. In Kenya, for example, AID insisted on the reimbursement procedure, even where some other donors were paying their contributions to the national population programme in the form of advances (SIDA, UNFPA).

As regards the actual mechanism for disbursement, AID maintains that it can get funds to the project quicker than almost any other donor. The first cheque is usually delivered within three weeks of signing the project agreement, and for subsequent payments, the minimum time elapsing between receipt of a request for reimbursement and the money arriving at the project is 4-6 weeks — assuming that the request is considered satisfactory.

AID has no standard requirements for the presentation of requests for disbursement. They are designed according to the country, the project, and even the individuals handling the project on the recipient side and in the Mission. In some countries, requests have to be carefully documented, showing what has been spent against the estimated expenditures for the period, with breakdown by item and budget line, and be supported by actual payment vouchers. Sometimes requests have to be submitted quarterly — sometimes whenever the money is actually needed. Not surprisingly, population officials in some countries find AID's procedures very exacting (particularly those that have to go through the difficult business of collecting vouchers), and in others, extremely accommodating.

In Indonesia, AID's procedures for authorising disbursement were very much easier than those of the Government. (The Government, for example, insisted on a detailed breakdown of expenditures, whereas AID did not). Indeed, BKKBN would turn to AID if it wanted money quickly and did not wish to wait for the Government of Indonesia's much lengthier and more complex approval process.

---

30. Although the evidence seems to suggest, not necessarily at the level of the staff who will actually be required to apply them.

That AID was able to be so accommodating in Indonesia was due primarily to the particularly close mutual confidence that had developed between it and the BKKBN ("a phone call to the Mission is all that is needed"). Eventually, the very flexibility of these arrangements became too much for the Government, which found that it was unable to check the progress of project expenditures against the national budget plan. It accordingly requested donor agencies to tighten up their respective procedures, where necessary, in the interests of stricter budgetary control. (This probably represents one of the few cases where a recipient government has found its donors' procedures too lax, rather than the reverse)[31].

Even in countries where the disbursement arrangements are much tighter, and call for requests to be accompanied by detailed financial statements and payment vouchers, AID may still show considerable latitude as a matter of practice. In some cases, where the government was not able to produce the required payment vouchers with its requests, AID nonetheless continued making disbursements for the population project for some considerable time, so as not to hold up the progress of the work.

Under U.S. regulations, all AID funds, although allocated to specific projects, remain in the U.S. Treasury for the account of the US AID Mission, until the latter, (in the case of population projects through either the Mission Chief or Population Officer), authorises disbursement to be made. The unspent balance remains automatically at the disposal of the project for one year after scheduled completion date after which it returns to the Treasury[32], unless special approval is given for extension. In cases where funds are paid out in the form of advance, a Congressional ruling insists that any interest that they may earn prior to being drawn down must be returned to the U.S. Treasury within 90 days after completion of the project[33].

AID's project agreements do not contain any exchange guarantee. However, there is usually sufficient lee-way in the aid allocation to accommodate any loss to a project occurring from a change in the value of the dollar. Should a project be found to require more funds than the amount approved by Congress, a procedure exists for obtaining Congressional approval for an increase.

Procurement

In the matter of procurement, AID's requirements are particularly strict. The project agreement will specify which particular items are to be purchased by AID direct, and which by the recipient country or an authorised agent on its behalf. Either way, most of the procurement financed by AID must follow the rules and procedures laid down by the U.S. Government.

The most important of these requires that aid-financed goods be of U.S. origin and transported in U.S.-owned carriers. The law allows for certain exceptions. Goods manufactured in the recipient country may be permitted, if significantly cheaper. (AID once agreed to buy cars made in Indonesia — where the Government does not allow the import of foreign vehicles — but changed its mind when it discovered that the engines had been manufactured in Japan). Goods from other developing countries are allowed under AID loan agreements, or in the case of very poor countries, under grant aid also. (Because of this provision, officials of the Bangladesh Ministry of Finance do not consider U.S. aid as being "tied"). Under these arrangements, the Philippines were able to buy contraceptives from S. Korea under its project agreement with AID. Overall, however, although there are cases where AID finances purchases of non-U.S. origin, they are neither frequent nor, generally, of significant size.

---

31. The AID Mission in Jakarta has now issued a new form for requesting disbursement, requiring more precise information (against a quarterly disbursement schedule). It will still make interim payments, however, if required).
32. AID reckons that the U.S. Government gets back $30-35 million each year in this way.
33. Most donors maintain that recipient countries cannot earn interest on their aid funds; it would seem, however, that the U.S. is one of the few to have an explicit ruling forbidding it.

There is probably less latitude in the application of U.S. rules about aid tying than of any other AID procedures. AID officials recognize that strict application of the rules can sometimes lead to absurd situations (such as insisting on U.S.- made vehicles for Morocco, a country which only has facilities for servicing French ones, or shopping for a manual typewriter for Egypt, when the U.S. has ceased to make them). Therefore, when commodities (of U.S. manufacture), are not available in the U.S., AID secures waivers for procurement elsewhere. It even agreed to finance contraceptive supplies from Japan, when it took over IPPF's Commercially-based Distribution Project in Egypt. Mission officers generally try to do their best to ease the inconveniences caused by U.S. tying rules, within the very narrow margin of flexibility allowed (e.g. trying to buy locally-made jeeps that would be much cheaper than those freighted from the U.S.)[34]. Cost, however, is not the priority consideration for AID. For supplies purchased in the U.S., AID is prepared to airlift, if necessary.

Under its loan agreements, AID gives the recipient country the right to choose the particular type of commodity to be supplied. In the case of contraceptive supplies, which AID buys by means of bulk purchase orders, countries have sometimes found themselves with a change of brand which they have not requested and may not want. Under U.S. Government rules, which require open tender and competitive bidding, AID had at one point to change its supplier, with resultant change in brand and dosage. In most countries, the officials responsible for the population programme recognize that, though unfortunate, it is the price to be paid for the cost advantage available to AID through this method of procurement.

AID allows local procurement for commodities on a small scale only (office supplies etc.). The recipient government (or implementing authority) does the purchasing, and in most cases the AID Mission helps with the procurement documents. For contract and technical support services, on the other hand (construction or supervision work), local contracting is common practice, and the recipient country is able to make contracts with local firms, using its own arrangements. The actual latitude allowed, however, is very limited, since U.S. rules about the size and capacity of the contractor have to be observed. The U.S. Government applies a number of standard criteria for assessing the suitability of a contractor for the job. Although, therefore, the choice is nominally that of the government, AID in fact intervenes at every point. In one case where the government wished to make a small contract with a particular firm of local architects to supervise a small hospital renovation job, two years elapsed before AID had successively checked the firm's credentials, drafted the contract, sent it to the country for approval and translation, and participated in the details of the contract negotiation. (The construction work involved represented some $1 million — a small component of the whole project — and the architect's fee represented only a very small part of that).

Monitoring, Reporting and Auditing

AID's arrangements for the monitoring and reporting of its projects, like its disbursement arrangements, are project-specific, and are worked out in discussion between the government and AID as part of the project agreement. Generally, the presence of a large AID Mission, part of whose job is to keep watch on the progress of AID-financed activities in the country, dispenses with the necessity for an elaborate system of formal reports for the benefit of Agency Headquarters in Washington.

There is, accordingly, wide variation as to actual practice. In some countries, the Mission's Population Officer will check continuously and closely on substantive progress and on the rate of disbursements on all AID-financed population activities, month by month. In others, a brief statement submitted half-yearly ("just sufficient to identify problems and budgetary solutions") is considered adequate. Sometimes,

---

34. In some countries, completely built-up jeeps freighted from the U.S. have been found to be actually less expensive than locally-assembled ones.

there is not even any special timing for the submission of these statements. As mentioned above, under the advance payments procedure, when the project needs more money, it will prepare a progress report and financial statement as the basis for receiving its next instalment. AID has deliberately chosen to avoid standardized reporting requirements in order to minimize paperwork. In Indonesia, for example, for many years AID had reporting forms for one project only (the Village Family Planning Programme), which, since it was to be replicated in the 10 Outer Islands, required some kind of limited standardization.

Not surprisingly, even some recipient country officials consider that AID's reporting arrangements are sometimes "very lax". There may, however, be special arrangements whereby some outside body is given the task of supervising the substantive progress of a project on AID's behalf. One area where this is sometimes done is in research (in India, AID gave the Indian University Grants Committee a mandate to supervise the progress of all AID-funded research in Indian institutions). Contracts with either national or local firms to supervise construction work have already been mentioned.

Any latitude shown by AID in its choice of implementation procedures or its manner of applying them ceases when it comes to the requirements for financial auditing. Itself dominated by the need at all times for accountability to Congress (which shows itself to be particularly interested in how aid funds are spent), AID, by its own reckoning, is probably more demanding and more likely to seek out malfeasance than other donor agencies. Every project has one or more routine audits during its life. Sometimes the agreement provides that these be done by local firms acceptable to AID, sometimes AID does them itself through its Regional Audit Offices. Generally, these arrangements are sufficient to get project accounts sorted out in due course (although on one occasion AID had to threaten to close the project account, before full and correct information was provided).

In addition to these regular audits, there is the constant possibility of a spot audit by the U.S. General Accounting Office. Its audits, generally undertaken by geographical area or functional sector, according to the current Congressional interest, are specifically designed to look for malfeasance. Under U.S. law, the accounts of all AID projects have to be open for possible audit for three years after the completion of the project. Not all projects, of course, will have to go through this ordeal, but AID feels that just the thought that it might happen has a salutary effect. AID, no more than any other donor, can ensure that every aid dollar is appropriately used. It considers, however, that its auditing arrangements go as far as is feasible in providing accountability to the taxpayer.

Evaluation

AID has long had comprehenisve and systematic arrangements for evaluating (ex-post) the activities undertaken under its aid programmes. All projects are subjected to a final evaluation of project performance against the expectation of project design; many receive a mid-term evaluation as well.

Inevitably, in a programme of the size and diversity of AID's, the very fact that the procedures for evaluation are a built-in part of project design means that there is a tendency for the exercise to have something of a routine nature. However, in addition to the routine evaluations ("Project Completion Reports"), AID has an Office of Evaluation which undertakes a wide range of evaluations of particular activities, analyses the results and publishes its reports. These are done for directly operational purposes, and there are highly-organised arrangements for feed-back. Evaluation results are fed into a central computer, and the standard guidance for the design of new projects specifically requires a statement of relevant past evaluation findings. AID's evaluation work in the field of population has undoubtedly played a part in shaping aid strategies. For example, it has highlighted the need to have country strategy statements for population. It also led to the finding that many population programmes are more effective in association with other programme activities.

In addition to project evaluations (some of which are undertaken by outside experts, particularly in the case of highly technical activities), AID occasionally undertakes some broader review. Examples are a "Study of Family Planning Effectiveness" (1979), "AID's Role in Indonesian Family Planning" (1979), and three evaluations of the National Family Planning Programme of Thailand. All such reviews are published documents.

VI. CO-ORDINATION

It is U.S. policy to conduct its foreign assistance in co-ordination with other donor agencies. In 1978, the importance of co-ordination for population assistance was underlined by a special report to Congress on this subject by the General Accounting Office. In response, AID, while reiterating its commitment to promote useful co-ordination, stressed that it was best done at country level.

AID, of course, participates at the headquarters level at all formal meetings of population assistance donors (e.g. the annual review of UNFPA's programme at the UNDP Governing Council, or occasionally, at specially-convened "Donor Co-ordination" meetings)[35], and these provide an opportunity for informal discussion of particular issues and programmes. Contacts with the World Bank and UNFPA, in Washington and New York respectively, naturally tend to be more frequent than with population donors whose agency headquarters are in Europe. The effectiveness of contacts between the three "great powers" among the donors of population assistance has naturally varied over the years, in response to changing policies and personalities in the agencies concerned. Today, all three are agreed that their contacts, formal and informal, provide adequate opportunities for a meaningful exchange of information as a basis for actual population programmes. Thus AID's (bilateral) country programme proposals discuss what the related activities of other donors are expected to be and how. AID's input will relate to their contributions[36]. Its proposals for worldwide projects, typically implemented through non-governmental agencies, also include information on the related initiatives of other donors. Moreover, AID's exchanges with UNFPA now not only cover implementation problems of specific projects, but extend also to future project proposals.

However, it is at the country level that AID, thanks to its strong field representation, is able to make the most effective contribution to the co-ordination of population assistance. Although it prefers not to itself take a lead in organising donor co-ordination initiatives (which it considers should properly be the responsibility of the country itself, or else be spear-headed by a multilateral donor), it is ready to participate in whatever co-ordination arrangements exist. It participates regularly, for example, in the UNFPA's tripartite country reviews. In Bangladesh, the AID Population Officer, following monthly meetings with the representatives of the other agencies providing the country with population assistance, together with the Population Officer of the World Bank and the UNFPA Co-ordinator, presents an oral report to the Deputy Secretary concerned at the Ministry of Health.

AID has not, to date, participated in any co-financing arrangements sponsored by the World Bank — not as a matter of principle, but for various practical reasons. (In Bangladesh and Kenya, AID had already formulated its own programme of aid for population). However, it is quite prepared to use part of the AID population programme in a country to complement the activities of other donors, where this appears useful. In some cases, AID has provided the equipment for health and family planning infrastructure built by the World Bank (in the Philippines, for example). In others, it has

---

35. Examples are the initiatives taken, first, by the World Bank in London and, later, by UNFPA in Geneva; meetings on population questions held at the OECD in Paris; the special meeting of donors arranged by UNFPA to discuss the resumption of population assistance to Pakistan.
36. UNFPA's Needs Assessment Reports and the World Bank's reports do something similar.

made good shortfalls in the assistance promised by other donors, in order to maintain project momentum. Examples are Egypt (the Commercially-based Distribution Project), and Bangladesh (sterilisation project).

To sum up, it would appear that in the matter of co-ordination, as in so many other aspects of aid implementation, the degree of effective collaboration and intermeshing of different donors' activities varies according to circumstances, and in particular, to the personalities involved at any given time.

US AID
AID FOR POPULATION ACTIVITIES

i) Total volume of assistance committed for population activities through 1981, US$ 1,733.6 million

ii) Annual expenditures on population assistance, 1975-1981 (US $ million)

1975	106.0
1976	119.0
1977	145.3
1978	166.6
1979	184.9
1980	186.2
1981	195.2

iii) Population assistance as a percentage of total (net) ODA, 1975-1981

1975	2.5
1976	2.7
1977	3.1
1978	2.9
1979	3.9
1980	2.6
1981	3.4

iv) Division of total commitments for population assistance as between bilateral, mulilateral and non-governmental organisations' programmes, 1975-1981

	Bilateral		Multilateral		Non-governmental Organisations		Total
	$ thousand	%	$ thousand	%	$ thousand	%	
1975	67.5	63.7	20.0	18.9	18.5	17.4	106.0
1976	78.4	65.9	20.0	16.8	20.6	17.3	119.0
1977	90.2	62.1	29.0	19.9	26.1	18.0	145.3
1978	104.7	62.8	28.0	16.8	33.9	20.4	166.6
1979	113.6	61.5	30.0	16.2	41.3	22.3	184.9
1980	121.8	65.4	32.0	17.2	32.4	17.4	186.2
1981	105.9	54.3	35.0	17.9	54.3	27.8	195.2

NON-GOVERNMENTAL ORGANISATIONS
THE INTERNATIONAL PLANNED PARENTHOOD FEDERATION[1]

I. INTRODUCTION

Some one-fifth of all international funding for population assistance is made available through the International Planned Parenthood Federation (IPPF), a voluntary organisation. The second largest voluntary body in the world (after the Red Cross), as its name indicates, it is federal in structure, encompassing a very large number of national voluntary Family Planning Associations (FPAs) in both developed and developing countries (currently 116). IPPF is a private, non-governmental organisation, and its funding is provided mainly to private sector programmes.

The IPPF grew out of the crusading movement for planned parenthood that sprang up in the United Kingdom and other western countries in the 1920s. As an international body, therefore, created (in 1952) to assist in the development of similar voluntary movements in other countries, its prime purpose has been to help *individuals*, and especially the very poor, by providing them with the knowledge and means of planning their families. IPPF's mandate includes also the "increase of awareness of demographic problems among both peoples and governments". Although its work over the years has encompassed both these purposes, the main focus has been on the needs of the individual and the ways in which family planning could best be promoted as an individual human right.

Since the mid-1970s, and notably since the World Population Conference at Bucharest, the emphasis of IPPF's activities has moved from family planning per se to the broader problems of population and their interrelationship with development. In the words of IPPF's Secretary-General, "IPPF was created to fight for the right to avoid unwanted pregnancies. It went on to help raise public consciousness about the need to create a balance between the population of the world and its natural resources"[2]. IPPF has accordingly come to extend the scope of its programme to include activities in such areas as general health care, parasite control, environmental sanitation and water supply, nutrition, raising the status of women, protection of children, youth clubs etc. In all these various activities, the family planning concern has always been actively pursued. The intention has been to show that family planning is a natural partner for other development efforts, and to test and demonstrate the many ways in which family planning can gain acceptance in a community[3].

IPPF differs from other agencies providing population assistance in that it provides funding not for specific projects but as *budgetary support* to its member FPAs to help them carry out their *total programme of activities*. The amount of support is decided annually for each FPA on the basis of a total programme mutually agreed upon each year. However, IPPF is rarely an Association's sole source of funding. Indeed the hope is that each Association will become increasingly able to lessen its dependence on IPPF support, attracting funds from the government, other international donors, and the communities served by its projects. Nonetheless, it requires to see details of all the projects that the member Associations are preparing to carry out each year, *including those which are to be funded from other sources*. This puts IPPF as a donor agency in

---

1. Statistical table, see page 170.
2. "IPPF in Action", 1980.
3. "Family planning" is not restricted to fertility limitation. Family planning programmes may in some contexts include also treatment for sub-fertility and sterility.

something of a unique position vis-à-vis its grant recipients, and one that other donors of aid, who deal with governments, might sometimes envy.

Each of IPPF's member FPAs has its own programme of activities, and IPPF has been providing financial support to 86 of them plus 6 other Associations which are not members. The amount of support varies widely with the circumstances of the Association and the nature of its programme. New and struggling FPAs in developing countries, particularly very poor countries, need a great deal of help; older established ones, particularly in European and North American countries, very much less. Some FPAs require IPPF financing for some or maybe even all of their projects; others need it only for supplies and equipment, or possibly simply to cover budget overheads.

The "IPPF Programme" which IPPF approves each year and of which it finances part of the cost is thus made up of the individual programmes of the member FPAs, and is based on the proposals that they put forward. It includes also, however, some activities for which the initial idea came from IPPF at the centre, and for which IPPF provides most or all the financing. These are, in effect, "IPPF projects", but they are still carried out within the framework of particular FPA programmes. In addition, there are activities undertaken at international and regional levels, such as project development workshops and training programmes.

The IPPF Programme is the outcome of two parallel paths of decision-making — through the volunteer structure and the Secretariat. The volunteer structure begins with the national FPAs, who are grouped into six regions and who elect two or three representatives (volunteer) to an annual Regional Council. The Councils review the proposals put forward by the FPAs of the region, discuss regional policies and sometimes also policies for IPPF as a whole — in which case they can make recommendations to the IPPF Central Council (also volunteer) which meets once a year in London and to which they send representatives[4].

The proposed programmes of the FPAs are discussed by IPPF's Budget and Finance Committee and the Central Council (similarly composed of volunteers). The Council has the major voice in the determination of IPPF policies. It can receive and approve specialist reports on particular issues as a basis for policy decisions (for example, it approved the report of IPPF's International Medical Advisory Panel on the question of the safety of the injectable contraceptive Depo Provera). It can also take important financial decisions, such as where the programme should be cut if income is found to be insufficient, usually on the recommendation of the Budget and Finance Committee.

Parallel with this voluntary structure is the Secretariat structure, which operates similarly at both regional and central levels[5]. The Secretariats have the twofold task of receiving ideas and instructions from the voluntary structure and of feeding its own ideas and suggestions to it. This delicate balancing act between Agency "voluntarism" and Secretariat "professionalism" is at the heart of the whole IPPF system, and in particular, the process of formulation of the annual programme. From all accounts, it seems to work remarkably well.

The third element that goes to make up the IPPF structure is the donors — the governments and other bodies which provide IPPF with its annual budget. About 90 per cent of IPPF's direct income is provided by the governments of some dozen DAC countries. A small amount comes also from donations from other countries and various

---

4. Both the Central and Regional Councils are supported by Executive Committees (also voluntary) which meet two or three times a year to provide continuity between the annual Council meetings.

5. The relative functions of the IPPF Regional Offices have changed from time to time. The decision has recently been taken to bring Regional Offices situated in different parts of the world to the premises of the International Office in London for reasons of greater operating efficiency. Technical assistance to FPAs will be provided by field offices which will be located in the field and which will serve a group of neighbouring FPAs. This reorganisation represents a decentralisation of programme responsibility to the field, while responsibility for administration, accounting and auditing is centralised.

private population bodies[6]. Despite its dependence on their financial contributions, IPPF has been concerned to maintain the voluntary character of the Federation, and not let the donors acquire a predominant voice in the formulation of policy or choice of programmes. IPPF's donors have come to appreciate the sensitivity of the Associations and also their wide diversity of situations and approaches. When they meet in London at the IPPF donors' meeting each December, they generally prove to be very supportive of whatever policies and projects have already been arrived at as a result of the interaction of volunteer and Secretariat views described above. IPPF is somewhat unusual in that its principal policy-making body (the Central Council) and its funding body (the donors) are separate and distinct (unlike say, UNFPA, whose donors, meeting at the Governing Council of the UNDP, decide both the budget and the policies that UNFPA is to follow). It is in large part this separation that has enabled the national Associations to preserve their independence as the grant-receiving bodies. IPPF takes no small pride in having established this entente with its donor governments. It feels that in consequence it is less vulnerable to changing donor whims and fashions in aid philosophies than many other population agencies.

Where of course the donors do have the ultimate say is in determining the *size* of IPPF's programme overall. In making up its annual programme, IPPF has always tended to budget conservatively — partly as a hedge against the possibility of donor contributions falling short of the promised amounts, and partly because of the limited absorptive capacity of some FPAs. As a consequence, it has rarely had to cut back on the commitments made to the Associations for their programme for the year. Nonetheless, IPPF today, like all aid agencies, is affected by the economic recession in the countries of its donors. Whereas previously, the proposals made each year by the Associations used to be cut in the interests of prudent financial management, they are now having to be cut to the point where it may be difficult to do much more than maintain the on-going projects.

The present budgetary situation aside, looking at IPPF's history as a whole, it would not seem that shortage of funds has been a significant constraint on the development of the programme; (although there has sometimes been a problem of local funding, especially for budgetary support, which the FPAs often find harder to raise within the country than money for projects). Overall, however, the main constraint was for many years rather the shortage of good projects. As the FPAs have gained in size and experience, this situation has changed. However, a major limiting factor has always been, and remains, the shortage of administrative and managerial skills, which means that some FPAs may be unable to carry out effectively even good projects which respond to important local needs.

Clearly, there are enormous differences between Associations. In Colombia or Singapore, for example, they benefit from the highly developed managerial talent of the country and from their now considerable Association experience. In very small countries like some of the Pacific islands, on the other hand, where some of the newer FPAs are to be found, managerial talent is limited, almost by definition. Most FPAs come somewhere in between, leaving IPPF to decide the delicate question of how much funding each one can realistically be expected to cope with.

II. APPROACH AND CRITERIA

In a number of ways, IPPF feels that it has a special role among the international agencies providing population assistance.

First, its private voluntary character enables it to by-pass governments and deal direct with people. (In Bolivia, for example, IPPF quietly sponsored six new initiatives

---

6. Primarily the FPAs of the United States, United Kingdom and Canada, the Japanese Organisation for International Co-operation in Family Planning (JOICFP) and the Population Crisis Committee (United States).

at a time when government opposition to family planning had forced all official population assistance agencies to withdraw). *Second,* and as a consequence, it is able to work wherever there is an effective nucleus of popular demand (a national FPA or even a few interested individuals), irrespective of prevailing official attitudes. (In Paraguay, for example, IPPF is providing the only subsidised family planning services available). *Third,* by sponsoring voluntary initiatives, IPPF hopes to bring about an eventual change of government policy. *Fourth,* IPPF, as something of a missionary for family planning, can bring family planning information and services to marginal groups in sometimes unlikely settings, who may be difficult to reach under other aid programmes. (Examples are its work with school drop-outs in Morocco, refugees from Viet Nam, disaster victims in Guatemala, and migrant workers in West Germany). *Fifth,* IPPF programmes are intended essentially to demonstrate that family planning programmes are *feasible,* but IPPF would not itself provide the major part of national family planning services.

In countries where there is no national family planning programme, the core of the FPAs' programmes is generally regular service activities (clinics, training courses, family planning information and education campaigns, etc.). These activities may themselves play a pioneer role and eventually be subsumed in a national family planning programme. This has happened, for example, in Egypt, and a number of countries in Asia. Alongside, and sometimes within these basic service programmes, IPPF is particularly interested in promoting pilot projects, innovative approaches and integrated family planning and development activities. The hope is that such "pathfinding" projects, once they have demonstrated their feasibility, will eventually be taken up by the government or some other donor agency and "go national". (In Jamaica, a project for pregnant adolescents, initiated in collaboration with the Women's Bureau, has now become a model used by the Government).

Sometimes the initiative for trying out some new approach comes centrally from IPPF itself and is developed by the FPAs with IPPF support. One case where such a central initiative has been notably successful is Community-based Distribution of Contraceptives (CBD). Having once proved itself a sound working proposition, this is now being applied in various forms and on a larger scale in nearly 40 countries, sometimes using contraceptives supplied by the government or other aid donors.

One of IPPF's best-known integrated projects similarly began not on the initiative of a national Association but at the suggestion of an outside body, the Japanese Organisation for International Co-operation in Family Planning (JOICFP), which got a number of Asian FPAs interested. The projects combine parasite control and environmental hygiene with family planning and improved nutrition. The idea has now been extended to eight countries in Asia and four in Latin America, with funding provided jointly by UNFPA, IPPF and JOICFP[7]. (IPPF calls such projects, incidentally, not integrated family planning projects, but "integrated community development strategies" — a significant difference of emphasis).

In some integrated projects, IPPF is prepared to finance not only the family planning component, but also the other development activities associated with it — if it feels that this will in time lead to increased demand for family planning. IPPF strongly favours any kind of mixed activity which offers the national FPA the possibility of association with other organisations and fields of interest. In this way, the FPA can sometimes benefit from the support and facilities of a more powerful and better-endowed partner. It also provides family planning with an entrée into new and different groups of the population. (In Afghanistan, for example, the Family Guidance Association is collaborating with the National Campaign against Illiteracy).

Through its local affiliates, the national FPAs, IPPF possesses an unusual "grass-roots" involvement in the life of a country. For this reason, it is probably better placed than many other donor agencies to effect a workable "symbiosis" between activities

---

7. Part of the Japanese Government's contribution to IPPF is used for these integrated projects. UNFPA also makes a contribution to the projects through the IPPF.

in its own immediate area of interest and those of other bodies which may serve as "carriers" for them. Indeed, by encouraging the FPAs to broaden their horizons and find new "partners" in different walks of life, IPPF is able to channel funds indirectly into activities that it may not be easy to promote directly. (In Indonesia, for example, the FPA has sponsored some "Women in Development" projects — an area outside of the immediate concern of the Government's family planning body, but in which other departments of the Government are now becoming interested).

IPPF's project criteria have, of course, to reflect its role as a private organisation. Thus it would not, for example, get involved in activities touching directly on the formulation of national population policy. On the other hand, it does not hesitate to support activities whose purpose is to influence policy. Many FPAs play an active advocacy and lobbying role to persuade their governments to adopt population and family planning policies. In Brazil, for example, the FPA (BEMFAM) runs seminars on population for civil servants, and has followed up the Colombo Conference of Parliamentarians on Population and Development by helping set up a Parliamentary group on population, with representation from the Central and State Parliaments; while in Kenya, the FPA conducted seminars for Parliamentarians even prior to Colombo, IPPF has supported initiatives in a number of countries for the reform of legislation which discriminates against women (Marriage and Family Laws), has tried to obtain better legal protection for children, and its member Associations in countries affected have helped to campaign against the practice of female circumcision.

IPPF differs significantly from other aid donors in that it eschews capital projects. Where many other donors like to see the results of their aid in the form of physical infrastructure, IPPF feels that its input should be applied for revenue expenditure rather than capital investment. Where, therefore, it has, exceptionally, agreed to assist a national Association to construct a building, it has done so by means of a building loan, whereas other IPPF funding is provided in grant form.

Apart from its dislike of infrastructure projects, IPPF has few "negative preferences". One concerns activities in the field of data collection and population dynamics, which it considers more suitable for the mandate of other donor agencies. IPPF would also be reluctant to take over an activity previously funded by another donor, although exceptionally, it has done so.

In addition to financial assistance, IPPF provides a large part of the contraceptives and other supplies used by the Associations. (IPPF is the only agency other than US AID to describe its role as including that of "supply agency"). Some FPAs receive supplies only (in some of the Pacific islands, Viet Nam). Others, which have other sources of supply, get only a part or none at all. (In Egypt, for example, the FPA is provided with all its contraceptive needs by the Government).

IPPF has no hard and fast criteria regarding project size. It depends on the local context and the nature of the activity. Some of the "Women's Projects" for example, are very small ($2-3,000). In countries where the national FPA is well established, projects may on the other hand be quite sizeable. Overall, the programme tends to include a large number of small-scale activities, since much of the funding is channelled to small, local branches of the FPAs whose implementation capacity is limited to small projects.

Changing Criteria for Resource Allocation

IPPF has until now tended to allocate its resources on a somewhat pragmatic basis, depending on the merits of the programmes proposed, the capacity of the Association concerned and the possibilities of funding available to it from other sources. It has recently been decided, however, that henceforward, priority should be given to "the poorest people in the poorest countries". The idea that the programme should move away from the countries of relative prosperity towards the areas of greatest need was first proposed by IPPF's Budget and Finance Committee (a volunteer not a Secretariat body, it will be remembered). This important shift of emphasis would seem therefore to have been prompted initially by largely financial considerations, which made it desirable to introduce a new selectivity in the use of the funds available. The implications of this policy, adopted in 1979, were intensively discussed over a period of two years in the various bodies making up IPPF's decision-making structure, before being put into effect in 1981. The new policy therefore represents the consensus view of IPPF's member Associations, i.e. the *recipients*. It has also received the support of IPPF's donors.

In order to put the new policy into effect, an assessment has been made of all countries. The criteria used are certain quantitative data (GNP per capita, poverty, contraceptive practice, crude birth rate, infant mortality rate, population below the age of 15), plus more general considerations such as the availability of family planning information and services, government commitment to family planning, the total financial resources available to the country for family planning (including those available from other donors) and the role and capacity of the FPA concerned (including *its* possibilities of raising funds from other sources).

IFFP's 1982 Programme already reflects these new criteria. The result is a small overall increase compared to the previous year in the amount allocated to what has now become the highest index group (i.e. the poorest), and a major decrease (16 per cent) in the amount for the countries of lowest need (Hong Kong, Cyprus, Singapore, Israel, Cuba, Ireland). The shift is not a radical departure, but rather a confirmation and strengthening of a trend that had been quietly evolving over several years. When, faced with a situation of shrinking budget resources, IPPF found itself obliged to make the hard choice between the conflicting criteria of *need* and implementing *efficiency*, it gave considerable weight to that of *need,* recognising that continuing priority to already efficient programmes tended to perpetuate the lack of capacity in others[8].

III. CONTRIBUTION TO SELF-RELIANCE

Financial Self-Reliance

For IPPF, the question of the contribution that its assistance can make to the self-reliance of its recipients presents itself in a more limited context than for most aid donors. Where other donors operate on a national level and provide their aid to national governments, IPPF is dealing with its volunteer member Associations. At the same time, the idea of financial self-reliance has perhaps a more direct reality for IPPF than for many other donors, in that a national FPA that can largely dispense with IPPF funding releases IPPF funds for other less well-situated Associations, and/or for more risk investment.

Obviously, the Associations are not advancing towards self-sufficiency simply by replacing IPPF funding by aid from other donors. Even government subsidies may create new bonds of dependency. Ideally, therefore, IPPF would like the Associations to develop local sources of income to the extent possible, including from the public directly concerned.

One way in which IPPF contributes directly to the self-sufficiency of the FPAs is by providing (free) the contraceptives they use in their programmes, and which they can, in turn, sell, usually through CBD. The income thus generated is used to cover project expenses[9], (although IPPF generally thinks of "self-reliance" in terms of the

---

8. A recent policy statement reads: "IPPF will give priority to supporting service delivery programmes which are directed towards the segments of the community that are most likely to be by-passed by the conventional facilities of governments. The under-privileged in rural and peri-urban areas, the poor, the illiterate, minority groups and immigrants and young people in all countries and societies should receive priority attention in service delivery programmes".
Source: IPPF's Involvement in Delivery of Family Planning Services; IPPF Policy Compendium, 2.0/01.

9. In Thailand, the Director of the CBD Programme is confident that the Programme can in time become self-supporting.

programme of the FPA as a whole and not of individual projects). Many FPAs, in addition, make a small charge for the contraceptives supplied in their clinics and for other family planning services. IPPF favours such changes as one way of increasing FPA self-reliance, but leaves each Association to decide its own policy.

Where IPPF is financing all or part of the costs of some particular project activity — a pilot project or some major "risk venture" — its support is usually provided for an initial testing period only, after which it is hoped that other sources of finance will be found. For example, in the case of the integrated parasite control/family planning/nutrition projects, it announced that it would limit its support in each country for six years. (The Indonesian project at Sawahlunto can now virtually stand alone, thanks to a partnership between government and private industry).

One aspect of financial self-reliance where IPPF practice differs significantly from that of other donor agencies concerns its attitude to recurrent costs. Unlike other donors, who tend to feel that these should be the responsibility of the recipient (i.e. in their case, the government), IPPF, being concerned to help its Associations with their total programme of activities, feels that its funding should more appropriately be applied to operating costs than to investment expenditure. In some countries it has at some time covered recurrent costs only. (In Iran and Southern European countries for short periods of time).

A considerable part of recurrent costs is for payment of salaries (an FPA's regular clinic staff and field workers would not normally be volunteers). FPA programmes, unlike those of foreign aid agencies, are essentially *domestic* programmes. Accordingly, they offer rates of pay that are at par or often below prevailing salary levels of the country. Nor, although they are private sector, would they want their pay scales to be far out of line with those of similar level staff in the public sector. (This has on occasion caused difficulties in the opposite sense: when the Government of Egypt introduced a generous system of incentive payments for doctors doing IUD insertion, the Egyptian FPA was obliged to follow suit). Although in certain cases, it might be useful to pay salary supplements as an inducement to staff to work on projects in the field, the FPAs, unlike international donors, are not going to want to pay higher salaries for rural service than they themselves receive at Association headquarters. At all events, the FPAs do not seem to have requested IPPF funding to cover salary supplements for project staff.

Technical, Managerial and Administrative Self-Reliance

Both IPPF itself and its member Associations in developing countries have the advantage of being able to draw on the considerable experience of the other FPAs, a number of whom ante-date the creation of the IPPF itself by many years. They thus have at their disposal a wealth of relevant technical, professional and operational expertise to help in the design of programmes and in their implementation. These "technical co-operation" resources exist on the national level also. As a volunteer organisation, the FPA may benefit from the advice and collaboration (also voluntary) of a wide range of professional skills and interests within the country — not only doctors, but lawyers, university teachers, sociologists, businessmen, marketing experts, media specialists, etc. This of course is not the case for all FPAs, particularly the smaller and newer ones. The other ones, however, have been growing steadily in professionalism, maturity and in standing in the community. Some (in Sri Lanka, for example) have ceased to be pioneers and have become a recognised part of the "establishment". Not only their technical competence, but their managerial and administrative capability has improved tremendously in the process.

Since, however, FPAs differ so greatly one from the other, overall, the problem of the "absorptive capacity" of the particular grant-receiving institution is as real for IPPF as for any other aid donor. In fact, in some respects more so, since many national Associations work through local branches in different parts of the country — all of them volunteer bodies and frequently lacking in administrative experience. IPPF leaves to the national FPA the responsibility for "educating" its branches in the basic administrative requirements involved in receiving IPPF funds. But the task is not easy. The Egyptian FPA, for example, has 22 branches of widely differing levels of competence, and in India, the Bombay Headquarters of the Family Planning Association of India makes grants to 30 different branches. Similarly, in cases where an FPA works with and channels IPPF funds to some other organisation within the country (the radio or TV service, for example), IPPF has to leave to its judgement the assessment of the efficiency of the intermediary.

In principle, the capacity to develop and implement programmes has been one of the criteria that IPPF has used for resource allocation. In practice, however, it has not always been realistic to stop and check on the administrative capability that is likely to be available, e.g. when the objective is to encourage some novel or provocative venture (such as CBD at the outset) or to get family planning started in a country where no programmes exist (say by trying to interest two or three doctors in opening a clinic — as has been the case in some African countries and the Gulf States). Some such activities have been going on quietly for years with IPPF support and without even submitting a report. Normally, however, once an operation is finally under way and has shown where the specific areas of administrative weakness lie, IPPF will try its best to provide technical help to strengthen them.

In recent years, IPPF has been paying increasing attention to the need to strengthen the administrative and managerial capacity of the FPAs[10]. Because it is dealing not with sovereign governments but with its own voluntary member Associations, IPPF is probably in a better position than most other donors of aid to look closely at this area of competence of its grant recipients. For example, it now carries out "management audits" of each FPA's programme — something that would be unthinkable under a government-to-government aid relationship. (See section below on Evaluation).

Most of the assistance provided is in the form of workshops and training. Thus a special Management Development Programme was set up in 1976 which organises regional (and occasionally multi-regional) workshops for FPAs to identify their management problems and plan such follow-up activities as may be indicated to help deal with them. A number of national workshops have accordingly been held with IPPF help — sometimes for management staff in such subjects as project formulation and evaluation, sometimes for field staff at district and even village level in basic record-keeping, accounting, clinic-patient management, etc. A method has been devised whereby one week's training is given in English, followed by the participants repeating the course to their colleagues in other parts of the country in their own language. (This "echo training" has been found very effective).

In some countries, the FPAs provide training not only for their own staff, but also for other family planning personnel. The Indonesian Family Planning Association at one time provided training for 20,000 government field workers, and in Colombia, the FPA opened a regional training centre for nurses and health auxiliaries from all interested Latin American countries. In Kenya, IPPF supports a Centre for African Family Studies which gives courses on the relationship between population and development to administrators and development specialists from all the anglophone countries of Africa.

IV. PROGRAMMING ARRANGEMENTS

As IPPF's donors make commitments for one year only, IPPF itself is only able to commit funds to the Associations on an annual basis. (SIDA has given IPPF a three-year Letter of Intent, but this is not accompanied by the funds for the period). However, once IPPF has approved a particular FPA programme, the assumption is that it will continue to provide the support required to carry it out for as long as may be reasonable.

---

10. It is significant that the 1981 Annual Report to Donors includes a section entitled "Self-reliance and Administration".

Exceptionally, a certain degree of advance commitment may be given for specific project activities. Thus the JOICFP integrated projects, as we have seen, were given a promise of IPPF funding for up to six years — though without specifying the amounts. The CBD projects were given similar assurances of support for a given period.

In theory, the FPAs are supposed to draw up a three-year plan of activities, but the programming has in fact been done on a purely annual basis[11]. In general, the FPAs can assume that the amount they will actually receive will be at roughly the same level as the previous year (allowing for inflation). If therefore they wish to propose some important new activity, they will need to cut back correspondingly in their requests for other projects.

Since IPPF financing is intended as budget support to help the FPAs carry out their total programme, the annual budget request which each Association has to submit must contain information on all the activities which it is proposing to carry out in the course of the following year, together with details of the funding expected for each from other sources, including the local currency funds. IPPF, after reviewing the proposals in the light of its overall aid criteria and the intrinsic merits of each activity, will fix a reasonable amount for each FPA intended to cover that proportion of its total requirements not already met from other sources (whether other donor agencies or the government). This said, IPPF is anxious to avoid giving the FPAs the idea that it is a bottomless purse, ever-ready to meet the gap between their plans and available resources. Sometimes it recommends that an FPA seek government financing for a particular project rather than always turn to IPPF. (FPAs have been heard to complain that new projects sometimes fall between two stools on this account). Sometimes it urges them to try other donors. (In Egypt, for example, IPPF ceased financing CBD after it was agreed that the project would be picked up by US AID).

The requests submitted to IPPF each year are shaped by the IPPF decision-making structure described earlier. That is to say, they include not only the needs of on-going projects and the suggestions of the FPA and its various local branches, but they also reflect the ideas discussed at the meetings of the Regional and Central Councils. (Some FPAs have been heard to complain that when they follow the policies recommended at these meetings, and design new activities accordingly, IPPF does not always support them — e.g. integrated projects have been rejected as containing too many non-family planning components!). In general, however, the consultation process ensures a broad harmony of approach.

The whole process of preparing the annual programme is very protracted. Until now, the FPAs have had to send their proposals to IPPF by April each year, in order to allow time for them to be considered successively by the various Committees meeting between then and November, and revised by the Secretariat accordingly. This means that the FPAs have had to start thinking about the next year's programme almost before the current year's programme has begun (IPPF works on the calendar year). While appreciating the constraints implied in IPPF's own programming time-table, the FPAs have, not surprisingly, criticised this arrangement as being not only burdensome but unrealistic.

In putting forward their annual programme proposal, the FPAs have to submit three forms for each project (a pro forma for on-going projects or a more detailed one for new requests, one for financial details, and a third combining the other two, presented under functional headings, i.e. training, information, CBD, etc.). Each project has to be presented separately — even the smallest. In addition, there is another form for budget overheads.

It takes variously from three to six weeks for the Head Office of the FPAs to prepare this documentation, after a lengthy process of consultation with their local branches, which are staffed often by volunteers untrained in project preparation or

---

11. Beginning in 1983, a new programming system will come into effect whereby the FPAs will be given an indicative figure (covering grants and supplies) each year as a frame for preparing their annual programme and budget request.

estimation of costs, who tend to send in either too little information or too much, and whose proposals have to be discussed, edited and finally translated into English or French. In many cases, the Head Office itself fills in all the report and budget forms for the branches, as being the only way of getting the material ready on time.

The FPAs get some IPPF help in the task of budget preparation from the Regional Offices, whose staff visit the Associations to discuss their proposals and advise on the way in which they should be presented. The proposals get further discussion at the Regional Councils. Most FPAs say that, although time-consuming, the whole process is in fact helpful to them — and a useful means of checking the exuberance of their local branches who often want to expand their activities unrealistically fast. (The visits of the Regional staff, in particular, are considered as a valuable form of technical assistance). After all these consultations have been completed and the budget request sent to London, the Associations may still find IPPF coming back to them with requests for further clarification.

IPPF has been considering for some time how the whole programming exercise could be streamlined, and has recently worked out a new system based on three-year planning, (henceforward to be taken seriously). The three-year plan becomes now the key programme document, but each FPA will be given an indicative figure for the first year, including cash and commodities, and a less firm figure for years two and three. The three-year plan will therefore be supported each year by a new set of documents setting out each Association's proposed work programme for the coming year and a report on the previous year's activities. In April each year, the three-year plan will be prepared as an up-dated rolling plan. The Work Programme for the forthcoming year will be submitted to the IPPF in October (instead of April under the present system), and the Annual Report will be presented in February. The new system is to be applied for the first time in the preparation of the 1984 Programme. Meanwhile, IPPF officials from London and the Regions have tested it out in the FPAs of 22 countries, in consultation with their volunteer as well as professional staff, and held a major training workshop to explain it. IPPF feels that the need to plan ahead will lead to improved management efficiency by obliging the FPAs to sort out their priorities[12].

Under present arrangements, once the annual programme has been agreed, the Associations have a limited discretion to make changes, keeping IPPF informed. (Flexibility within a 10 per cent margin is allowed in budget management). For significant reallocations as between budget categories or any major change, IPPF has to be consulted. (For example, when the Bangladesh Family Planning Association wished to change the site of one of its clinics in Old Dacca, because another clinic had since been set up nearby, the resulting budget increase required them to get IPPF authorisation). Often, however, changes are made and IPPF is only notified afterwards.

It should perhaps be pointed out in this connection that the national FPAs do not stand in the same relation to IPPF as do local aid missions to the headquarters office of the major donor agencies. The FPAs are neither branch offices of IPPF, nor are they themselves donor agencies. IPPF considers them as "service agencies" for channelling IPPF funds to certain agreed activities, and for which they have the implementing responsibility. They do not "represent" IPPF in the country but are independent, within IPPF's federal structure.

Regional Offices, now to be supplanted by Field Offices responsible to Regional Bureaux, have delegated authority to exercise full responsibility on behalf of the International Office. Substantively, they are actively involved in assisting Associations in programme planning by providing technical assistance for the purpose, if necessary calling on specific professional qualifications from the International Office.

---

12. The fact that the system will be introduced just when IPPF's budgetary situation may not allow it to do more than accept a minimum of new proposals may be unfortunate in terms of timing.

Exchange Rate Variations

The amount of each Association's annual allocation is determined in US dollars. If the dollar falls in the course of the year, the FPA will suffer an exchange loss, and where this has been considerable, may ask IPPF to make up the difference. IPPF gives sympathetic consideration to exchange losses. In 1980, a number of African countries included the amount of the exchange loss as an expenditure item in their budget request for the following year, and in some cases, IPPF agreed to make up the difference.

More often, variations in the exchange rate work the other way, and the Association receives additional local currency funds — which must be returned to IPPF. (One FPA, when making out its budget request, slightly under-values the dollar, as a hedge against a subsequent drop. If the dollar maintains its value, the FPA considers the increased local currency funds thus accruing as additional income).

In some cases, complications have arisen where there is a significant difference between the official exchange rate and the unofficial value of the dollar. In Egypt, for example, the FPA succeeded in inducing IPPF to use the unofficial rate, which at one time was 30 per cent higher. The difference was taken to represent the Egyptian Government's contribution to the EFPA programme.

V. IMPLEMENTATION PROCEDURES

Disbursement Arrangements

Until the beginning of the 1980s, IPPF has always funded the FPAs by means of quarterly advances. The payments are made on receipt of a summary financial statement showing all income and expenditure during the past quarter, cash balance and expenditure forecasts. IPPF remits the amount estimated as needed, up to a maximum of the approved grant[13]. The funds are transferred to the Association's account in a local bank within one week. Should an Association be late in receiving its advance, the reason is usually that the local branches have been slow in submitting their quarterly financial reports.

Recently, however, IPPF has found itself with a serious cash flow problem. The donors have begun providing their contributions to IPPF in the form of several instalments throughout the year, and in consequence, IPPF is no longer able to provide funds for all the FPAs together at the beginning of each quarter. It is therefore obliged to spread a number of small payments over the year (six at the minimum) as funds are received from the donors. (FPA financial staff are of the opinion that this arrangement should be more efficient rather than less). The requirement for the FPAs to submit quarterly requests and financial statements still applies.

If at the end of the year, an Association should have any of its IPPF allocation still unspent (i.e. not yet commited in the form of orders placed), the following year's remittance is reduced by that amount. The Associations do not like this arrangement, because if projects are slow in starting, they feel that they lose out. In Bangladesh, for example, where the Association's programme is beset practically every year by some national disaster such as flood, drought or famine, the start of activities is often considerably delayed, and the Association feels that it is losing part of its budgetary allocation for the year in consequence.

Where an FPA receives funding for certain activities from other donors of aid, the arrangement is often made in the context of existing aid agreements between the donor and the government of the country concerned. For example, the Bangladesh Family Planning Association gets some minor funding from US AID under its Programme Agreement with the Government of Bangladesh, and some from the World Bank under

---

13. IPPF may occasionally advance cash to meet project expenditures where projects are funded by other agencies who will only pay after the project has been carried out.

the IDA Health and Family Planning Project. The Association accordingly receives these funds not from the donor agencies direct but through the Government of Bangladesh. Funding from voluntary private bodies, on the other hand, does not go through the government but can be paid direct. (In Indonesia, the Pathfinder Fund provided money direct to one of the *local branches* of the Indonesian Family Planning Association, simply keeping the Association Headquarters in Jakarta informed).

IPPF is itself, of course, in the category of voluntary, private funding agencies, and its allocations to the FPAs are accordingly paid direct to the account of the Associations[14]. This is a very real advantage that IPPF enjoys over official donor agencies, whose programmes are with governments. In many countries, all foreign aid inputs have not only to be first approved by the central planning or co-ordinating body, but have then to be channelled to the implementing body concerned through the Treasury Department. This can, and in many cases does, result in significant delays before the destined recipient actually gets the money — a problem which IPPF programmes are happily spared.

Procurement Arrangements

As already mentioned, the major commodity which IPPF supplies to its member Associations is contraceptives. Some 30 per cent of these, it itself receives free from the United States over and above the latter's cash contribution to the IPPF programme. The rest it buys through bulk purchase by its central purchasing office in London. At one time, IPPF was supplying 17 different brands of oral contraceptives, largely for historical reasons, as each FPA came to request its particular preferences. On the whole, the FPAs seem to get the brands they want, regularly and in adequate quantities[15]. IPPF also has a joint commodity grant arrangement with Japan for JOICFP projects under which one-third is provided by the IPPF and two-thirds by Japan.

The FPAs send to IPPF each year lists of the supplies and equipment needed, as part of their annual budget requests. After due review, the requests are met either by procurement by IPPF's purchasing office or, occasionally, by goods supplied by a donor country, or by authorising the Association to make the purchase locally.

The bulk of the requests are for contraceptives, which IPPF buys at "best price" on the basis of previous experience. Because of its large bulk purchases, the supplies give IPPF very favourable prices. The principal other request that IPPF receives is for vehicles. These are purchased either by the FPA itself, if the bid appears reasonable, or by international competitive bidding (ICB). Overall, however, IPPF does not use ICB very much.

For the FPAs, local purchase (which includes purchase by the Regional Office) is often more convenient. For one reason, it is likely to move much faster. In many countries, although foreign goods supplied by IPPF are free of customs duties, it takes a very long time to process them and get them off the dock, because of *national* import procedures.

The overall amount which each FPA can purchase locally is agreed each year, after review of the specifications of the items required and comparison of prices with those that IPPF could obtain by bulk purchase from London. But before each purchase can be made, the supplier's pro forma invoice has to be sent to London for approval. Sometimes the FPA finds this requirement slightly absurd, as when the Family Planning Association of Kenya needed to send for approval the pro forma invoice for a locally-made steel cabinet costing $2,000 and which was already in the budget. For IPPF, however, it is the only way that it is able to follow what its money is actually being

---

14. This policy has been challenged with some frequency, but IPPF has insisted on adherence to direct funding of FPAs.

15. Recently, IPPF's International Medical Advisory Panel reviewed the currently supplied formulations and brands of oral contraceptives, and recommended against provision of identical formulae under different brand names. Some oral contraceptives are also being phased out for technical reasons, and the current list of orals supplied by the IPPF is now reduced to about half.

spent on, since its regular reporting arrangements (see below) do not provide this kind of detailed information.

For local purchases, whatever the amount, IPPF requires to see comparative prices from domestic suppliers. "Local purchase" may, however, include foreign goods already in the country (or region), or foreign goods manufactured in the country (or region). (Thus in Indonesia, where the Government has banned the import of cars, the FPA was nonetheless able to buy Japanese vehicles). Once the purchase has been agreed by IPPF, the Association will place the order, and IPPF will pay the supplier direct from London.

By and large, IPPF favours local purchase, for reasons of convenience, provided the price differential is not too great[16]. Although IPPF has to keep its own donors assured that its financial management is sound, it is perhaps freer than many donors of aid to make its procurement decisions on an essentially pragmatic basis. For one thing, it has the advantage of not being bound by constraints of aid tying. It is also free of the procedural obligation to call for international competitive bidding (with its attendant delays), and the moral one to share out orders equitably amongst its various donor countries. One reason, of course, is that apart from the supplies of contraceptives, IPPF's individual purchase orders tend to be relatively small. The pressures, therefore, both external and internal, tend to be correspondingly lighter also.

Reporting, Accounting and Auditing Arrangements

Under its system of quarterly advances, IPPF, as mentioned above, has been requesting the FPAs to send in regular reports showing the status of expenditures. The first quarterly report is a summary financial statement, but at the end of the second quarter, a half-yearly report has to be submitted giving information on income and expenditures (actual and projected) and receipts of cash and commodities; for the third quarter, a report (financial information only) is optional; at the end of the fourth quarter, a financial and a programme report must be prepared for the whole year.

The quarterly reports, perhaps inevitably, have come to be something of a pro forma requirement, and it is doubtful whether IPPF has been able to make a great deal of substantive use of them. They have not provided the detailed information necessary to make it possible to follow how the programmes are actually progressing, how the funds are being spent — nor even what they are being spent on. At the same time, the FPAs for their part have found the quarterly reports a great strain, despite the fact that all that IPPF is asking for is a consolidated statement covering the programme as a whole — largely because of the difficulty of getting correct and timely information from the local branches.

Moreover, if an FPA has support from, say, the government and several different donor agencies in addition to IPPF, each one will require a separate report on the use of its money, presented according to *its* particular rules, format and timing. Sometimes the reporting requirements of the different donors coincide — more often they do not. The fact, therefore, that IPPF does not require a breakdown of expenditures and a progress report for each separate project is not so much of a bonus, since the other donors do. Similarly, although the other donors probably do not require their financial statements to include details on the status of funding received from IPPF, this does not make reporting that much easier, since IPPF wants to know the details of expenditure of *their* funds.

To meet IPPF's need for more detailed information and, at the same time, to take into account the very real difficulties of the FPAs in coping with reporting requirements, new reporting arrangements have been worked out in conjunction with the new programming procedures. A new Handbook explaining the new procedures, and

---

16. Price considerations may not be the most important. Other factors to be taken into account are lead time and the greater difficulty of reimbursement at the local level. Local purchase with IPPF funds counts as part of global IPPF purchases, thus enabling IPPF to get the benefit of bulk purchasing.

replacing the current Handbook on Planning, Programming, Budgeting and Reporting is to be issued in 1982[17].

Under the new system, FPAs will report briefly on all projects in their annual reports. Where projects are funded by other agencies, a copy of the report required by the donor, although in a different format and even for a different financial year, will be acceptable to IPPF. The purpose of the new reporting system is, of course, to provide IPPF with a better basis for informed decision-making throughout the implementation of the programmes. To make effective substantive use, however, of a regular flow of substantive information, a considerable effort of analysis will be required at the receiving end – representing additional burdens on IPPF's already slimmed-down Secretariat.

The FPAs recognise IPPF's concern for accountability of the funds it receives from its donors and dispenses worldwide. Their accounts officers have learnt to keep several different sets of accounts for each of their several donors, together with a consolidated budget to record cash flow. Many go to considerable effort also to keep check on the accounting capability of the local branches. (When officers visit the branches, they will normally examine the accounts, and if something seems wrong, an accountant from the Association's Head Office will be sent to look into it).

IPPF does an internal audit of each FPA's accounts once every two years for large grant-receivers (less frequently for small ones), by sending an auditor from London and/or the Regional Office. IPPF requirements, however, demand in addition an annual audit by an external auditor (chosen by the Association and approved by IPPF). The results of the external audit have to be presented within six months of the close of the preceding financial (i.e. calendar) year. Most FPAs meet this requirement without undue difficulty. (Even the FPA of war-torn Afghanistan recently sent in its auditors' report only a few weeks late, with apologies for the delay!).

Evaluation and "Management Audit")

IPPF attaches great importance to evaluation, which it views as an integral part of the programming, budgeting and reporting process, and as a valuable means of providing direct opportunities of learning from experience. (During the past few years, evaluation workshops have been held in a number of countries for FPA staff and volunteers). IPPF's evaluation work covers both global analyses of the activities of the Federation, as a basis for policy-making and management, and field evaluations of particular FPA programmes. In the latter case, the FPA concerned does not supply a team member, although it participates actively in the work. Normally it will be invited to discuss the preliminary findings of the study before the team leaves the country, and the final report is intended to take into account its reactions and comments.

IPPF recognises that these evaluation studies, although highly professional, have certain basic limitations as an operational tool and means of improving management efficiency. One is the impossibility of studying the activities of all the FPA's local branches, which are likely to be widely scattered throughout the country. Another is the difficulty of ensuring effective arrangements for follow-up. (The formal mechanism for follow-up gives this responsibility to the Regional Offices, who sometimes pursue the matter with vigour, sometimes less so: IPPF is trying to create a mechanism which will effectively follow up on the measures taken for follow-up).

Some FPAs are unenthusiastic about the whole idea of a one-time country evaluation study, and find much more useful IPPF's regular practice of "management audits". These exercises are considered by most of the FPAs less as an "inspection" than as a valuable opportunity for discussing particular management problems while their incidence is still fresh. (The audit will cover such matters as organisational

---

17. The earlier Handbook was issued in 1975. One has sympathy for some of the FPAs who have not long since completed the task of translating it into the national language and educating its volunteer staff in its use.

structures, planning, budgeting, personnel policies, commodity control, etc.). IPPF and the Association consider together what practical measures might help strengthen any particular deficiencies and what IPPF could do to assist.

IPPF's management audits are something of an unusual donor exercise in that they bring funding agency and grant-receiving body together on a regular basis to consider the "nuts and bolts" of programme administration, not related to specific projects — elements that tend often to get overlooked in the press to get new programmes approved. The aim is to carry out 25-30 evaluation missions a year. FPAs which receive large grants are visited every two years: others every five.

VI. RELATIONS WITH OTHER AID DONORS

Collaboration with United Nations Agencies

IPPF has a Memorandum of Understanding with WHO which covers consultation on matters of joint interest, such as the safety and effectiveness of contraceptive methods; representation at each other's scientific and technical meetings; exchange and development of training materials and documents; joint work in the area of family life education; and joint projects in which each organisation has an agreed role, (examples are a research project on adolescent fertility, a project for day-care centres, etc.). Both IPPF and WHO support individual country projects after having agreed in principle on whether and at what level funding should be provided. Funds are then transferred directly to the projects. IPPF and WHO keep each other informed of the progress of these projects by sharing financial and other reports and through annual review meetings.

IPPF has recently had an exchange of letters with FAO to identify areas for collaboration. Consultations which followed have emphasized such areas as rural development, women's development, co-operatives and nutrition.

Joint Financing with Other Non-Governmental Organisations

Sometimes, IPPF joins with some other non-governmental body for the financing of particular projects. For example, a number of projects were financed by the Population Crisis Committee (United States), under an arrangement whereby IPPF had the substantive project responsibility, and the Population Crisis Committee contributed the funding. (One such project was to train traditional healers in Bangladesh in modern methods of contraception).

Occasionally, the co-financing partner is a small private body not normally engaged in the population field. IPPF welcomes this kind of association as a means of getting a new interest group involved in the work of furthering family planning knowledge and acceptance.

Ear-Marked Donor Contributions

For the past several years, IPPF has been receiving a certain amount of funding from some of its donor countries, ear-marked for specific projects. In addition, the US AID introduced the practice of "negative" ear-marking a few years ago by requesting of all recipients of its funds that these should not be used for abortion-related activities. Recently, Canada has followed suit[18]. AID has always been extremely vigilant in this matter, and at one point tried to get the AID missions to check on the programmes of the national FPAs to be sure that no abortion work was being carried out. This is normal practice for AID in respect of its "intermediary" institutions, but IPPF has

---

18. AID's concern on this point has involved tremendous accounting complications for IPPF. For example, if an IPPF staff member has attended a conference where abortion was discussed, AID would need to be shown that the expenses were met entirely from a budget account which received no United States contribution.

resisted it in the case of the FPAs, as constituting an infringement of their independence. Today, the AID missions maintain working contacts, often very helpfully, with the FPAs of the countries concerned, but have no say in their programmes.

IPPF is not entirely happy about the practice of donors ear-marking part of their contributions for specific purposes, in that it goes against the whole principle of the independence of the national FPAs vis-à-vis the donor agencies. It also creates an additional administrative burden for the FPA concerned in the form of additional reporting requirements, etc. (For example, the Government of Canada, which had financed the printing of a handbook for the Family Planning Association of Bangladesh, required a special financial report as soon as the work was completed).

To date, the extent of such ear-marking is still limited. However, if the aid funding situation overall continues to be difficult, IPPF thinks it possible that the practice may increase as a means of giving donors more identification with the activities financed by their money, as well as greater possibilities of checking directly on progress. Should this come about, IPPF would probably not be in a position to resist.

Another form of ear-marked funding, however, is welcomed by the IPPF. This comes from member FPAs in some developed countries such as Canada and the United Kingdom, and is provided to support projects of FPAs in developing countries. These funds are raised through public campaigns from private sources, and are sometimes matched by government agencies wishing to encourage NGO fund-raising.

Exchange of Information with Other Donors

As one of the major international institutions concerned, IPPF participates at high level in most of the international gatherings at which the donors of population assistance assemble to discuss policies and programmes. In between conferences, contacts are maintained on a more informal and ad hoc basis, sometimes concerning particular countries or programmes.

At the country level, IPPF cannot directly participate in whatever co-ordination may take place between aid missions or embassies, in that it does not itself have representation in the country. The national FPA may have established working contacts with one or more of the donor aid missions in the country, but such arrangements are likely to be ad hoc and related to specific project possibilities. Occasionally, the FPA will participate in broad donor discussion of population programmes on a national basis (e.g. in Egypt, the FPA and IPPF participate in the donor meetings organised each year by the Co-ordinator of the UNFPA), but this is not yet the commonly accepted practice.

INTERNATIONAL PLANNED PARENTHOOD FEDERATION
EXPENDITURES ON POPULATION PROGRAMMES

Year	Expenditure ($US million)
1975	29.6
1976	31.7
1977	38.3
1978	45.3
1979	45.2
1980	48.2
1981	49.0

Source: IPPF Finance Department.

THE PATHFINDER FUND[1]

I. INTRODUCTION

A small, private sector foundation, the Pathfinder Fund was one of the earliest bodies in the United States to provide contraceptive services for people in developing countries. Based in Boston, it was initially part of the pioneering family planning movement in America in the 1920s, and began to extend its activities to Third World countries in the early 1950s. It was established as the "Pathfinder Fund" specifically for this purpose in 1957[2]. In terms of international population assistance, Pathfinder's programme is modest ($8.5 million in 1982). Its significance lies rather in the innovative and exploratory nature of many of the activities that it has chosen to support.

At the end of the 1960s, Pathfinder began to receive an annual grant from US AID. Since then, AID has provided approximately 80 per cent of Pathfinder's budget, and uses it as one of its principal intermediary agencies for innovative work in the population field. In addition, Pathfinder receives annual donations from a variety of other (private) sources, either for specific projects or unrestricted use. Pathfinder considers the availability of these private source funds (currently amounting to nearly $1 million) as "one of its greatest assets", enabling it to respond quickly to new opportunities as they arise and to take "pathfinding" risks[3].

Pathfinder describes the purpose of its programme as "to encourage innovative solutions to population problems", and by "population problems", it means primarily those caused by unrestrained fertility. Most of its work, therefore, has traditionally been concerned with some form of family planning activity (fertility control methods, delivery systems, contraceptive supply, training of personnel, etc.). In common, however, with other agencies providing population assistance, in the latter part of the 1970s, it began to feel that a broader approach was indicated, so as to include activities designed to help tackle the "demand" side of the family planning equation. Today, therefore, Pathfinder's programme formally comprises three separate (though inter-related) elements. By far the largest is still what it terms "fertility services", and of which family planning is still the "centerpiece". Second is a new programme entitled Women in Development, which aims to try to improve the status of women in developing countries (with a view to offering them alternative options to multiple child-bearing) and to increase their involvement in the management of family planning programmes). The third element consists of a new emphasis on activities likely to have an impact on population *policy*. Intended primarily to build up commitment in developing countries to the need for lower fertility and the small family norm, these "policy" activities do not represent a new departure for Pathfinder, but they are now being promoted as part of a deliberate programme strategy.

Pathfinder projects do not now necessarily have to include a family planning element, although in most cases the hope is that directly or indirectly they will lead to an improved climate for family planning, either on the national/societal or on the individual level. In financial terms, however, all but a small part of Pathfinder's budget continues to go for the support and development of family planning programmes, most of its other activities being still experimental and/or small-scale[4].

---

1. Statistical table, see page 183.
2. Pathfinder began as the vision of one man, Dr. Clarence James Gamble, and was funded primarily by the family of the founder until its incorporation as a public foundation in 1970.
3. Pathfinder "Proposal (to AID) for a specific support grant", January 1982.
4. The preponderance of family planning in Pathfinder's budget is in part due to the fact that some of the family planning projects are large-scale — and thus expensive. Morveover, some of the "women's projects" ultimately become fertility projects" and end up being listed as such.

As the scope of its activities has expanded, Pathfinder's staff has also grown, both in numbers and in diversity of background. Pathfinder remains a small institution (and takes pride in being so) — with now some 20 professional staff at Headquarters and 9 in the field. To the earlier core of physicians and public health specialists, however, have now been added staff from other disciplines, social scientists, management specialists etc.[5]. It has, in addition, a Board of Directors (22) drawn from a variety of professions and including four members of the founding family.

Despite its new interests (and its growing experience), Pathfinder does not presently envisage any substantial expansion in the size of its programme. The constraints are partly, of course, budgetary: both AID support and private funding (which has tended to grow, together with the size of the AID grant) are now getting tighter[6]. But they are also partly administrative. As a small foundation, Pathfinder has a capacity for rapid decision-making which might be lost if it had to handle a significantly larger number of projects. Rather than seeking to do more, therefore, its preference is to aim for greater impact. Pathfinder sees a number of ways in which this might be achieved — for example, by greater strategy coherence in the choice of projects, by more systematic study and application of the lessons of past experience, and by greater effort to ensure that "pathfinding" activities have a suitably propitious cadre in which to work. (A programme, for example, to train non-physicians to insert IUDs will not be effective if the medical profession remains hostile). Pathfinder recognises that where its path-finding activities have not been acted upon by the government or other appropriate body, it has often been for lack of the necessary commitment in the host country — but this it considers as something that should be foreseen and to the extent possible planned for.

On the other hand, Pathfinder does not seem unduly troubled by some of the practical constraints to project implementation at the recipient end that are frequently cited by other donors. (Failure to provide local currency counterpart, for example). Nor does it stress the problems posed by administrative and technical weakness. This is perhaps because Pathfinder has anticipated them, since it is in the nature of "pathfinding" activities that the technical and administrative skills required for project implementation may not yet be in place[7]. Indeed, in many cases, one of the purposes of the project will be to help provide them.

II. APPROACH AND CRITERIA

Pathfinder's preferred activity is, by definition, "pathfinding", i.e. pilot projects or the provision of seed money to try out some new approach. A large part of the activities that it supports, however, are in fact continuing service or training programmes that may have begun as exploratory activities but which continue into the development stage. Indeed, the proper balance between the pioneering and the proven in Pathfinder's total programme is a matter that is under constant and careful review.

Being always on the look-out for innovatory approaches, Pathfinder is prepared to consider proposals from virtually any source, if the initiative seems intrinsically promising. As a consequence, one of the most striking features of the Pathfinder programme is the variety of the activities that it has chosen to support, and corresponding variety of "grantees" or implementing bodies that carry them out. These latter may sometimes be departments of government, sometimes private bodies (including some that at first glance appear unlikely partners for population work), and sometimes even individuals, if they are deemed to be doing particularly valuable work of a pioneering nature.

---

5. The Boston staff are all U.S. nationals, although there is no actual policy on this.
6. The AID annual grant was cut by 30 per cent in 1980.
7. Perhaps in part also because it designs its projects to circumvent them as far as possible. (Viz, the local Pathfinder officer who said that he always arranged for clinic projects to include a small sum for building maintenance, knowing that "it takes three years for the Ministry of Health to change a light bulb").

Moreover, as a private agency, Pathfinder does not have to sit back and wait for requests for its assistance. Many projects, in fact, originate with ideas advanced by members of its own staff. The formal grant "request" is then put forward by the particular implementing body that has agreed to collaborate in trying it out.

The AID Grant

Although the bulk of its programme is financed out of the annual grant from AID, Pathfinder remains a strictly independent body, with its own policies and criteria. If AID puts forward suggestions for activities which Pathfinder considers do not conform with its policies, Pathfinder can and does reject them.

On the whole, however, the relationship that has developed between Pathfinder and AID works well and is to the advantage of both parties. AID, which has always made extensive use of intermediary non-governmental bodies in all sectors of its development programme, finds that in the field of population assistance, Pathfinder, with its close and varied contacts in developing countries, offers possibilities for action that it would often be difficult for it to take itself, operating on a direct government-to-government basis. Thus it has been able to finance some modest population work in countries where government population policies are still ambivalent (Tanzania, Zaire), or are in the very early stages (Rwanda, N. Yemen), or even are overtly negative (Bolivia, Paraguay)[8]. Sometimes the AID grant may even enable Pathfinder to make a first contact in a country that has hitherto been opposed to any kind of family planning activity (Pathfinder is hoping to discuss possibilities in both Burma and Malawi, for example). In other cases, while there may be no problem about the government's sympathies, it may still be desirable to undertake some particularly controversial activity on a purely private basis (for example, training in sterilisation techniques in Indonesia).

In addition, Pathfinder provides AID with useful possibilities for trying out innovative projects for women. Part of the annual AID grant to Pathfinder is specifically designated for this purpose. The actual projects to which it is applied are occasionally AID's own initiatives, more often Pathfinder's, and sometimes those of a variety of other private agencies in the country concerned.

Where Pathfinder finances an activity out of the AID grant, it is AID's criteria that must be applied. This means that because of the prohibitions that apply to the U.S. aid programme, Pathfinder cannot support with AID money any family planning programme that includes abortion, nor can it provide Depo Provera among the contraceptives it supplies. Moreover, in the area of women's projects, there is a fundamental difference of approach. AID requires that the women's projects that it finances must include a family planning component, whereas Pathfinder, while it has a preference for "integrated projects with a family planning centerpiece"[9], is sometimes willing also to support projects designed solely for income generation. However, when these constraints become particularly irksome, Pathfinder is always free to use its private source funds for activities that AID will not support. In Ecuador, for example, when AID rejected a women's project that had no family planning component, Pathfinder went ahead anyway, using its private funds. Similarly, in Bangladesh, Pathfinder is financing some clinics, under the AID grant, that do not provide abortion services, and others, out of its own funds, that do: it simply takes care that the two sets of project accounts are kept separate.

This does not mean, however, that it is only in the disposition of its marginal private source funds that Pathfinder is able today to play a genuinely "pathfinding" role. Some of its AID-financed activities are themselves of an exploratory nature — indeed not infrequently, or else AID would be doing them itself as part of its bilateral programme. A number of the projects which Pathfinder submits to AID, and which AID agrees to fund, are "ad hoc" activities which have no particular relationship with

---

8. Pathfinder is at present the only agency doing family planning work in Bolivia.
9. "Pathfinder on Pathfinder", 1980.

any current programme strategy (they may be in a country in which Pathfinder has no on-going programme), but which both agencies agree, nonetheless, look worth a try.

Types of Assistance and Preferences

Pathfinder's support for an activity may include virtually all of the usual types of population assistance. That is to say, it will supply commodities and equipment[10], provide technical assistance in the form of foreign expertise and training, organise seminars and conferences, publish population literature, and occasionally sponsor research. It prefers, however, not to finance infrastructure (chiefly because this is likely to represent a costly element of what are often very small projects), nor basic bio-medical research (although it might be prepared to, if done in a developing country and related to the specific country conditions). It does, however, make two important exclusions, as a matter of principle. One is budgetary or "core" support. Pathfinder prefers a discreet and identifiable project, for which it will itself have the recognised donor responsibility. The other is that it will not support the activities in developing countries of non-national bodies, except for occasional projects funded through missionary groups.

In its *fertility-related* work, Pathfinder has a number of preferences. These include demonstration projects; the decentralisation of family planning services (notably through community-based distribution, but in Colombia, Pathfinder is financing a mobile minilap service); special efforts for high-risk groups, notably adolescents; education and motivation of key family planning personnel (Pathfinder has been instrumental in a number of cases in introducing family planning into the curriculum of medical schools and schools of nursing); and, of course, technical training for both physicians and para-medical staff. Pathfinder is also concerned to show that family planning acceptance can be improved by making the services more attractive to the client – what it calls the "user perspective" – an aspect of service delivery that government programmes often tend sadly to overlook. (Pathfinder's efforts in this direction include family planning counselling as well as clinical services – e.g. a seven-country project in Latin America for training drug-store employees, to enable them to provide informed advice with the sale of contraceptives over the counter).

Many of Pathfinder's *women's projects* are frankly exploratory, since so little is known for certain as to how best to organise women's groups in a manner that will be both viable and eventually replicable on a larger scale. The women's programme consequently includes some novel and varied undertakings (e.g. support for a group of women vegetable growers in Niger; training of day-care workers in Brazil), as well as projects linked with health and family planning activities.

Under the heading of "policy development", Pathfinder is pursuing one of its long-term preferred activities – namely that of developing a "constituency" in favour of family planning. Aimed at "opinion-leaders" in all walks of life, the work takes the form mainly of conferences, seminars, study visits, etc., but may include also arrangements designed for a single individual. Such activities are generally limited to those countries where the motivation is high and where the timing seems appropriate. (The constant assessment of a country situation and the identification of key individuals represents an important part of Pathfinder's work). It also gives high priority to work in the area of law and population, which it undertakes by means of research, conferences and publications.

One underlying purpose that runs through Pathfinder's programme in all areas is to help fill what it considers as critical gaps in available services or knowledge. It is with this in mind that it publishes a wide variety of population literature, and makes occasional training films. Pathfinder publications, or support for publications, in addition to the more conventional reports of conferences, technical literature, training manuals, etc., include some more unexpected items also, such as contributions to

---

10. Pathfinder is prepared to supply contraceptives for a government or other agency's family planning programme, as well as for its own projects.

feminist magazines or information to promote greater awareness of Third World problems. Some Pathfinder publications appear in French, Spanish, Portuguese and also Bengali.

Geographical Criteria and Size

In its choice of countries, Pathfinder's first preference is for those where other population donors are not yet active. The "AID connection", however, while it does not distort this preference, inevitably brings with it a certain modification. Thus we find Pathfinder supporting projects in, for example, Egypt, Turkey and Kenya, as well as in Indonesia and in Bangladesh, where it has had important programmes for many years. Generally, however, Pathfinder's priority countries (currently some 15) tend primarily to be in Latin America and in Africa, where the need for pioneering work is greatest. In Asia, where national population programmes are already well-established (and other donors also), its activities are presently limited to Bangladesh and Indonesia. In the Middle East, it is keen to support any initiative that looks promising, and currently has activities, for example, in Jordan and N. Yemen.

Unlike most agencies in the population field, Pathfinder does not, a priori, rule out support for occasional activities in the developed world. Some of its publications dealing with general development or the status of women are not only produced in the U.S., but are intended for Western audiences. Pathfinder is also supporting some family planning work in Italy[11].

Since it is not Pathfinder's purpose to finance large-scale service programmes, but rather to direct its support selectively to specific *target* activities (say, changing the negative attitude of a particular country's physicians), its projects are often modest in size — sometimes very modest (they may be for as little as a few hundred dollars). Pathfinder takes the line that nothing is too insignificant, if it looks like being potentially useful — nor too much trouble, although small projects involve the same administrative requirements as big ones. (In Indonesia, for example, the total programme, amounting to some $200,000 in 1980, covered 16 separate projects ranging from $110,000 to $1,000[12]. Pathfinder is prepared to fund a "project" which consists of sending some key individual to study abroad, or simply to attend a conference, or meet with his colleagues in another country. (It sent the administrator of an AID project in Zaire to observe the management of the CBD project in Southern Sudan). Pathfinder considers that these small "one-off" activities can have an important catalytic effect, and that its ability to pick them up quickly is one of the special contributions of its programme.

On the other hand, Pathfinder has some very large projects. In Brazil, it is funding CBD projects with BEMFAM (the Brazilian Family Planning Association) in four states, a total of some $700,000 per year, and in Nigeria, is supporting family planning efforts in medical schools to the tune of nearly $500,000. In Bangladesh also, although the individual projects are not on the scale of those in Brazil, Pathfinder has a major programme of family planning service and training activities that complements and supports the national programme of the Government.

III. CONTRIBUTION TO SELF-RELIANCE

Financial

Although the likely duration of its own involvement is one of the important factors to be taken into account before deciding on any new project proposal, Pathfinder, in common with other donor agencies, nonetheless sometimes finds itself

---

11. Including the publication of comic-book type "novellas" carrying a family planning message.
12. The $1,000 project provided for a journalist to write a monthly profile of a career woman for a popular magazine for a year, to be followed by a survey of the readers and their reactions.

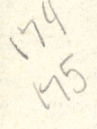

staying with a particular activity considerably longer than originally envisaged. Some of its projects have in fact been very long-term (viz, an MCH project in Liberia, begun in collaboration with the Peace Corps in 1977, and for which it is still providing assistance in 1983). In principle, where Pathfinder is supporting a continuing service programme, it tries to reduce its contribution on a phased basis, specifically in order to encourage self-reliance. (In Bangladesh, for example, it has been supporting for years a number of family planning satellite clinics in Metropolitan Dacca, but is now hoping that the Government will incorporate them in the national programme in the next five-year plan). In cases, however, where it appears difficult for the government to assume responsibility, Pathfinder, again in common with other donors in like situations, usually takes a pragmatic view, and will either continue to help out, or find other donors to do so[13]. Where it continues its own support for a protracted period, it usually tries to do so on a selective basis, say, by supplying specific elements that the government will find it difficult to provide itself (imported equipment, for example), or by helping to improve the technical quality of the service.

Pathfinder support for a project makes no distinction between local and foreign exchange costs. Some Pathfinder projects (training, seminars etc.) may be all local currency costs. Some may be in large part recurrent costs (salaries and regular service operating costs).

Where Pathfinder pays salaries, (e.g. for the staff of the clinics that it supports), they are not infrequently slightly higher than on the corresponding government scale[14]. It has also on occasion paid small honoraria to doctors as incentive/bonus for family planning work, particularly sterilisation. The local Pathfinder representatives usually maintain that this pays off in terms of improved performance; although opinion at Headquarters is somewhat divided as to the principle. In practice, it is the view of the man-on-the-spot which prevails.

Administration and Management

With its close knowledge of local conditions, Pathfinder is well placed to identify the specific weaknesses in a country's capability for carrying out population activities. As a consequence, its projects include attention to the need to strengthen public management (at all levels), as well as to improve the purely technical skills required. The emphasis tends to be on the practical. Like most aid donors, Pathfinder will occasionally send programme managers for extended fellowships abroad: it is more likely, however, to send them to see how programmes are being run in other countries. Pathfinder is also well aware of the difficulties caused by the lack of experience in basic administrative support functions. Many of its projects, therefore, also include training for middle-level staff in such simple but essential functions as opening a bank account, operating a budget, managing personnel, ordering supplies etc.

Pathfinder is making a special effort to provide training in these skills for women, in order that they may be able to have a greater say in the design and running of family planning programmes. One of the special features of its Women's Programmes consists of the identification of individual women leaders, or potential leaders, who can be trained to assume management responsibility for their own programmes. Pathfinder recognises that many of these women will have had no training in even the simplest kinds of administrative work, nor possibly any previous experience of community activity. It is therefore trying to find ways to give them the necessary practical training and also the confidence to enable them to play leadership roles in the programmes that most concern them. (Whether by design or by chance, the project managers of nearly all Pathfinder's projects in Bangladesh have been women[15]).

---

13. For example, of Pathfinder's 8 pilot sterilisation projects in Indonesia, 3 eventually became well established, and Pathfinder was successful in finding another outside agency, the International Project of the Association for Voluntary Sterilisation (IPAVS) to take over the others.

14. It claims that this does not, in fact, distort the government salary structure since Pathfinder doctors do not get the pensions etc. of government servants.

15. Or at least they were at the time of the author's visit there in 1981.

IV. PROGRAMMING ARRANGEMENTS

Programme Formulation

Despite its traditional predilection for pioneering activities — many of which arise unexpectedly or are taken up as ad hoc risk ventures — Pathfinder plans its overall programme through a regular programming exercise, just like any other donor agency.

Every two years, Pathfinder's Headquarters and international staff, and the Board of Directors assemble in Boston for a two-week meeting to discuss the overall directions that the organisation should follow for the next 3-5 years. Plans for the regions and for each of the countries in which Pathfinder is most active are worked out with the field representatives who come to Boston once a year for this purpose. The plans, which take into account the overall country situation and needs, what other donors are doing, and where it appears that Pathfinder can make the most impact, include an indicative figure for each country. They also incorporate detailed one-year projections for individual projects.

One aspect of this whole process which should be noted is that although Pathfinder's Board of Directors participate in it, the body that is its major source of funds does not. It is accordingly complemented by a second and at least equally important exercise, namely the preparation of the necessary submissions to AID.

This is done on three levels. A "comprehensive grant application" is presented every five years, setting out Pathfinder's programme priorities and plans on a country-by-country basis. This enables AID to decide on an approximate total for its support to Pathfinder for the period covered by the presentation. This is followed by an annual "Submission for incremental funding" (under the current grant), which contains abbreviated reviews of the broad strategies that Pathfinder is following in the different areas of its programme, and lists of on-going and prospective projects[16]. Finally, each individual project proposal has to be submitted to AID for concurrence. AID is thus kept informed at every stage of Pathfinder's priorities and intentions, and has ample opportunity to comment and suggest modifications.

To what extent in making up its programme, Pathfinder cuts its coat to best fit the AID cloth is a difficult matter to determine. Certainly, the general directions of programme strategy are laid down by Pathfinder's own staff and Directors. At the same time, knowledge of AID's priorities and interests is something that cannot be ignored. In fact, the country-level strategies will most likely have been discussed with the AID Missions in the country concerned, prior to the in-house discussions in Boston. Moreover, in some cases, as previously mentioned, the initiative for a particular project is that of AID, which indicates to Pathfinder, in advance, its interest in Pathfinder's collaboration in carrying it out.

Pathfinder's programme does, however, have numerous other sources of inspiration, in addition to AID. The most frequent is likely to be the Family Planning Association of the country concerned. In Latin American countries, in particular, much of Pathfinder's programme consists of support for activities proposed by the Family Planning Associations. There are also a host of smaller private bodies with ideas which they hope Pathfinder may agree to support. In some cases, the initiative may come from the government, though this is less likely. There are some notable exceptions, as in Indonesia and Bangladesh, where Pathfinder is actively collaborating with the government in the national population programme. There have also been some cases where a government has turned to Pathfinder for assistance at the very beginning of its national programme (as in Mexico and Rwanda)[17].

---

16. The activities which Pathfinder finances from its other sources of funding do not, of course, have to be included in this submission.

17. The low profile of a small *private* outside agency would have obvious advantages at the politically delicate early stages of a new government programme.

Project Approval

The time taken for Pathfinder to approve a new project request can be anything from 24 hours to 6 months or more. At the shorter end of the spectrum are for the most part small "ad hoc" projects (under $10,000) which Pathfinder finances out of its private source funds — which, it will be remembered, it likes to keep available for just such purposes[18]. Many of these projects which Pathfinder may consider worthy of support are not eligible for AID funding, either because the notice is too short (as will be seen below, AID needs a certain amount of time for its review process, and does not like to fund projects retroactively), or because the subject matter is something that AID's own rules forbid it to assist. Occasionally, even if the request falls within the broad outline of activities that AID has already approved for that country, Pathfinder will still use its "own" funds, if it is necessary to act speedily. Requests for a training programme or a seminar, for example, can sometimes get approval from Boston within 24 hours.

On the other hand, if Pathfinder is considering some new project of particular importance, the whole process of project preparation and approval will be correspondingly more important also. The development of some of Pathfinder's bigger projects has thus taken as much as two years from the time when the proposal was first mooted to the actual start of implementation. This is, however, unusual.

As a general rule, Pathfinder does not require an elaborate production in the way of project preparation, although it has, of course, specific requirements in respect of the information to be provided, and will be more rigorous in the case of larger projects than smaller ones. The process of project appraisal is similarly reduced to the minimum consistent with responsible decision-making and the size of the proposed activity. Thus after the initial project idea has been discussed at the weekly meeting in Boston of Pathfinder's Project Review Committee, and its comments and queries have been returned to the prospective grantee (normally in about two weeks), the latter will then prepare the full project proposal (often with substantial assistance from Pathfinder's local staff) in, on average, about four weeks. Boston will then review the proposal, and unless there are further queries, will re-write it in the appropriate form for submission to AID.

AID approval involves getting three separate clearances: from AID's Office of Population in Washington; from the Regional Bureau of the State Department; and from the AID Mission in the country concerned. If the project is for more than $50,000[19], the approval of AID's Contracts Office is required as well. If there is no problem, AID's concurrence can be obtained in about 6 weeks. (Clearance from the Contracts Office adds another 2-4 weeks to the process).

Pathfinder normally hopes that the whole process from original inception of the project to final AID concurrence can be done in 6 months or less. In certain circumstances, approval may be obtained more quickly — for requests for project renewal, for example, (although approval will depend on past performance and is not automatic). A straightforward travel or training grant can probably be processed through all stages (Pathfinder's and AID's) in as little as 4 weeks. And in some cases, where the initial project idea comes from AID, its concurrence is, in effect, guaranteed in advance. For projects of modest size, approval may then take only 2-3 weeks.

Sometimes AID will return a project to Boston for further clarification or for modification. (A major project in Kenya was held up for two months, pending the development of a specialised evaluation plan requested by the AID Mission). If there are difficulties, it is very often at the Mission level that they occur. (In some Latin American countries, for example, the U.S. Ambassador has been opposed to sterilisation programmes)[20]. And, of course, each AID Mission has its own operating style. Some work

---

18. Certain private donations are for specially designated activities, but these are usually minor.
19. $75,000 after June 1, 1983.
20. Sometimes, of course, the views of the Ambassador may work the other way. If he throws his weight behind a particular proposal, it is likely to go through easily and quickly.

closely with the Pathfinder Representative, welcome discussion of new initiatives, and will frequently give their unofficial blessing to a proposal before it is formally submitted to Boston. Some others like to think of the Pathfinder programme as something of an adjunct to AID's own, and to look at each Pathfinder proposal in that light.

Once a project has been approved by AID, Pathfinder takes over responsibility for its administration. If modifications are required in the course of implementation, Pathfinder can amend a project for up to 25 per cent of its cost (maximum $10,000) without reference to AID. Above this limit, AID approval is required.

International Staff

Pathfinder maintains nine field offices (their number has recently been increased). Regional offices cover Latin America North, Latin America South, and sub-Saharan Africa. There are also country offices in Brazil, Egypt, Turkey, Bangladesh, Indonesia and Nigeria. The size of these field offices naturally varies with the nature of the programme. The biggest, the Bangladesh office, has a staff of 20.

Pathfinder's field representatives differ from those of most other aid agencies in that the senior officers are either nationals of the countries in which they serve or of the region. Many of them hold senior government or university positions as well as working for Pathfinder. (Others are full-time Pathfinder staff). The supporting staff (all full-time Pathfinder employees) are also nationals of the country.

Being themselves part of the establishment of the country, Pathfinder's international staff contribute much of the special character of the Pathfinder programme. It is their intimate knowledge of the local situation (and personalities) that enables Pathfinder to identify such a wide range of specific needs and possibilities for action, and to tailor its programme so as to support them.

The senior international staff are Pathfinder's accredited representatives in the country. Their role is to explain Pathfinder's programme priorities and manner of operation to potential grantees, to keep in close touch with the AID Missions and those of other donors, and most important of all, to be constantly on the look-out for new ways in which Pathfinder might assist[21]. They also, as previously mentioned, have a major hand in the preparation of project requests, assist the project officers to comply with Pathfinder's reporting and accounting requirements, keep an eye on project implementation, and help smooth out difficulties where necessary. These functions they perform for all projects alike, whether funded out of the AID grant or from private funds. In most cases, the population staff on the AID Missions find the presence of a local Pathfinder representative a valuable practical asset.

Where the field staff are somewhat restricted, however, is in decision-making authority. Pathfinder's management style tends to be centralised, with all decisions of any consequence taken at Headquarters. All requests for change in a project, for example, even a slight modification as between project categories, has to be referred to Boston. In practice, however, this requirement is not too burdensome, since Boston is usually disposed to accept the advice of its man-on-the-spot, and a telephone call is sometimes all that is needed. Pathfinder has had under consideration for some time the possibility of allowing the field officers a 10 per cent margin of flexibility for approving changes in the course of project implementation, and also a small discretionary fund. AID apparently would welcome such a development. However, Pathfinder's senior field officers are not necessarily all that keen on having a wide authority for decision-making delegated to them. If a request has to be turned down, there are obvious advantages for the local man to be seen as simply transmitting a negative decision taken at headquarters, rather than himself be responsible for it.

---

21. At one time, they had virtually quotas for new project proposals to be submitted each year — an approach that disappeared automatically as funding became tighter.

V. IMPLEMENTATION PROCEDURES

Disbursement

Pathfinder is usually unable to commit funds for an activity for more than one year at a time. Where a project is expected to continue for several years, it gives an assurance of renewal *in principle* (usually for three years but sometimes for more), and this has generally been found to be good enough. Renewal is not automatic however — it is implicitly understood to be conditional upon project performance — and as the funding situation becomes more difficult, this condition is, of necessity, tending to be taken more seriously than it has sometimes been in the past.

Pathfinder's funding (always grants) is paid in the actual currency of the country of implementation, except in Latin America, where payment is made in U.S. dollars. Since the grants are made (and calculated) annually, projects are unlikely to suffer significantly from any fall in the exchange value of the dollar. However, should there be a substantial drop, Pathfinder would be prepared to make a mid-year amendment to the grant.

Although its projects vary enormously in size, the same procedural arrangements apply. Each has its own Letter of Agreement defining the scope of the activity (although in the case of very small projects, the Letter will be simpler). In addition, each Letter will be accompanied by a standard set of printed instructions setting out the arrangements for implementation and Pathfinder's procedural requirements.

Pathfinder funds its projects entirely by means of advances, except for equipment and supplies from the U.S., for which it pays the supplier direct. Advances are made quarterly — unless some very major purchase is involved, in which case, all or most of the grant can be paid at once.

It is not Pathfinder's practice to lay down very tight conditions to be met by the grantee before disbursements can begin (although Pathfinder staff agree that in some cases it might have been prudent to have done so). The first disbursement is accordingly made immediately following receipt by Boston of the signed Letter of Agreement. The second quarter's instalment follows automatically, but thereafter disbursements are conditional upon receipt of pro forma quarterly statements of expenditure from the project director. These show expenditure by project category, but do not have to be accompanied by actual payment vouchers, which are kept against possible visit by the auditor (see below).

Pathfinder is unusual in that it is able to send funds direct to the project or individual grantee. In Indonesia, for example, projects located in a city receive funds direct from the bank in Boston: for projects in rural areas, the money goes to the Pathfinder Representative in Jakarta, who sends it to the nearest post office.

In Bangladesh, where there is a particularly close collaborative relationship between the Pathfinder office and the AID Mission, Pathfinder receives a certain amount of funding direct from the Mission, instead of via the usual Washington-Boston-project route. This obviously makes for a very considerable measure of flexibility and saving of time in dealing with new situations. Pathfinder's senior representative in Bangladesh says that he can get funds for a new activity in two months from the AID Mission in Dacca, as against six from Boston. Pathfinder representatives in other countries would naturally like to have the same possibilities. The idea has been under discussion for some time, but has not so far been extended elsewhere.

Procurement

For AID-financed projects, AID's procurement rules apply. That is to say, goods must be of U.S. manufacture[22], and be transported in U.S. carriers etc. By the same token, however, AID's waiver possibilities also apply[23].

In practice, although Pathfinder can take advantage of AID's possibilities of waiver to purchase goods and supplies from Third World countries, it generally prefers not to, on grounds of quality. All goods financed out of U.S. aid funds have to be vetted by the relevant standards agency in the U.S. Nevertheless, Pathfinder maintains that often the medical supplies, equipment etc. made in Third World countries are of inferior standard to those made in the U.S., and it accordingly prefers to stick to U.S. makes, with which the medical men on Pathfinder staff are familiar and in whose quality they have confidence.

For projects funded from outside the AID grant, on the other hand, there are no restrictions as to the country of origin of goods to be supplied. The director of the project can do the purchasing himself from whatever source he considers the most advantageous (using the funds he will have already received as advance). He will, however, have to submit to Pathfinder the specifications of what he is proposing to buy. There is thus a certain amount of third country procurement (e.g. surgical equipment required for Bangladesh was purchased in Japan), but this is relatively minor in the context of Pathfinder's programme overall.

Under the privately-funded projects, procurement can also be done locally — always assuming that the items are available on the local market and are of the requisite standard. The actual procurement is done by the local Pathfinder office. For AID-funded projects, local purchase follows AID's rules. These allow a ceiling of $5,000 local procurement per project in any one year. In addition, office supplies, gasoline etc. and other items required for normal programme operations may also be purchased locally. Overall, however, Pathfinder projects, whether AID-funded or other, include only a small amount of local purchase — mostly for relatively minor items.

Reporting and Auditing

In addition to the quarterly pro forma statement necessary to obtain the next quarterly advance, Pathfinder requires its projects to submit, also quarterly, a more substantive report setting out the progress of implementation as against the goals envisaged (e.g. numbers of people trained, sterilisations performed etc.). Boston is strict about these reports, which have to be sent in within 15 days of the end of the corresponding period. Reports go also to the local Pathfinder office which is expected to comment to Boston on any problems raised (or successes achieved).

To complement the reports from the projects, Pathfinder requires its international staff to monitor progress by personal visits to the more important project activities. There is no set time-table for these visits and subsequent reports to Boston, but if too long a period elapses, Boston will likely send a reminder.

For projects financed out of the AID grant, AID does not require Pathfinder to submit reports on progress, but likes to be kept informed (some AID Missions choosing to keep a closer watch than others). Frequently, when the Population Officer on the AID Mission travels to visit AID's own projects, he will visit Pathfinder's also (but only after checking with the local Pathfinder representative). Similarly, when Pathfinder's staff visit Pathfinder projects, they sometimes invite the AID officer to come too. Some-

---

22. Or they may be goods assembled in the U.S., provided at least 51 per cent of the components are of U.S. origin.

23. Pathfinder could thus supply non-U.S. made vehicles, if it chose to: usually, however, it prefers not to provide vehicles at all, unless there is very strong justification, because of the problem of maintenance and spares.

times, AID will suggest to Boston that a visit by Pathfinder's Headquarters staff would be timely[24].

In respect of auditing, Pathfinder's requirements are obviously influenced by its large number of small projects. It would clearly be unrealistic to require auditing of each one, and only those costing over $25,000 usually get audited in practice. Below that, projects are selected for audit on a random basis. (Pathfinder's rules specify that a minimum of 10 per cent of these smaller projects must be audited annually[25].

Evaluation

Pathfinder is very serious both about doing evaluation and about using the results as a practical management tool. Where possible, therefore, it tries to include an evaluation plan and a system for monitoring and feedback as part of the initial project design.

In addition to these built-in evaluation arrangements, Pathfinder is increasingly interested in trying to assess the long-term results of its projects, either in particular areas of activity, or as a means of testing the validity of some new approach, or simply where it has invested an important and continuing effort. Studies of this kind are done largely by outside consultants. Indeed, when Pathfinder engages a consultant, it is more likely to do so for the purpose of evaluating its own activities than of providing expert services for the project itself. In Indonesia, for example, it commissioned three consultants to examine the results of its five-year involvement (social and motivational activities) with the religious group, Mohammediyah, in order to see the impact, not only on the public, but on the agency itself and the Government of Indonesia. In Bangladesh, Pathfinder itself received a special grant from the Ford Foundation to evaluate the results of its training programme in menstrual regulation techniques.

Pathfinder's evaluation efforts have not in every case come up with wholly positive conclusions, but as Pathfinder's staff rightly recognise, there are important lessons to be learnt from this too.

VI. CO-ORDINATION WITH OTHER DONORS

The need for donor co-ordination is particularly keenly felt by Pathfinder, as a voluntary agency, because of the very large number of small private agencies of all kinds doing population work in developing countries. In Latin America and Africa, especially, where there are fewer national population programmes, and hence fewer opportunities for the major population donors, Pathfinder would like to see some attempt to bring a measure of order into the many and various family planning initiatives of the private agencies (beginning with a better geographical distribution within the country). It sees little likelihood of it however — since in the absence of any particular interest on the part of the government, the question immediately arises as to *who* should do the co-ordinating. Where the government has its own population programme, the prospects for co-ordination of private voluntary efforts are brighter. The establishment by the Government of Bangladesh of an official committee to which all population projects proposed by voluntary agencies must be submitted for approval is welcomed as an encouraging step in the right direction.

---

24. Headquarters staff travel to Pathfinder's most important project countries and to new countries to explore possibilities. A country with an active Pathfinder programme is likely to receive a visit from Headquarters at least twice a year.

25. Some Pathfinder staff would like to see a more uniform arrangement, whereby all donors would agree to impose an annual auditing requirement on all projects, so that the recipient would have the same obligations (and need to observe the same financial discipline) irrespective of the funding source. Pathfinder has in fact reached an informal agreement of this kind with the Family Planning Associations in several countries in which both agencies are active.

Sometimes Pathfinder and other private agencies look upon each other as potential rivals: more often they help each other out. Thus in some countries, Pathfinder and the Family Planning Association are competitors, but often Pathfinder provides support for the activities of the local Family Planning Association. (In one case, Pathfinder provided bridging financing for two years for a programme of Community-based Distribution of Contraceptives started by the Family Planning Association and for which funding promised by UNFPA was not yet available). Occasionally, a Family Planning Association has taken over a project started by Pathfinder, but this is less common.

Exchanges of information as between the larger private agencies vary as to frequency and coverage. IPPF Western Hemisphere has always shared its mission reports, and Pathfinder now exchanges reports with a number of other agencies also; FPIA[26], IFRP[27], Development Associates[28], AVS[29]. Today, these exchanges frequently include reports on proposals under consideration, which would not have been the case a few years ago.

Pathfinder does not have (or require) much regular consultation with the larger population assistance donors at the headquarters level. At the country level, however, its international staff are in a position to maintain the unofficial contacts with other donor representatives that make for real co-ordination where the action is. It is by means of these contacts that Pathfinder is able very often to find follow-up financing for the development of experimental activities begun with its support.

THE PATHFINDER FUND

AID FOR POPULATION ACTIVITIES

i) Total volume of population assistance expenditures through 1981, $ 58.933 million

ii) Annual expenditures on population assistance, 1975-1981 (US$ thousand)

1975	4.366
1976	4.816
1977	5.414
1978	5.455
1979	7.210
1980	7.055
1981	7.204

iii) Division of total expenditures on population assistance by major population sectors, 1975-1981 (US$ thousand)

	1975	1976	1977	1978	1979	1980	1981	Total	%
Population Policy	—	—	—	0.181	0.290	0.332	0.442	1.245	3.0
Family Planning	4.366	4.816	5.414	4.938	6.304	5.837	5.604	37.279	89.8
Women's Programmes	—	—	—	0.336	0.616	0.886	1.158	2.996	7.2
Total	4.366	4.816	5.414	5.455	7.210	7.055	7.204	41.520	100.0

26. Family Planning International Assistance.
27. International Fertility Research Programme; Chapel Hill, North Carolina.
28. A private body providing training and consultant services; Washington D.C.
29. Association for Voluntary Sterilisation.

OECD SALES AGENTS
DÉPOSITAIRES DES PUBLICATIONS DE L'OCDE

ARGENTINA – ARGENTINE
Carlos Hirsch S.R.L., Florida 165, 4° Piso (Galería Guemes)
1333 BUENOS AIRES. Tel. 33.1787.2391 y 30.7122

AUSTRALIA – AUSTRALIE
Australia and New Zealand Book Company Pty, Ltd.,
10 Aquatic Drive, Frenchs Forest, N.S.W. 2086
P.O. Box 459, BROOKVALE, N.S.W. 2100

AUSTRIA – AUTRICHE
OECD Publications and Information Center
4 Simrockstrasse 5300 BONN. Tel. (0228) 21.60.45
Local Agent/Agent local :
Gerold and Co., Graben 31, WIEN 1. Tel. 52.22.35

BELGIUM – BELGIQUE
Jean De Lannoy, Service Publications OCDE
avenue du Roi 202, B-1060 BRUXELLES. Tel. 02/538.51.69

BRAZIL – BRÉSIL
Mestre Jou S.A., Rua Guaipa 518,
Caixa Postal 24090, 05089 SAO PAULO 10. Tel. 261.1920
Rua Senador Dantas 19 s/205-6, RIO DE JANEIRO GB.
Tel. 232.07.32

CANADA
Renouf Publishing Company Limited,
2182 ouest, rue Ste-Catherine,
MONTRÉAL, Qué. H3H 1M7. Tel. (514)937.3519
OTTAWA, Ont. K1P 5A6, 61 Sparks Street

DENMARK – DANEMARK
Munksgaard Export and Subscription Service
35, Nørre Søgade
DK 1370 KØBENHAVN K. Tel. +45.1.12.85.70

FINLAND – FINLANDE
Akateeminen Kirjakauppa
Keskuskatu 1, 00100 HELSINKI 10. Tel. 65.11.22

FRANCE
Bureau des Publications de l'OCDE,
2 rue André-Pascal, 75775 PARIS CEDEX 16. Tel. (1) 524.81.67
Principal correspondant :
13602 AIX-EN-PROVENCE : Librairie de l'Université.
Tel. 26.18.08

GERMANY – ALLEMAGNE
OECD Publications and Information Center
4 Simrockstrasse 5300 BONN Tel. (0228) 21.60.45

GREECE – GRÈCE
Librairie Kauffmann, 28 rue du Stade,
ATHÈNES 132. Tel. 322.21.60

HONG-KONG
Government Information Services,
Publications/Sales Section, Baskerville House.
2/F., 22 Ice House Street

ICELAND – ISLANDE
Snaebjorn Jónsson and Co., h.f.,
Hafnarstraeti 4 and 9, P.O.B. 1131, REYKJAVIK.
Tel. 13133/14281/11936

INDIA – INDE
Oxford Book and Stationery Co. :
NEW DELHI-1, Scindia House. Tel. 45896
CALCUTTA 700016, 17 Park Street. Tel. 240832

INDONESIA – INDONÉSIE
PDIN-LIPI, P.O. Box 3065/JKT., JAKARTA, Tel. 583467

IRELAND – IRLANDE
TDC Publishers – Library Suppliers
12 North Frederick Street, DUBLIN 1 Tel. 744835-749677

ITALY – ITALIE
Libreria Commissionaria Sansoni :
Via Lamarmora 45, 50121 FIRENZE. Tel. 579751/584468
Via Bartolini 29, 20155 MILANO. Tel. 365083
Sub-depositari :
Ugo Tassi
Via A. Farnese 28, 00192 ROMA. Tel. 310590
Editrice e Libreria Herder,
Piazza Montecitorio 120, 00186 ROMA. Tel. 6794628
Costantino Ercolano, Via Generale Orsini 46, 80132 NAPOLI. Tel. 405210
Libreria Hoepli, Via Hoepli 5, 20121 MILANO. Tel. 865446
Libreria Scientifica, Dott. Lucio de Biasio "Aeiou"
Via Meravigli 16, 20123 MILANO Tel. 807679
Libreria Zanichelli
Piazza Galvani 1/A, 40124 Bologna Tel. 237389
Libreria Lattes, Via Garibaldi 3, 10122 TORINO. Tel. 519274
La diffusione delle edizioni OCSE è inoltre assicurata dalle migliori librerie nelle città più importanti.

JAPAN – JAPON
OECD Publications and Information Center,
Landic Akasaka Bldg., 2-3-4 Akasaka,
Minato-ku, TOKYO 107 Tel. 586.2016

KOREA – CORÉE
Pan Korea Book Corporation,
P.O. Box n° 101 Kwangwhamun, SEOUL. Tel. 72.7369

LEBANON – LIBAN
Documenta Scientifica/Redico,
Edison Building, Bliss Street, P.O. Box 5641, BEIRUT.
Tel. 354429 – 344425

MALAYSIA – MALAISIE
University of Malaya Co-operative Bookshop Ltd.
P.O. Box 1127, Jalan Pantai Baru
KUALA LUMPUR. Tel. 51425, 54058, 54361

THE NETHERLANDS – PAYS-BAS
Staatsuitgeverij, Verzendboekhandel,
Chr. Plantijnstraat 1 Postbus 20014
2500 EA S-GRAVENHAGE. Tel. nr. 070.789911
Voor bestellingen: Tel. 070.789208

NEW ZEALAND – NOUVELLE-ZÉLANDE
Publications Section,
Government Printing Office Bookshops:
AUCKLAND: Retail Bookshop: 25 Rutland Street,
Mail Orders: 85 Beach Road, Private Bag C.P.O.
HAMILTON: Retail Ward Street,
Mail Orders, P.O. Box 857
WELLINGTON: Retail: Mulgrave Street (Head Office),
Cubacade World Trade Centre
Mail Orders: Private Bag
CHRISTCHURCH: Retail: 159 Hereford Street,
Mail Orders: Private Bag
DUNEDIN: Retail: Princes Street
Mail Order: P.O. Box 1104

NORWAY – NORVÈGE
J.G. TANUM A/S Karl Johansgate 43
P.O. Box 1177 Sentrum OSLO 1. Tel. (02) 80.12.60

PAKISTAN
Mirza Book Agency, 65 Shahrah Quaid-E-Azam, LAHORE 3.
Tel. 66839

PHILIPPINES
National Book Store, Inc.
Library Services Division, P.O. Box 1934, MANILA.
Tel. Nos. 49.43.06 to 09, 40.53.45, 49.45.12

PORTUGAL
Livraria Portugal, Rua do Carmo 70-74,
1117 LISBOA CODEX. Tel. 360582/3

SINGAPORE – SINGAPOUR
Information Publications Pte Ltd,
Pei-Fu Industrial Building,
24 New Industrial Road N° 02-06
SINGAPORE 1953, Tel. 2831786, 2831798

SPAIN – ESPAGNE
Mundi-Prensa Libros, S.A.
Castelló 37, Apartado 1223, MADRID-1. Tel. 275.46.55
Libreria Bosch, Ronda Universidad 11, BARCELONA 7.
Tel. 317.53.08, 317.53.58

SWEDEN – SUÈDE
AB CE Fritzes Kungl Hovbokhandel,
Box 16 356, S 103 27 STH, Regeringsgatan 12,
DS STOCKHOLM. Tel. 08/23.89.00
Subscription Agency/Abonnements:
Wennergren-Williams AB,
Box 13004, S104 25 STOCKHOLM.
Tel. 08/54.12.00

SWITZERLAND – SUISSE
OECD Publications and Information Center
4 Simrockstrasse 5300 BONN. Tel. (0228) 21.60.45
Local Agents/Agents locaux
Librairie Payot, 6 rue Grenus, 1211 GENÈVE 11. Tel. 022.31.89.50

TAIWAN – FORMOSE
Good Faith Worldwide Int'l Co., Ltd.
9th floor, No. 118, Sec. 2,
Chung Hsiao E. Road
TAIPEI. Tel. 391.7396/391.7397

THAILAND – THAÏLANDE
Suksit Siam Co., Ltd., 1715 Rama IV Rd.
Samyan, BANGKOK 5. Tel. 2511630

TURKEY – TURQUIE
Kültur Yayinlari Is-Türk Ltd. Sti.
Atatürk Bulvari No : 77/B
KIZILAY/ANKARA. Tel. 17 02 66
Dolmabahce Cad. No : 29
BESIKTAS/ISTANBUL. Tel. 60 71 88

UNITED KINGDOM – ROYAUME-UNI
H.M. Stationery Office, P.O.B. 276,
LONDON SW8 5DT. Tel. (01) 622.3316, or
49 High Holborn, LONDON WC1V 6 HB (personal callers)
Branches at: EDINBURGH, BIRMINGHAM, BRISTOL,
MANCHESTER, BELFAST.

UNITED STATES OF AMERICA – ÉTATS-UNIS
OECD Publications and Information Center, Suite 1207,
1750 Pennsylvania Ave., N.W. WASHINGTON, D.C.20006 – 4582
Tel. (202) 724.1857

VENEZUELA
Libreria del Este, Avda. F. Miranda 52, Edificio Galipan,
CARACAS 106. Tel. 32.23.01/33.26.04/31.58.38

YUGOSLAVIA – YOUGOSLAVIE
Jugoslovenska Knjiga, Knez Mihajlova 2, P.O.B. 36. BEOGRAD
Tel. 621.992

Les commandes provenant de pays où l'OCDE n'a pas encore désigné de dépositaire peuvent être adressées à :
OCDE, Bureau des Publications, 2, rue André-Pascal, 75775 PARIS CEDEX 16.
Orders and inquiries from countries where sales agents have not yet been appointed may be sent to:
OECD, Publications Office, 2, rue André-Pascal, 75775 PARIS CEDEX 16.

OECD PUBLICATIONS, 2, rue André-Pascal, 75775 PARIS CEDEX 16 - No. 42625 1983
PRINTED IN FRANCE
(41 83 04 1) ISBN 92-64-12524-8